Ethical Practice in
Small Communities

Psychologists in Independent Practice

Leon VandeCreek, Series Editor

Michael J. Murphy, Series Editor

Ethical Practice in Small Communities

Challenges and Rewards for Psychologists

Janet A. Schank

and

Thomas M. Skovholt

AMERICAN PSYCHOLOGICAL ASSOCIATION

WASHINGTON, DC

Published by
American Psychological Association
750 First Street, NE
Washington, DC 20002
www.apa.org

To order
APA Order Department
P.O. Box 92984
Washington, DC 20090-2984
Tel: (800) 374-2721; Direct: (202) 336-5510
Fax: (202) 336-5502; TDD/TTY: (202) 336-6123
Online: www.apa.org/books/
E-mail: order@apa.org

In the U.K., Europe, Africa, and the Middle East, copies may be ordered from
American Psychological Association
3 Henrietta Street
Covent Garden, London
WC2E 8LU England

Typeset in Palatino by Stephen McDougal, Mechanicsville, MD

Printer: Data Reproductions Corporation, Auburn Hills, MI
Cover Designer: Minker Design, Bethesda, MD
Technical/Production Editor: Genevieve Gill

Library of Congress Cataloging-in-Publication Data

Schank, Janet A.
    Ethical practice in small communities: challenges and rewards for psychologists / Janet A. Schank and Thomas M. Skovholt.— 1st ed.
        p. cm. — (Psychologists in independent practice)
    Includes bibliographical references and index.
    ISBN 1-59147-346-2
    1. Psychologists—Professional ethics. 2. Small groups. I. Skovholt, Thomas M. II. Title. III. Series.

    BF76.4.S33 2006
    174'.915—dc22   2005017081

British Library Cataloguing-in-Publication Data
A CIP record is available from the British Library.

Printed in the United States of America
First Edition

To all of the psychologists and other social service professionals who live and work in a range of small communities. Their generosity, wisdom, and compassion are inspiring to me and to all who benefit from their work.

—Janet A. Schank

To my brother Glen and sister Jane, with love and appreciation.

—Thomas M. Skovholt

Important Notice

The statements and opinions published in this book are the responsibility of the authors. Such opinions and statements do not represent official policies, standards, guidelines, or ethical mandates of the American Psychological Association (APA), APA's Ethics Committee or Ethics Office, or any other APA governance group or staff. Statements made in this book neither add to nor reduce requirements of the APA "Ethical Principles of Psychologists and Code of Conduct" (2002a), hereinafter referred to as the *APA Ethics Code* or the *Ethics Code*, nor can they be viewed as a definitive source of the meaning of the Ethics Code Standards or their application to particular situations. Each ethics committee or other relevant body must interpret and apply the Ethics Code as it believes proper, given all the circumstances. Any information in this book involving legal and ethical issues should not be used as a substitute for obtaining personal legal and/or ethical advice and consultation prior to making decisions regarding individual circumstances.

Contents

Acknowledgments

I, Janet, want to thank the many people who offered valuable assistance and support throughout the lengthy process of bringing this book to publication. They added humor and goodwill along the way. My sister, Gail Schank Hafer, and brother-in-law, John Hafer, knew when to ask and not ask about the work and how to offer encouragement from afar. LaVon Lee, John Poupart, and Howard Rainer understood and supported small-community work and me as their struggling-author friend. They served as role models and inspiration through their lives, and they shared their well-timed humor and their contributions to their own small communities. Paul Rosenblatt, the late Martin Snoke, Ray Conroe, Dorothy Loeffler, Annie Baldwin, and the late Alton Raygor helped me early on to believe that I would succeed. Jeff Leichter, Kay Slama, Kathy Harowski, Penny Giesbrecht, Lavorial Salone, Melissa Mussell, Beth Haverkamp, Laurie Johnson, Jaine Strauss, Carol Hasegawa, and especially Janet Thomas believed in this work as friends and professional colleagues. Each gave me the opportunity to expand my knowledge and professional experience. Thanks also go to the members of the Minnesota Psychological Association Rural and Greater Minnesota Division for their insights and encouragement. I would not have had the background to even begin this work without the support of Gary Schoener, whose own career in the field of ethics and whose generosity to me over the past 20 years set a high standard for me personally and for all of us who have been fortunate enough to be associated with his work and the mission of the Walk-In Counseling Center.

A heartfelt thank-you goes to Tom Skovholt. His boundless patience as my graduate school advisor and his support of my qualitative research when it was risky to do so within our department meant everything to me. Tom continued to be gracious in involving me in projects after the completion of my degree and was the catalyst for this book from the very beginning. Few former graduate students have had the opportunities that Tom has offered to me. Through his body of work within psychology and his unique style of questioning and encouragement, he has served as a role model for me and countless other current and former students at the University of Minnesota.

Judy Nemes, Genevieve Gill, and the staff in the Books Department at the American Psychological Association (APA) were patient, reassuring, and eminently knowledgeable in the long process of bringing this work to print. Their contributions made this a much better work throughout all its iterations until we reached the final result.

Special thanks and gratitude go to Leon VandeCreek. He was the person who took the idea of this book forward to APA and who advocated on our behalf. VandeCreek patiently waited for the drafts, read and edited them with great care, and provided encouragement and leadership in this project.

Finally, thank you to all of the mental health practitioners in small communities—rural, small colleges, communities of color, gay/lesbian/bisexual/transgender, suburban, deaf, disability, feminist, religious, corrections, military, chemical dependency, therapists who see other therapists, and others—who took the time to share their insights and lives with us. Their work enriches the field of psychology and the lives of the clients and communities with which they work.

I, Tom, want to acknowledge and thank important ethics teachers in my life: my parents, Joe and Elvera Skovholt; Esther Swenson; Ms. Gratz; Alvin Lewis; Ronald Soderquist; Ross Snyder; Phyllis Epley; Harry Grater; Jacquie Resnick; Norman Moen; Bill Cuff; and the many clients I have had during the past 30 years who have taught me and shown me about being courageous and ethical in the face of adversity. I also want to thank Janet for the opportunity to work with her on this important topic during the last 10 years, first as her advisor and now as her colleague. Interacting with her during this time has made my professional life richer and more meaningful.

Ethical Practice in
Small Communities

Introduction

This book came out of the experience of my colleague and this book's first author (Janet A. Schank) growing up in rural Nebraska. As a child and adolescent, Janet watched how professionals and their clients related. They interacted smoothly in a complex variety of roles. Later, with the distance of time and place, she realized that interacting in multiple ways is a natural part of small-community culture.

Years later, after finishing an MA in counseling psychology at an urban university, Janet spoke with a friend from her small town who had returned to practice as a clinical social worker. She asked him how he would be able to manage the overlaps between his life and the lives of his clients. This dilemma was strong, because his family had lived in town a long time, and everyone remembered him as the son of the rural mail carrier. At the time, her friend told her how much he loved the work and how meaningful it was to contribute to, and be part of the fabric of, this rural area.

During a trip home a few years later, Janet was surprised to hear that her friend had closed his practice and taken a job, unrelated to mental health, in a nearby town. When she asked him why, his answer was both poignant and illuminating. He said, "Janet, I have a wife and daughter to support. I could only take so many chickens in payment." To those of you who have never been a part of a small community, his answer may seem amusing. To those of us who have, it speaks to the complexity and poignancy of living and working in the helping professions within a small community. As time went on, Janet's awareness of the split between optimal rural culture and urban-based ethics codes continued and grew.

As Janet's advisor, I (Thomas M. Skovholt), wholeheartedly supported her enthusiasm for a qualitative interview study of this issue for her doctoral dissertation. Janet was fortunate to be able to interview rural psychologists at their practice sites. When others in the large metropolitan area of Minneapolis–St. Paul asked about her interviews, she was reluctant to share much information, fearing that they would not understand or be truly interested. She soon found out that small communities existed everywhere. Other mental health and social services professionals were interested, because many of them lived and practiced in small communities. Theirs were just different small communities than Janet's—although she was, at that time, in her second small community, as a psychologist for 14 years in the counseling center of a liberal arts college. She heard over and over from friends and colleagues, "That's just what it's like for me in the Native community"—or the gay community, the deaf community, suburbs, communities of color, the corrections system, therapists who see other therapists as clients, and others. These serious, well-meaning professionals identified with the challenges and rewards of living their personal and professional lives within their small community and strove to practice ethically while their lives overlapped with those of their clients and with those of other members of their communities.

The work on this topic went from the dissertation, to an article, to many presentations and consultations. At the same time, the topic broadened from rural communities to a more inclusive group of small communities and psychological practice in these small communities. In time, this long evolution of effort formed this book. Janet and I hope that her experience has helped energize this topic so that the book will be of value to practitioners, researchers, and policymakers in their work on ethical practice.

In this book Janet and I emphasize optimal professional conduct while recognizing that the culture of a small community has its own demands. The advantages of small-community practice, along with suggestions to enhance ethical practice in small communities, are included to provide a more complete picture of the lives and worlds of those who practice in these communities. We ask that readers do not misuse our work. We do not endorse the stance that multiple relationships are always acceptable. Although we describe in this book the challenges of small-community practice, we do not endorse the abandonment of boundaries. After all, in our professional and personal lives, "good fences make good neighbors." This proverb led the poet Robert Frost to ask *why* they make good neighbors and to suggest that "Before I built a wall, I'd ask to know what I was walling in or walling out."

As Behnke (2005) noted, "Ethical dilemmas arise not by virtue of a flaw or defect in our profession; they are rather a comment on the richness and complexity of what we do" (p. 77). The vibrancy found in small communities gives people hope, helps them come together and endure in trying times, and contributes to the safety net of small-community life. To be credible, fit in, and be accepted involves multiple relationships across people. The psychologist is part of this community too—indeed, he or she must be—to be trusted with others' personal data and drama.

The ambiguity of the human condition makes us all yearn for rules and recipes for life, but fine-tuning them for the culture is a difficult chore. As the writers of this book, we realize that the questioning of rigid guidelines can lead to an unfastening and misuse of standards. We are advocating not a lessening of ethical guidelines but rather more and better guidelines. The paradox is that ethical guidelines, adopted without the inclusion of cultural intelligence, are of questionable ethics. The 2002 American Psychological Association "Ethical Principles of Psychologists and Code of Conduct" (American Psychological Association, 2002a) are about doing the greatest good for the most people. We hope that this book, in its small way, does just that. We hope, too, that small-community clients can be better helped with the use of appropriate small-community guidelines. Helping vulnerable people in distress is, after all, the central purpose of clinical practice.

In this book, we address the central dilemma for small-community psychologists: how to practice, at a high ethical level according to ethics codes, and how to also be an engaged member of the small community. Practitioners in small communities often do not follow the model of many of their urban colleagues: practicing in one community and living in another.

This book contains chapters that address the challenges and advantages of small-community practice. The map of the tour starts with chapter 1, in which we examine broad issues, including a discussion of the 2002 APA Ethics Code. Chapter 2 covers the historical development of ethics codes and how codes help provide professional identity. The map goes on to chapter 3, in which the density of the terrain increases. Here, we explore multiple relationships, the factors in unethical conduct, how traditional large urban and small communities are alike and different, how multiple relationships become problematic, the concept of treatment boundaries, and the varieties—from very damaging to affirming—of dual relationships. The map then leads to chapter 4, in which rural practice is illuminated as an example of small-community practice. The chapter includes interviews with rural psychologists. They describe earnest attempts to be both engaged community members—in part because it gives them professional credibility—and highly ethical practitioners. The map then escorts the reader to the vista of chapter 5. There, we look at the vast expanse of small communities: communities of color and cultural–ethnic communities; small colleges; military; disability cultures; religious communities; gay, lesbian, bisexual, transgender (GLBT) communities; feminists; criminal justice, corrections, and law enforcement; therapists who see other therapists; suburbs; and people with addictions. Chapter 6 presents strategies to minimize risk. The map takes a final turn to chapter 7. Here, the focus is on the great opportunities in small communities for psychologists to serve and grow.

Chapter

1

Ethics in a Broad Context

Psychologists train and practice in an area rife with ambiguity. There are often no "right" answers in dealing with the complexities of human problems and interactions. Guidelines are necessary, but frequently not sufficient, in promoting ethical choices and behavior (Pedersen, 1997b). Yet there must be some guidelines, both in formulating and in treating the issues that clients present to psychologists. A critical component of those guidelines is a set of ethical standards, both internally and externally imposed. What one psychologist sees as an ethical problem may be viewed by others as a practical problem or a political problem (MacKay & O'Neill, 1992). Thus, the process of ethical reasoning and decision making requires a complex combination of higher level thought and deep reflection, along with the ability to choose a course of action in spite of doubt and uncertainty (Neukrug, Lovell, & Parker, 1996).

As we review these complex concerns, we want to remind the reader that the focus of this book is on the challenges and rewards for psychologists in small communities. Small communities are defined as spaces where, as Purtilo and Sorrell (1986) say, there is an "intricate web of professional-personal roles" (p. 23). The safety of large metropolitan areas permits the practitioner to disappear from the work role and to enter personal life. Boundaries appear automatically in New York City, Cairo, Singapore, or Toronto. They do not occur as easily for the small-community

7

psychologist in rural Idaho, where the psychologist must exist within a web of roles to be professionally and culturally competent. This means working within the existing community system of support networks, politics, and informal communication connections. Examples of small communities that share limited space include ethnic groups, deployed military units, small colleges, gay and lesbian populations, and farm or frontier towns and surrounding areas.

Pope and Vasquez (1998) indicated that, regardless of the setting, psychologists must be especially careful to fulfill their enormous responsibilities to help others change their lives and to help without hurting. Stress resulting from the lack of a "right" way to respond compounds the anxiety that we as psychologists often feel when faced with the pain and problems of clients. A professional response to that stress and anxiety includes educating oneself, minimizing denial, and being accountable for one's own professional behavior.

Pope and Vasquez (1998) pointed out that the field of psychology is expected to provide a professional code to promote the welfare of clients and to protect them from harm. Professional ethics committees, state licensing boards, and criminal and civil courts provide additional means of ensuring at least minimal standards of practice. What is unethical may not be illegal, and so mechanisms for accountability sometimes overlap. Standards may conflict, leaving professionals to resolve the dilemma of what is in the best interest of clients. Pope and Vasquez (1998) stressed that each clinical situation brings with it new ethical demands, and the rote application or following of codes is not adequate or sufficient.

External and Internal Standards

The guidelines and standards that guide psychological practice are both internally and externally imposed. External standards come from legal statutes, professional codes of conduct, and regulating boards. Internal standards come, in part, from a psychologist's own values, environment, and life experience (Haas, Malouf, & Mayerson, 1988; Jordan & Meara, 1990). However, the opportunities to examine these standards and their interaction are often confined to a limited amount of relevant graduate school training and to occasional workshops or seminars. Psychologists may hesitate to discuss more immediate ethical dilemmas with their colleagues, fearing judgment or exposure. Thus, they may ignore the problem, struggle in isolation, or rationalize the choices they make (Schank & Skovholt, 1997).

Ethical and values issues in therapy are often made intuitively and automatically, as a result of the internalization of an ethical stance (J. D. Woody, 1990). Dilemmas or conflicts result from uncertainty or from conflict among values, principles, or obligations. Psychologists need to "reflect on the unique problem, weigh the various factors and risks, and make the 'best' decision possible, perhaps seeking consultation in doing so" (J. D. Woody, 1990, pp. 133–134).

Licensure boards, courts, and professional codes provide both frameworks and safety nets in shaping professional practice and protecting client interests. Now, some psychologists are attempting to look beyond this traditional viewpoint to examine whether these standards are sufficient in meeting the needs of small-community psychologists. In their article on clinical ethical decision making, T. S. Smith, McGuire, Abbott, and Blau (1991) suggested that what appears to be inconsistent or confusing in the practical application of ethics is really "a complex balancing act that clinicians face as they attempt to resolve ethical dilemmas" (p. 236). They claimed that "there is widespread agreement that the development of additional guidelines, examples, and casebooks will not solve the complex problems that ethical decision making poses" (T. S. Smith et al., 1991, p. 236).

Ethics is more than simply adhering to standards or the rote application of rules. To be most beneficial to clients and psychologists, ethics should be not static but rather constantly examined and evolving. To do otherwise would be what Pope and Vasquez (1998) identified as mindless rule following, a poor substitution for a more thoughtful and concerned approach. However, the interpretation of these rules relies on the psychologist's professional judgment—bias, experience, professional and theoretical orientation, personality, and values (Koocher & Keith-Spiegel, 1998) and "is subject to individual bias or perspective" (Jordan & Meara, 1990, p. 109).

Virtues and Character

Whereas principles serve as "guides for decision and action, rules, and codes of conduct, virtues reflect the internal composition of character" (Jordan & Meara, 1990, p. 109). Character is not so much a question of what one ought to do as who one ought to be.

Meara, Schmidt, and Day (1996) provided a comprehensive discussion of virtues and principles as a foundation for ethical decision making, including policies and personal character. An important part of such decision making involves being able to deal with the ambiguity inherent in many ethical dilemmas and necessitates "practice to develop the abilities to discern the subtleties and nuances of a problem" (Meara et al., 1996, p. 30).

The ability to discern such nuances is an important step, but not the only step, involved in the decisions that psychologists make. After deciphering the subtleties, psychologists are then faced with even more of a dilemma. In situations in which we are pulled by competing demands or even challenged to take the "right" action, we must be able to rely on our own ability and the ability of our colleagues to make difficult decisions. Making difficult decisions is frequently uncomfortable, and sometimes those decisions come at a great personal cost for psychologists who strive to practice ethically and virtuously. For example, small-community psychologists may be faced at some time in their careers with the ethical demand to report misconduct by another person in the community, either a mental health colleague or another person who is well known and respected within that small community. A psychologist who is faced with the dilemma of having to report a friend or even a mentor for misconduct usually agonizes over the impact that such an action will have on the friend, the friend's family, and the small community in general. It is not unreasonable to expect that the psychologist will also agonize over the impact that such a course of action will have on his or her own family, professional practice, and personal life.

Principles, skills, and knowledge of relevant legal and ethical codes are necessary, but usually not sufficient, in choosing a course of action when one is faced with an ethical dilemma. What is needed is a professional character that is "formed and informed by the profession" (Jordan & Meara, 1990) and that aspires to the ideals of the profession, including conscientious decision making with an emphasis on what is preferred rather than just what is permitted (Jordan & Meara, 1990).

Meara et al. (1996) described the characteristics that are necessary to become what they term *a virtuous agent*, that is, a person who

> (a) is motivated to do what is good, (b) possesses vision and discernment, (c) realizes the role of affect or emotion in assessing or judging proper conduct, (d) has a high degree of self-understanding and awareness, and perhaps most importantly, (e) is connected with and understands the mores of his or her community and the importance of community in moral decision making, policy setting and character development and is alert to the legitimacy of client diversity in these respects. (p. 29)

These characteristics may be difficult to assess, particularly in oneself, and they do not lend themselves to facile discussion or automatic application of standards. Training programs in psychology and ongoing continuing education efforts can address knowledge and application but are rarely able to teach one how to be the kind of person who has the courage and integrity to make difficult choices among competing demands. Psychologists must be able not only to make those choices but also to determine the possible consequences of those choices for a wide range of people.

The basis for these personal qualities or virtues may be relatively stable character traits, although Anderson and Kitchener (1998) suggested that "practice and work may further develop aspects of them" (p. 97). They identified five traits that they deemed central to what they described as *therapeutic psychology*: "practical wisdom, integrity, respectfulness, compassion, and trustworthiness" (Anderson & Kitchener, 1998, p. 98). The ability to take into consideration the perspectives of others and what they deem important, along with compassion grounded in empathy and concern for the well-being of others, lays the groundwork for these virtues.

Principles and Guidelines

It is inevitable that broader principles and narrower guidelines sometimes come into conflict, and it is vital that psychologists possess the requisite knowledge and skills to make the best possible decisions in ambiguous situations. Unlike the manuals that are used to interpret various standardized tests, there are no parallel guidebooks in ethics that provide "a set of expected behaviors or universally acceptable solutions to moral dilemmas and ethical conflicts" (Bersoff & Koeppl, 1993, p. 346). Thus, psychologists must actively seek out relevant principles and guidelines by which to anchor and evaluate their psychological practice.

The Hippocratic Oath has stood for centuries as the basis for safeguarding the behavior of health care professionals, including confidentiality of communication between provider and clients/patients in Western medicine (Backlar, 1996). Other schools of moral and ethical thought have also contributed to codes of conduct and ethical standards for psychologists. Western legal and ethical codes are based on the work of Aristotle in identifying one definition of the truth, "decided upon by those in power to be followed by others" (Ivey, 1987, p. 196).

Bersoff and Koeppl (1993) provided an overview of relevant philosophies, beginning with descriptive ethicists, who "are concerned with uncovering and delineating the moral beliefs of particular groups" (p. 346). Normative ethicists then "attempt to transform these principles into concrete and behaviorally prescriptive paradigms designed to guide, if not dictate, correct behavior" (Bersoff & Koeppl, 1993, p. 346).

Kant and other proponents of deontology, the study of moral obligation, believed that "actions are right or wrong regardless of their consequences" (Bersoff & Koeppl, 1993, p. 346) and based their formulations on an unfaltering respect for the dignity of the individual. Lloyd and Hansen (2003) stated that deontology "provides us with a method by which we can think about our behavior in an ethical manner" (p. 30) but does not specify what that behavior should be. This theory views ethical decision making as "the rational act of applying universal principles to all situations irrespective of specific relationships, contexts, or consequences" (Fisher, 2003, p. 243).

Utilitarianism or teleology, closely linked to the philosopher John Stuart Mill, holds that an action is most correct when its results are more positive than those of its alternatives and thus end up "balancing the possible costs and benefits of an action" (Fisher, 2003, p. 347). Utilitarianism views the consequences of an act as more important than universal principles and posits that the greater good supersedes the obligations to individuals with whom a psychologist may work directly (Fisher, 2003). According to utilitarian theory, "an action is ethical if it results in production of more good than harm" (Haas & Malouf, 1989, p. 3).

W. D. Ross, a 20th-century English philosopher, proposed a set of duties for ethical conduct that "include nonmaleficence [do no harm], fidelity [faithfulness to a pledge or duty of what is right], beneficence [doing good], justice [to treat fairly], and autonomy [moral independence]" (Bersoff & Koeppl, 1993, p. 347). Because this concept of *prima facie* (legally sufficient and evident) duty "provides an array of moral choices" (Bersoff & Koeppl, 1993, p. 347) to be applied to an ethical dilemma, it has gained wider acceptance than most other theories. However, each principle is not completely binding and "may be superseded by an equal or more applicable principle" (Bersoff & Koeppl, 1993, p. 347).

Bersoff and Koeppl (1993) pointed out that the existence of these and other such divergent and relevant ideologies suggests that neither alone "provides adequate solutions for all moral conflicts" (p. 347). They suggested that the foundation of ethical duty is nonmaleficence—above all, "do no harm." In this return to the Hippocratic Oath, in addition to the incorporation of various philosophical ethicists, one sees how complex a process it is to develop principles and guidelines to guide the practice of psychology and protect the public served by the profession. For example, the concept of "do no harm" may mean that psychologists who practice in an urban area specialize in a particular area of practice and frequently refer clients to psychologists who specialize in other areas (e.g., eating disorders, sexual abuse, sexual orientation). However, their small-community colleagues may not have that luxury and may struggle with how to balance the conflicting standards of "do no harm" and practicing outside their areas of true competency.

Any such code of ethics is only a validation of

the most recent views of a majority of professionals empow-
ered to make decisions about ethical issues. It is inevitably
anachronistic, conservative, protective of its members, the
product of political compromise, restricted in its scope, and
too often unable to provide clear-cut solutions to ambiguous
professional predicaments. (Bersoff & Koeppl, 1993, p. 348)

The need for ethical guidelines to go beyond describing options and to move toward what Pedersen (1997b) identified as
helping psychologists "deal with the moral dilemma of contrasting cultures" (p. 27) will become increasingly more essential in
our ever-changing society and technologically more accessible
world.

The Five General Principles of the 2002 American Psychological Association Ethics Code

Five General Principles provide the foundation for the American
Psychological Association's (APA's) 2002 Ethics Code (APA,
2002a; see also APA Web site version at http://www.apa.org/
ethics/). Although the principles are not enforceable rules, these
aspirational characteristics represent the moral vision and ethical ideals of a common purpose for the field of psychology. The
principles are not arranged in order of importance, and their priority is dependent on particular ethical dilemmas (Fisher, 2003).
    These principles encourage psychologists to live their profes-
sional lives in the best way possible, and they "represent the ethical ceiling for psychologists, instead of the ethical floor" (Knapp
& VandeCreek, 2003, p. 27). If the principles seem in conflict with
each other, or if a particular decision is unclear, psychologists are
urged to balance their application toward compassionate, beneficial behavior (Knapp & VandeCreek, 2003).

Principle A: Beneficence and Nonmaleficence

Psychologists strive to benefit those with whom they work and
take care to do no harm. In their professional actions, psychologists seek to safeguard the welfare and rights of those with

whom they interact professionally and other affected persons, and the welfare of animal subjects of research. When conflicts occur among psychologists' obligations or concerns, they attempt to resolve these conflicts in a responsible fashion that avoids or minimizes harm. Because psychologists' scientific and professional judgments and actions may affect the lives of others, they are alert to and guard against personal, financial, social, organizational, or political factors that might lead to misuse of their influence. Psychologists strive to be aware of the possible effect of their own physical and mental health on their ability to help those with whom they work. (APA, 2002a, p. 1062)

Beneficence directs one to contribute to the welfare of others, and *nonmaleficence* directs one to do no harm. If psychologists find themselves in situations in which their interests conflict with those of others, they seek to resolve those conflicts in a manner that "avoids or minimizes harm." As a part of this obligation, psychologists are expected to be aware of and deal with personal problems that may affect their work in ways that could harm or exploit the persons with whom they work (Fisher, 2003; Knapp & VandeCreek, 2003).

Principle B: Fidelity and Responsibility

Psychologists establish relationships of trust with those with whom they work. They are aware of their professional and scientific responsibilities to society and to the specific communities in which they work. Psychologists uphold professional standards of conduct, clarify their professional roles and obligations, accept appropriate responsibility for their behavior, and seek to manage conflicts of interest that could lead to exploitation or harm. Psychologists consult with, refer to, or cooperate with other professionals and institutions to the extent needed to serve the best interests of those with whom they work. They are concerned about the ethical compliance of their colleagues' scientific and professional conduct. Psychologists strive to contribute a portion of their professional time for little or no compensation or personal advantage. (APA, 2002a, p. 1062)

The overarching principle of *fidelity* directs psychologists to hold service to clients and to society as primary. Fidelity also involves respectful and collegial interactions with colleagues and maintenance of appropriate professional relationships and high standards of competence. This includes consulting with other professionals and avoiding exploitive or harmful conflicts of interest (Fisher, 2003; Knapp & VandeCreek, 2003).

Principle C: Integrity

Psychologists seek to promote accuracy, honesty, and truthfulness in the science, teaching, and practice of psychology. In these activities psychologists do not steal, cheat, or engage in fraud, subterfuge, or intentional misrepresentation of fact. Psychologists strive to keep their promises and to avoid unwise or unclear commitments. In situations in which deception may be ethically justifiable to maximize benefits and minimize harm, psychologists have a serious obligation to consider the need for, the possible consequences of, and their responsibility to correct any resulting mistrust or other harmful effects that arise from the use of such techniques. (APA, 2002a, p. 1062)

Integrity means "internal consistency in behavior, words, action, and intent" (Knapp & VandeCreek, 2003, p. 32). Behaving with integrity includes minimizing deception and correcting deleterious effects of research and clinical interactions. Integrity calls for honesty, truth, and accuracy and following through on commitments, along with the responsibility to correct misrepresentations of, for example, oneself or one's research (Fisher, 2003; Knapp & VandeCreek, 2003).

Principle D: Justice

Psychologists recognize that fairness and justice entitle all persons to access to and benefit from the contributions of psychology and to equal quality in the processes, procedures, and services being conducted by psychologists. Psychologists exercise reasonable judgment and take precautions to ensure that their potential biases, the boundaries of their competence, and the limitations of their expertise do not lead to or condone unjust practices. (APA, 2002a, pp. 1062–1063)

Justice refers to equal treatment, equitable distribution of services, and "appropriate access to treatment and to the benefits of scientific knowledge" (Fisher, 2003, p. 21). It calls for psychologists to guard against biases and prejudices, both their own and those of others, that may harm others or promote injustice (Fisher, 2003; Knapp & VandeCreek, 2003).

Principle E: Respect for People's Rights and Dignity

Psychologists respect the dignity and worth of all people, and the rights of individuals to privacy, confidentiality, and self-determination. Psychologists are aware that special safeguards may be necessary to protect the rights and welfare of persons or communities whose vulnerabilities impair autonomous decision making. Psychologists are aware of and respect cultural, individual, and role differences, including those based on age, gender, gender identity, race, ethnicity, culture, national origin, religion, sexual orientation, disability, language, and socioeconomic status and consider these factors when working with members of such groups. Psychologists try to eliminate the effect on their work of biases based on those factors, and they do not knowingly participate in or condone activities of others based on such prejudices. (APA, 2002a, p. 1063)

This broad principle has considerable overlap with the four previous ones. It highlights client autonomy, knowledge about and protection of the rights of vulnerable persons, and respect for differences (Fisher, 2003; Knapp & VandeCreek, 2003).

The five aspirational principles just described are reassuring because they provide a blueprint for professional behavior. However, an absolute sense of reassurance in the profession of psychology is like a mirage: It is clearly there, and then it disappears. In this first chapter, we offer both moral absolutes and the limits to these moral absolutes. After all, we are guiding our own professional behavior and those around us within the context of the human world as a global village with the paradoxes, ironies, and complexities of human life in the murky world of the 21st century.

In the chapters that follow, we explore the absolute importance of high professional ethical standards within the world of small-community psychology. We describe at length how the ethical decision-making process in this context can, at times, be very challenging. Higher order thought and reflection are two necessary ingredients for practitioners during this ethical navigation.

2

Development of an Ethics Code

A s practitioners of psychology, we are preoccupied with the pragmatics of the ethics code of the profession: what it is, what it really means, and how to use it. On occasion, we have asked "Where did all of this come from?" In this chapter, we explore the historic roots of the profession's ethics code, and how the code helps shape who we are and what we hold sacred, and then we discuss how an ethics code cannot be a "solve-everything cookbook."

Philosophical Basis

Ethical codes "establish a framework for professional behavior and responsibility" (Mabe & Rollin, 1986) and function as a medium for professional identity. Ethics codes are necessary but not sufficient. These codes define the role of the profession and guide its practice so that clients can trust the professionals in whose hands they place their lives (Hecker, 2003). Pope and Vasquez (1998) proposed that ethics is more than the mindless following of rules. Instead of simply listing the "dos and don'ts" of behavior, ethics codes clarify what is and is not acceptable practice, identify areas that are agreed on as concerns for the profession, and identify standards to which the profession agrees to be held accountable. Codes and rules "are not a substitute for an active,

deliberative, and creative approach to fulfilling our ethical responsibilities" (Pope & Vasquez, 1998, p. 17). Professionals in a
given field are still responsible for struggling with competing
demands, multiple perspectives, situations that are continually
evolving, and consequences that are often uncertain.

Pope and Vasquez (1998) further elaborated that ethics codes

> cannot do our questioning, thinking, feeling, and responding
> for us. Such codes can never be a substitute for the active pro-
> cess by which the individual therapist or counselor struggles
> with the sometimes bewildering, always unique constellation
> of questions, responsibilities, contexts, and competing de-
> mands of helping another person. . . . Ethics must be practical.
> Clinicians confront an almost unimaginable diversity of situ-
> ations, each with its own shifting questions, demands, and
> responsibilities. . . . Ethics that are out of touch with the prac-
> tical realities of clinical work, with the diversity and constantly
> changing nature of the therapeutic venture, are useless. (pp.
> xiii–xiv)

The right and wrong answers that many graduate students learn
in ethics classes are just the beginning. They are an important
beginning, yes—but just a beginning. When applying codes of
conduct to practice, psychologists have a responsibility to take a
wider and deeper viewpoint that responds to the needs of clients
while respecting the enormous power and trust inherent in the
psychologists' position.

Vehicle for Professional Identity

A code of conduct provides a way for psychologists entering the
profession to define themselves and to become part of a larger
identity of like-minded professionals. A code of conduct is a vehicle by which psychologists can be known to the general public
and to other professions. It must also be a means of letting others
know "that it is more than just a paper document, that it is enforced, and that members who violate the code are disciplined"
(Mabe & Rollin, 1986, p. 295). Mabe and Rollin (1986) wrote that
it is through a code of conduct that the profession has the oppor-

tunity to set the standards by which its members will interact with clients and to regulate itself.

A code of conduct may serve as an anchor in struggling with what MacKay and O'Neill (1992) termed *mixed dilemmas*—those in which ethical considerations may be blocked or challenged by obstacles such as legal systems, demands of employers, other professional relationships, and inadequate resources. Although it may be difficult to take a stand in mixed-dilemma situations, psychologists can reassure themselves that their choices and behaviors are bound by a profession-wide set of standards to guide their practice.

Limitations in Using a Code to Explicate Professional Responsibility

An ethics code provides an essential framework; however, it cannot foresee every possible dilemma and situation. Standards may come into conflict, leaving psychologists to resolve this conflict.

In the last 30 years there has been increased regulation of psychology and other psychotherapeutic professions through federal and state law, licensing boards, and legal means of redress through criminal and civil law. Although professional codes of ethics and laws may have some overlap in content, neither is exhaustive in providing for the safeguard of clients. Both serve important functions in providing protection for consumers and in providing parameters of practice for psychologists.

MacKay and O'Neill (1992) identified two distinctions within the larger concept of ethical dilemmas: (a) the perceived conflict between ethical values that seem to point toward different courses of action and (b) a conflict between what seems to be the right ethical course of action and obstructions such as employment constraints, laws, or other impediments. Unlike the Canadian Psychological Association's (2000) Code of Ethics, which contains four broad principles arranged in order of priority in considering decisions related to competing principles, the American Psychological Association's (APA's) Ethics Code (APA, 2002a) and other ethical decision-making models do not include assistance in making difficult choices.

T. S. Smith, McGuire, Abbott, and Blau (1991) surveyed 102 mental health practitioners, asking them to respond to 10 ethical dilemma vignettes developed from clinical cases. The authors found that practitioners do evaluate what should be done in dealing with an ethical conflict but may not be willing to follow through. Practitioners look to formal codes for what they *should* do but to personal values and practical considerations for what they *would* do. Respondents offered several rationales for should–would choices in the vignettes: upholding the law; upholding a code of ethics; no specific reason identified (intuition); upholding personal moral values and standards; financial need; fear of legal action; fear of verbal or social reprisal by colleagues, clients, or supervisors; and protection of personal or professional reputation. When professional codes and their application were relatively clear and were supported by legal statutes, should–would choices tended to be more consistent.

J. D. Woody's (1990) article on ethical conflicts in clinical practice is applicable to ethical dilemmas in small-community psychology. She said that rules are not absolute but subject to interpretation. The examples she offered included dilemmas of competence, integrity, client welfare, client self-determination, and confidentiality. Codes of ethics, being imperfect, do not always acknowledge conflicting obligations or offer instructions on weighing the importance of conflicting obligations.

In her discussion of personal and professional identity, J. D. Woody (1990) identified areas of importance:

□ consideration of the therapist as a person as well as an expert:
> The clinician can draw from many sources to fortify critical thinking, but the personal/professional identity ultimately chooses on the basis of a vision or beliefs about life, reality, and one's own character, that is, the kind of person one is or wants to be through this choice. (p. 143)

□ in addition, therapists must also weigh their own knowledge, competence, and integrity;

□ the expectation that helping professionals will be able to evaluate themselves clearly and with great insight; this

includes monitoring one's own competence, skills, knowledge, self, needs, and life stresses;

☐ situational factors (burnout, isolation, life crises) that can
play a part in unethical behavior;

☐ personal conscience as a basis for professional conscience,
composed of thinking, emotions, and behavior; and

☐ the human aspect of counseling; professional training of
therapists sets limits on, but does not do away with, personal influence; the therapist is a participant–observer but
cannot be completely objective; "the goal, however, is to
integrate the personal and professional identities so that
one's own knowledge, integrity, and judgment can be scru-
tinized as a factor in the process of arriving at an ethical
decision" (p. 144); this goal involves personal character,
not just professional values or skills.

Theories of ethics, professional codes of ethics, professional
theoretical premises, socio–legal context, and a therapist's personal and professional identity are all decision bases for resolving ethical concerns. Therefore, it is especially important that clinicians know the content and limitations of codes of ethics so
that their decision making can become second nature, automatic,
and intuitive (J. D. Woody, 1990).

In the final analysis, ethical decision making is a mix of intuition and rationality, along with competing values. Therapists
need to learn to pinpoint sources of the conflict and get more
information before they can make a good ethical decision (J. D.
Woody, 1990). A code with a primary focus on values may not
offer sufficient guidance, yet a code that primarily focuses on practical application "will fail to place the professional's work in a
larger context and inevitably fall short of addressing the myriad
of complicated situations that arise in a professional's life"
(Behnke, 2004, p. 58). Therefore, "the drafters of an ethics code
must achieve a balance between the general and the specific"
(Behnke, 2004, p. 58).

Evolution of the Ethics Code

Ethical codes are by nature temporary, "since they need timely
revisions which reflect changes in the culture, society and devel-

opments within the field" (Green & Hansen, 1989, p. 150). The 2002 APA Ethics Code evolved from nine previous versions, beginning 64 years earlier, in 1938, with a temporary Committee on Scientific and Professional Ethics (Bersoff & Koeppl, 1993). Although the 1938 committee did not recommend a formal ethics code, it did recommend the formation of a committee (created in 1940) to investigate unethical conduct and devise rules or principles to be considered by the larger association. As the tasks of this committee became increasingly complex, and the advice somewhat subjective, the need arose for a more formal board, the Committee on Ethical Standards for Psychologists, initiated in 1947 (Canter, Bennett, Jones, & Nagy, 1994; Pope & Vasquez, 1998).

This Committee on Ethical Standards for Psychologists used a critical-incident method of surveying the 7,500 members of APA, asking them to describe ethical decisions and relevant ethical issues from their first-hand experience. The resultant drafts, which had already been revised by a variety of groups, were published in the journal *American Psychologist*. A final version was published in 1953 (APA, 1953a). The more familiar summary document did not include incidents or elaboration, focusing instead on 19 pages of ethical principles and subprinciples (APA, 1953b). Several revisions were adopted in the next 40 years, including changes in content regarding sexual misconduct, dual relationships, advertising, and research (Canter et al., 1994; Pope & Vasquez, 1998).

The type and frequency of ethical complaints increased over the intervening years, partly because of the increase in APA membership and partly because of increased awareness and education of consumers of psychological services. Limitations because of the broad language of the Ethics Code were one of the primary motivators behind the 1992 revision, begun by a 1986 task force (Canter et al., 1994). This task force strove to create an Ethics Code that would be more easily understood and used by "psychologists, students, consumers, and ethics committees" (Canter et al., 1994, p. 18). The process included soliciting member input and publishing drafts in the *APA Monitor*. The APA Council of Representatives adopted the final version in 1992 (Canter et al., 1994).

The 1992 Ethics Code (APA, 1992) was a dramatic change from previous codes, including distinctions between ideals of practice and minimal standards of conduct "with as much specificity as possible" (Canter et al., 1994, p. 21). The 1992 Ethics Code also sought to address the dilemmas inherent in daily practice—a shift from the previous codes, which were more aspirational. The 1992 Ethics Code was a response to the need for a more practical approach in meeting the increasingly broader and more complex "knowledge base and scope of practice" (Gottlieb, 1994, p. 288) within the profession of psychology.

The next major innovation occurred with the 2002 Ethics Code. The task force that authored it (APA, 2002a) solicited comments from more than 1,300 respondents—individual APA members, state and provincial psychological associations, and APA divisions (Knapp & VandeCreek, 2003)—and the Ethics Code was "updated to reflect changes to the discipline and evolving societal needs" (Martin, 2002, p. 56). The 2002 revision process took many months. The focus was on brevity and clarity (Knapp & VandeCreek, 2003).

This latest APA Ethics Code includes "New standards on the release of test data. . . . Expanded protection of student privacy. . . . more information on informed consent in research. . . . More guidance on using new therapies. . . . (and) Clarity on terminating therapy" (Martin, 2002, pp. 56–57). References to APA practice guidelines, which are aspirational rather than enforceable, were deleted from the 2002 Ethics Code. This eliminated some confusion that was involved when disciplinary bodies attempted to use practice guidelines as a basis for disciplinary actions (Vasquez, 2003). A standard-by-standard comparison on the 1992 and 2002 Ethics Codes is available on the APA Web site (http://www.apa.org/ethics/codecompare.html) and makes clear precisely what was changed, added, and deleted in formulating the latest Ethics Code.

The 2002 APA Ethics Code comprises two major categories: (a) General Principles and (b) Ethical Standards. The General Principles attempt to assist psychologists in making decisions when faced with ethical difficulties involving conflicting standards of the Ethics Code (Fisher & Younggren, 1997) and are intended "to guide and inspire psychologists toward the very highest ethical ideals of the profession" (Knapp & VandeCreek, 2003, p. 25). The General Principles, to which psychologists should aspire, cannot be enforced; however, the Ethical Standards, which specify minimal standards of practice, can. The Ethics Code emphasizes the necessity of preventive action for the ethical practice of psychology, in an attempt to prevent possible harm to students, clients, and others who may interact with psychologists (Canter et al., 1994). There are few moral absolutes beyond the prohibition of sexual contact with current clients, sexual contact with former clients within 2 years of termination, and client abandonment (Bersoff & Koeppl, 1993).

Multiple Relationships, Bartering, and Informed Consent

The 1992 revision focused on several areas: forensic activities, sexual relationships and sexual exploitation, advertising and public statements, teaching, fees for service, third-party requests for information and services, research, publication, and continuity and confidentiality of records. The 2002 APA Ethics Code takes this focus further by clearly defining what is meant by a *multiple relationship* and by indicating that not all multiple relationships are unethical. For the purposes of this book, we focus more specifically on those areas that may be most relevant to psychologists working in small communities: sexual relationships and sexual exploitation, multiple relationships, bartering, and consent to treatment.

Changes From the 1992 Ethics Code

The 1992 APA Ethics Code more clearly defined prohibitions against sexual relationships with students or supervisees in training, even if the students or supervisees are the instigators of the relationship. In addition, the prohibition against sexual harassment was further defined and detailed (Canter et al., 1994). The latest revision of the Ethics Code (APA, 2002a) continues similar provisions (7.07 Sexual Relationships With Students and Supervisees, 3.08 Exploitative Relationships, and 6.05 Barter With Clients/Patients).

3.08 Exploitative Relationships

Psychologists do not exploit persons over whom they have supervisory, evaluative, or other authority such as clients/ patients, students, supervisees, research participants, and employees. (APA, 2002a, p. 1065)

The 1981 Ethics Code made an even broader prohibition (6a), noting that "Psychologists make every effort to avoid dual relationships that could impair their professional judgment or increase the risk of exploitations." Ten years later, the 1992 APA Ethics Code "revised and expanded the guidelines regarding dual relationships" (Sonne, 1994, p. 336). This revision provided a broader definition of *dual relationships* and acknowledged that some overlapping relationships are not necessarily harmful. Although the definition did not address the distinction "between multiple problematic relationships and accidental or incidental contacts" (Sonne, 1994, p. 339), it clearly stated that multiple relationships may not be avoidable. It did, however, urge psychologists to examine the potential risk in such relationships, particularly when there is the likelihood of exploitation or other forms of harm. It also specified that psychologists must act on behalf of clients, attempt to anticipate possible harm, and limit or change their own behavior if necessary to preserve objectivity (Gottlieb, 1994).

The 2002 Ethics Code (APA, 2002a) attempts to provide even more clarity through the language used in Standard 3.05, Multiple Relationships. This is especially important in light of the fact that about half of the complaints that came before the APA Ethics Committee involved boundary or role conflicts (Knapp & VandeCreek, 2003). This standard delineates the possible roles that may constitute multiple relationships; however, it also clearly states that "multiple relationships that would not reasonably be expected to cause impairment or risk exploitation or harm are not unethical" (APA, 2002a, p. 1065).

The issue of bartering for services was explicitly addressed for the first time in the 1992 Ethics Code, which acknowledged the necessity for bartering under certain circumstances, as long as it does not interfere with therapy or exploit clients in any way. This was an acknowledgement that bartering is widely practiced and acceptable in some cultural and situational contexts (Plaut, 1997).

The 2002 Ethics Code substantially improved the standards to state the following:

> 6.05 Barter With Clients/Patients
> Barter is the acceptance of goods, services or other nonmonetary remuneration from clients/patients in return for psychological services. Psychologists may barter only if (1) it is not clinically contraindicated, and (2) the resulting arrangement is not exploitative. (APA, 2002a, p. 1068)

This revision was an attempt to balance the reality of bartering as a practice in some small communities with protection of the client from exploitation and other related problems that may occur within the therapeutic relationship (Vasquez, 2003).

Informed consent became a critical component of the 1992 Ethics Code and of the 2002 revision:

> 3.10 Informed Consent
> (a) When psychologists conduct research or provide assessment, therapy, counseling, or consulting services in person or via electronic transmission or other forms of communication, they obtain the informed consent of the individual or individuals using language that is reasonably understandable to that person or persons except when conducting such activities without consent is mandated by law or governmental regulation or as otherwise provided in this Ethics Code. (APA, 2002a, p. 1065)

Informed consent, based on the principles of dignity and respect for client autonomy, means that clients are full and active participants in their treatment. This is both an ethical obligation and a reflection of good clinical practice. This standard defines what is required for clients to give true informed consent, both at the beginning and throughout the treatment process (Knapp & VandeCreek, 2003). Psychologists are now required to inform clients at the beginning of therapy about fees, confidentiality, procedures, and the ability to consent, and they must provide documentation of such. Psychologists in training or those who are supervised must inform clients of that fact, along with the name of the supervisor (Canter et al., 1994). Similar requirements remained in the 2002 Ethics Code.

Specific Prohibitions Against Multiple Relationships Reconsidered

The prohibition of dual relationships was first addressed by APA in 1953 (Canter et al., 1994). Boundary guidelines (including prohibitions against multiple relationships) were established to guard against the personal needs of the psychologist getting in the way of therapy (Gabbard, 1994b). The 1992 Ethics Code applies several tests to determine when a multiple relationship will be prohibited: the likelihood that (a) the psychologist's objectivity may be impaired, (b) the relationship will interfere with the psychologist's ability to effectively deliver services, and (c) the multiple relationship can lead to harm or exploitation of the client (Fisher & Younggren, 1997). These principles are also contained in the 2002 Ethics Code but are further clarified by the specific definition of *multiple relationships* included in this chapter and are addressed in more detail in chapter 3.

The 1992 Ethics Code addressed the relevant difficulties inherent in small-community practice in Standard 1.17a, Multiple Relationships, which indicates that "in many communities and situations, it may not be feasible or reasonable for psychologists to avoid social or other nonprofessional contacts with persons such as patients, clients, students, supervisees, or research participants" (APA, 1992, p. 1601). The 2002 Ethics Code does not include a similar reference. It does, however, admonish psychologists to clarify role expectations and limits on confidentiality that may arise as a result of conflicting roles. The 2002 Ethics Code purposefully defines *multiple relationships* as follows:

> (a) A multiple relationship occurs when a psychologist is in a professional role with a person and (1) at the same time is in another role with the same person, (2) at the same time is in a relationship with a person closely associated with or related to the person with whom the psychologist has the professional relationship, or (3) promises to enter into another relationship

in the future with the person or a person closely associated with or related to the person. (APA, 2002a, p. 1065)

Treatment boundaries serve the essential function of defining the roles for both psychologists and clients. This framework "includes both the structural elements (e.g., time, place, and money) and the content" (D. Smith & Fitzpatrick, 1995, p. 499) of therapy relationships. D. Smith and Fitzpatrick (1995) went on to say that proper maintenance of therapeutic boundaries ensures the objectivity of psychologists and the autonomy of clients while fostering a foundation of safety and trust essential to the quality of the therapeutic alliance. It is what Lyn (1990) referred to as "the borders of the therapeutic relationship"— the times in between sessions when psychologist and client should not interact. In the 2002 Ethics Code, these times were reconsidered, especially within small communities.

However, it is essential that psychologists, even in small communities, not justify multiple relationships as necessary or inevitable (Borys, 1992). The 1992 Ethics Code took context into consideration but did not clarify what characteristics of the relationship should be considered and may have, in fact, confounded the situation by referring to outcome rather than type of relationship (Brownlee, 1996). As we mentioned earlier in this section, the 2002 Ethics Code contains more specific language, in Standard 3.05(a), Multiple Relationships.

Some difficulties may occur when dealing with vagueness and use of qualifiers in the Ethics Code, especially in application to multiple relationships. Bersoff (1994) cautioned that such ambiguity may lead to the enforcement of only the most serious lapses, or what he termed "behavior that is so egregiously wrong that no code would be necessary to condemn it" (p. 384).

The emphasis on avoiding multiple relationships that have the potential for impaired objectivity, competence, or effectiveness places greater responsibility on individual psychologists to make decisions about future possibilities for exploitation or harm to clients. There is an intense need to teach ethical decision making and to open up discussion of the complex realities of its application. An important addition to the 2002 Ethics Code was a specific definition of *multiple relationships* and a clarification that not all multiple relationships are inherently unethical as long as the relationships would not cause harm to clients or impairment by the psychologist (D. Smith, 2003a; Vasquez, 2003). This change is an acknowledgment that in some situations and communities, multiple relationships may be "unavoidable or might benefit the client or both" (Vasquez, 2003, p. 566).

It is important to keep in mind that provisional consideration of the acceptability of some multiple or overlapping relationships does not mean that the second relationship is without rules or limitations. Behavior that is incompatible within a therapeutic relationship should not always or automatically be acceptable within an outside relationship (Kagle & Giebelhausen, 1994). As Lazurus (1998) suggested in the following,

> The therapist is to be fully accountable and must ponder issues such as potential risks of harming the patient, possible conflicts of interest, whether or not a dual relationship will impair the therapist's judgment, if the patient's rights or autonomy will be infringed upon, and whether the therapist will gain a personal advantage over the client. (p. 24)

Multiple relationships have the potential to erode and distort the therapeutic relationship, to create conflicts of interest, and to compromise the objectivity that is essential to sound professional judgment (Pope, 1991). However, most small-community psychologists welcomed the recognition in the 1992 Ethics Code that their practice settings did not always lend themselves to the preclusion of all multiple relationships—an issue that is addressed with more specificity in the 2002 Ethics Code. The 1992 Ethics Code recognized that such therapeutic relationships may be concurrent or consecutive and acknowledged that it may not be reasonable to expect that small-community psychologists avoid all out-of-therapy contact with their clients (Sonne, 1994). A good example is the small community of a university training program in which one is teacher, supervisor, mentor, evaluator, and research collaborator to students and is also expected to socialize with those same students.

In this chapter, we have explored the complexity of ethical behavior within the context of the professional code of conduct for psychologists. The task is much more difficult than just following a few simple rules. Regulating human behavior in a way that maximizes positive human interaction and behavior, both professional and personal, is a complex and difficult process. The practice of psychology within a small community necessitates a deeper understanding of professional conduct and decision making, while taking into account context, culture, and community values.

3

Current Concerns in Small Communities

In this chapter and those that follow, we focus more specifically on the challenges and strengths inherent in small-community practice. In this chapter, we examine ethical and unethical conduct, traditional and small-community similarities and differences, the problematic nature of overlapping relationships, sexual and nonsexual dual relationships, and other areas of ethical concern.

Definition of Multiple Relationships

The 2002 American Psychological Association (APA) Ethics Code (APA, 2002a) is the first iteration of the code to explicitly define multiple relationships. It also clarifies that not all multiple relationships are unethical if such relationships are not prohibited by the rule. This clarification recognizes that "individual psychologists may perform a variety of roles" (Fisher, 2003, p. 65). Incidental encounters and some social contacts are not considered unethical unless these contacts or relationships could reasonably be expected to impair the psychologist's objectivity or harm the client (Fisher, 2003).

Another addition to the 2002 Ethics Code is what Behnke (2004) identified as the "consideration-of-the-future aspect"—an indication from the psychologist that another relationship will occur at a later date. Behnke (2004) went on to note that the code includes criteria for unethical multiple relationships—impaired objectivity or competence and a risk of harm—along with the touchstone of what a reasonable psychologist would do. The following is from the 2002 Ethics Code:

3.05 Multiple Relationships

(a) A multiple relationship occurs when a psychologist is in a professional role with a person and (1) at the same time is in another role with the same person, (2) at the same time is in a relationship with a person closely associated with or related to the person with whom the psychologist has the professional relationship, or (3) promises to enter into another relationship in the future with the person or a person closely associated with or related to the person.

A psychologist refrains from entering into a multiple relationship if the multiple relationship could reasonably be expected to impair the psychologist's objectivity, competence, or effectiveness in performing his or her functions as a psychologist, or otherwise risks exploitation or harm to the person with whom the professional relationship exists.

Multiple relationships that would not reasonably be expected to cause impairment or risk exploitation or harm are not unethical.

(b) If a psychologist finds that, due to unforeseen factors, a potentially harmful multiple relationship has arisen, the psychologist takes reasonable steps to resolve it with due regard for the best interests of the affected person and maximal compliance with the Ethics Code.

(c) When psychologists are required by law, institutional policy, or extraordinary circumstances to serve in more than one role in judicial or administrative proceedings, at the outset they clarify role expectations and the extent of confidentiality and thereafter as changes occur.

3.06 Conflict of Interest

Psychologists refrain from taking on a professional role when personal, scientific, professional, legal, financial, or other interests or relationships could reasonably be expected to (1) impair their objectivity, competence, or effectiveness in performing their functions as psychologists or (2) expose the person or organization with whom the professional relationship exists to harm or exploitation.

3.08 Exploitative Relationships

Psychologists do not exploit persons over whom they have supervisory, evaluative, or other authority such as clients/ patients, students, supervisees, research participants, and employees. (APA, 2002a, p. 1065)

One of the most significant statements in the 1992 APA Ethics Code, carried forward in the 2002 Ethics Code, is the attention given to the pervasive nature of multiple relationships in many small communities. Multiple relationships are also referred to as *dual relationships* or *overlapping relationships*. The relationships, which can be concurrent or consecutive, occur when psychologists have other connections with clients in addition to the therapist–client relationship. Examples of such roles include a therapist who is also the business partner of a client, a supervisor who is also the therapist of a supervisee, and a therapist who has previously been a longtime friend of a client (Welfel, 1998).

Any number of other overlapping roles can potentially occur, particularly in a small community. Even when a relationship is not prohibited by the Ethics Code, psychologists still have the responsibility to guard against impaired objectivity, especially in small-community settings, where overlapping relationships may be a frequent occurrence. Although many overlapping relationships do not raise ethical questions, they may "provide fertile ground for the development of problematic situations and, therefore, caution is in order" (Haas & Malouf, 1989, p. 57).

An ongoing social relationship between a psychologist and client may limit the client's freedom to self-disclose. Also, it is unlikely that a psychologist can maintain the simultaneous roles of friend and therapist, especially as the process of therapy usually prevents a truly equal social relationship. With a posttherapy social relationship, the client is also precluded from ever returning to the original therapeutic relationship (Haas & Malouf, 1989).

Lamb, Catanzaro, and Moorman (2004) recommended that several factors be considered in evaluating nonsexual overlapping relationships: context, history, current status of the relationship, the client's reaction, and the psychologist's explanation of the purpose of the boundary-crossing within the context of therapeutic goals. However, Lamb et al. (2004) identified an important point—the ambiguity of determining whether a particular action is likely to cause impairment, exploitation, or harm.

What Makes Multiple Relationships Problematic?

Gabbard (1994b) provided one of the most effective and descriptive examples of the problems inherent in multiple relationships: "The problem lies in knowing when to disregard boundaries and when to honor them. Clinical judgment in this regard is highly variable from one therapist to another. Though many musicians can play the scales, not all can improvise" (p. 283). To add to the confusion, the ethical codes across the helping professions, such as psychology, social work, and counseling, are not consistent. According to Moleski and Kiselica (2005),

> A comparison of the ethics and standards of practice of the American Counseling Association (1995), APA (2002), the American Association of Marriage and Family Therapists (AAMFT, 2001), the National Association of Social Workers (NASW, 1996), and the American Mental Health Counselors Association (AMHCA, 2000) supports the position that there are variation, ambiguity, and ambivalence regarding dual relationships. (p. 5)

In spite of the confusion, as Herlihy and Corey (1992) stated, multiple relationships can be problematic. They may be pervasive, difficult to recognize, sometimes unavoidable, the subject of conflicting advice, potentially harmful, and a risk to consumers and professionals, and they may affect a range of others (consumers, other professionals, the profession of psychology, and society).

They Are Pervasive

The potential for overlapping relationships may come from a variety of roles and people. Bartering, counseling friends or family members of clients, socializing with former clients, and supervising former clients are just a sample of the possibilities (Herlihy & Corey, 1992).

Life in small communities, which have fewer inhabitants and the possibility of less access to a wide range of professional services and service providers, often means that psychologists must consider almost every person in the community a prospective client (Faulkner & Faulkner, 1997). Johnson, Ralph, and Johnson (2005) described such a small community when they wrote about being a psychologist on an aircraft carrier:

> As a result of the embedded psychologist's multiple identities, he or she can be said to maintain dual-role relationships with every client to whom professional services are rendered. . . . One area of particular ethical difficulty for the embedded psychologist is the management of perpetual and inescapable multiple-role relationships. (pp. 73, 74)

Even if each person in a small community is not a prospective client, it is likely that clients or prospective clients are connected to others through business, social, or familial relationships.

They Are Difficult to Recognize

Dual, multiple, or overlapping relationships are often easier to define than to recognize. Does the degree of involvement affect the definition? How do the dynamics of the relationship define it? What kinds of posttherapy relationships—if any—are acceptable or ethical?

It may also be difficult to know whether the potential for a dual or multiple relationship exists. Psychologists cannot always predict who will come for therapy in the future or even who might be related to whom, particularly in a small community. This may prove especially difficult for psychologists who relocate to a small community in which the established community members are more familiar with extended family relationships and with patterns of allegiances, alienations, and friendships.

Steinman, Richardson, and McEnroe (1998) outlined a set of traps into which helping professionals may fall when making decisions related to ethical dilemmas. The most relevant of these include

- [ ] confusion among ethical codes, personal values and standards, and religious convictions;
- [ ] the belief that ethical questions do not have right or wrong answers because "the circumstances under which they occurred (rather than the behavior itself) must be taken into consideration in making the decision" (p. 7), and
- [ ] the difficulty of "taking sides from among two or more conflicting interests" (p. 9).

A heightened awareness of these potential traps and possible conflicts is a part of everyday practice for psychologists in small communities. They are more likely than their traditional urban counterparts to face such dilemmas and thus must be continually aware of such potential conflicts.

They Sometimes Are Unavoidable

The distinction of *sometimes* unavoidable is an important one. The argument put forth by some psychologists, particularly within small communities, is that multiple relationships *are* unavoidable. Without careful consideration of alternatives, this argument can lead to the mistake of widespread acceptance of any and all multiple relationships. Psychologists who view multiple relationships as unavoidable in small communities risk the unfortunate mindset that they have little control over situations and therefore have no responsibility to maintain appropriate professional relationships (Pope, 1991). Herlihy and Corey (1992) also pointed out that boundaries between overlapping relationships—for example, the distinction between a friendship and a professional therapy relationship— may be unclear. It may be all too easy for the conversation within a therapy session to shift to a more casual and mutual level, or for a psychologist to let information shared within a therapy session affect the dynamics of an out-of-therapy friendship.

They Are the Subject of Limited Advice

The 2002 APA Ethics Code offers broad relevant principles but little specific guidance regarding nonsexual posttherapy relationships with former clients. Kessler and Waehler (2005) described the complexity of the issue:

> We strongly believe that the decision to negotiate multiple relationships with clients always depends on context and most times must be avoided. However, we hope to challenge the inflexible, knee jerk reaction to avoid all multiple relationships that we and others (e.g., Behnke, 2004) have personally observed among many practitioners. (p. 66)

There are no easy answers that can be applied to decisions regarding the advisability of multiple relationships (Anderson & Kitchener, 1998). However, "Psychologists are not relieved from acting morally toward a person just because the person is no longer a client" (Anderson & Kitchener, 1998, p. 98).

Many mental health professionals, including participants in a study conducted by Salisbury and Kinnier (1996), are in friendships with former clients and view those friendships as appropriate under some circumstances. Although not specifically prohibited, psychologists must avoid nonsexual posttherapy relationships that would create a risk for harm, a possibility that is not easily or accurately predictable. An important factor in the ethical success of these relationships is the degree to which psychologists can differentiate between themselves and their clients in the maintenance of appropriate interpersonal boundaries. If compounded by significant life stress on the part of a psychologist, it is likely that the risk of less insightful and more harmful decisions will increase (Baer & Murdock, 1995).

According to Herlihy and Corey (1992), all ethics codes for the helping professions warn against dual relationships. Disagreement arises, however, over how those codes should be interpreted and whether they serve as guidelines or as rigid prohibitions.

They Are Potentially Harmful

Overlapping relationships may not always be abusive or exploitive, but the potential is heightened by the existence of a second relationship (Herlihy & Corey, 1992; Pearson & Piazza, 1997; D. Smith & Fitzpatrick, 1995). The addition of a personal relationship to a professional relationship creates the potential for harm because of the power differential between professional and client (Pearson & Piazza, 1997). For example, a psychologist who enters into a business or close personal relationship with a former client may not be able to counteract, and may even subtly enjoy, the transference of "expertness" from the previous therapy relationship. The position of respect that psychologists hold (i.e., hearing privileged information, advising, counseling) makes it even more important that psychologists not use their position to advantage themselves, both socially and professionally (Vasquez, 1991).

In an article on seeing acquaintances as clients, Roll and Millen (1981) identified possible complications as a potential loss of friendship, problems with transference, and the "support of grandiosity" (p. 181). The inequity of roles between therapist as "expert" and client as "inadequate" (p. 181) can lead to disequilibrium in both the professional and friendship relationships. As Koocher and Keith-Spiegel (1998) pointed out,

> Successful personal relationships satisfy mutual needs, are not necessarily goal directed, and are emotionally involving for all parties. Professional relationships, on the other hand, serve the needs of the client and are emotionally involving for all parties. Friendships and family relationships aspire to longevity, whereas professional relationships are designed to progress as rapidly as possible and terminate once the therapeutic goals have been achieved. (p. 182)

Borys (1992) addressed the difficulty of psychotherapy with friends and family members by noting that "Friendships and family relationships have histories which often include expectations, loyalties, and assumptions which may conflict with actions taken by the therapist within the context of the therapeutic relationship" (p. 444). The potential for damage and misunderstanding exists for both the therapeutic relationship and the friendship or family relationship.

Borys (1994) used the example of a therapist who attends a client's wedding as a gesture of support but then observes behavior that illuminates issues yet to be addressed in therapy. The therapist is left with the conflict of bringing up the wedding observations in therapy or keeping them private. Either choice could be damaging to the client.

Kitchener and Harding (1990) suggested that psychologists should enter into dual relationships only when the risks of harm are small and the potential benefits are great. They identified three factors to consider: (a) incompatible expectations, (b) divergent responsibilities, and (c) the power and prestige of the psychologist. Divided loyalties, loss of objectivity, and vulnerability of clients are possible obstacles, with the responsibility falling on the psychologist to make sure that the client is not harmed or injured.

They Involve Risk to Clients and to Psychologists

Clients who feel exploited by overlapping relationships may feel confused, hurt, angry, and betrayed. This betrayal may have long-lasting consequences and may preclude such clients from ever seeking help from other professionals. Alternatively, they may feel trapped and dependent on the relationship, in spite of feelings of anger and confusion (Herlihy & Corey, 1992).

A nonsexual posttherapy relationship between a psychologist and former client precludes the client from ever returning to that psychologist for therapy in the future. Because it is difficult to predict the path, length, depth, or importance of the posttherapy relationship, it is not easy to assess whether it is worthwhile for the client to give up the possibility of a future therapeutic relationship. It can also be awkward to shift the dynamics of a therapy relationship to a posttherapy relationship of more mutual advice-giving and support.

Although psychologists are not legally obligated to take someone back as a client, Pipes (1999) suggested that the nature of the therapy relationship is of utmost consideration. He advised that many clients may remain vulnerable following termination of therapy or may continue to have very strong feelings about their psychologist or about therapy. Pipes (1999) also reminded readers that former clients may request records or require court testimony from a psychologist. It would be difficult in such a situation to argue that a psychologist's objectivity was not impaired by the occurrence of a nonsexual posttherapy relationship. Many therapy relationships could be further strengthened if the possibility for posttherapy contact did not exist, leaving clients with fewer inhibitions about what they might say in therapy or with fewer fantasies about the possibility of an outside-of-therapy relationship.

Psychologists who are involved in overlapping relationships that turn negative or acrimonious risk loss of professional credibility and professional reputation, possible litigation, complaints to licensing boards, and possible restrictions to or loss of licensure. For example, a psychologist who enters into a posttherapy personal relationship with a client may be the subject of conversation among others in the community if the relationship ends badly. Even problematic overlapping relationships that are undetected or unreported affect the psychologist involved, may lead the psychologist to doubt his or her competence and sense of self, and may make it easier for him or her to perform further violations (Herlihy & Corey, 1992).

They Have Effects on Other Consumers, Other Professionals, the Profession, and Society

Clients who are not involved in an overlapping relationship with a particular psychologist may resent that other clients have the opportunity to be involved in more than a professional relationship with the psychologist. Although it may be difficult for those other clients to openly question overlapping relationships between their psychologist and other clients, they may be resentful and thus less likely to refer others to that psychologist (Chapman, 1997; Herlihy & Corey, 1992).

It is not only clients who might be damaged. The resultant negative publicity can spread to other professionals, other individuals within the community, and the larger society (Chapman, 1997; Herlihy & Corey, 1992; Pipes, 1999). Nonpsychologist colleagues may be reluctant to work with such psychologists and may resent having to explain negative fallout from overlapping relationships that those psychologists have with clients. Sell, Gottlieb, and Schoenfeld (1986) suggested that the effects of unethical and criminal actions by psychotherapists have had a profound effect on all mental health professionals, in terms of both negative publicity and increased liability insurance premiums.

It is difficult to confront psychologists who are engaging in damaging overlapping relationships. For example, a psychologist may confront a colleague who is involved in an out-of-therapy relationship with a client. The confronting psychologist may be criticized by the colleague, by the client, and by others in the community who do not realize the potential problems such a relationship can cause. Ignoring what is happening, and therefore condoning it through default, can create morale problems within an agency and promote an unfortunate image of psychology among nonpsychologists who may be unfamiliar with the standards of the profession (Herlihy & Corey, 1992).

Ill-considered behavior can be deleterious to the reputation of particular psychologists and to the entire profession of psychology, especially in some small communities in which psychology is already regarded with suspicion and distrust. If psychologists do not take on the responsibility of regulating their own profession, then regulatory agencies may increase their efforts to do so, and potential clients may hesitate to seek assistance (Herlihy & Corey, 1992).

What Constitutes Unethical Conduct?

While prohibiting sexual relationships between psychologists and former clients for at least 2 years after the end of the professional relationship, the APA Ethics Code contains "no explicit statements regarding the appropriateness of engaging in post-termination social, business or professional relationships" (Lamb et al., 1994, p. 270). Koocher and Keith-Spiegel (1998) concluded that "Psychologists are more likely to be judged culpable when a small-world hazard was perceived in advance *and alternatives were clearly available*. The psychologists undertook a professional relationship anyway, which later resulted in charges of exploitation, prejudice, or harm" (p. 192; italics in original).

The concept of impaired objectivity as a barrier to possible multiple or overlapping relationships is important to consider in deciding whether a particular situation conforms to the ethical standard. However, it is much more difficult when psychologists try to anticipate factors that could possibly impair their objectivity at a later date. Although most of us would like to think that we could anticipate any possible challenges to our objectivity, none of us can ever guarantee that unforeseen circumstances or situations will not arise. In addition, Koocher and Keith-Spiegel (1998) suggested that "For psychologists already predisposed to blend roles, rationalization processes are probably well under way, thus subverting the caliber of any risk assessment" (p. 173). The authors also pointed out that the private, intimate nature of the therapy relationship, along with the power inherent in the role of the therapist, combine to provide "an almost ideal environment for emotionally or morally precarious professionals to attempt to fulfill their personal needs" (Koocher & Keith-Spiegel, 1998, p. 173).

Younggren and Gottlieb (2004) indicated that a psychologist who enters into an overlapping relationship with a client must manage the relationships so that the therapeutic relationship is not damaged by the other relationship. They pointed out the need for both an initial conversation with the client before entering into an overlapping relationship and ongoing examination and discussion throughout the course of the overlap. The obligation to safeguard the therapeutic alliance falls on the psychologist, especially as it is unreasonable to expect that the client would recognize potentially damaging situations.

The burden of proof ultimately falls on psychologists to prove that they are able to be objective in their professional interactions with clients. There should be little difficulty, however, in agreeing that some behaviors—for example, sexual relationships with clients, exploitation and manipulation of clients for personal gain, jeopardizing client welfare, and breaking confidentiality—are clearly unacceptable (Lazarus, 1998). It is also important that the psychologist consider whose needs are being met by an overlapping relationship while considering professional standards and cultural norms (Barnett, 2004). The responsibility lies with the psychologist to know which behaviors may help clients and which behaviors may harm them (Vasquez, 2003). Haas and Malouf (1989) included three guidelines to consider before entering into an overlapping relationship: (a) Will the relationship inhibit the client's ability to make autonomous decisions? (b) Will the relationship restrict the psychologist's actions and responses within therapy? and (c) What are the motivations of the psychologist?

Traditional Urban and Small-Community Similarities and Differences

The issue of ethical dilemmas and decision making is compounded for psychologists working in small communities and rural areas. Prevailing standards in training, ethical codes, and regulations are not so easily applied in rural and small-community practice, in which it is essential to understand what Gutheil and Gabbard (1998) described as "the critical role of the context in which behavior occurs" (p. 411). Cultural differences, along with what Purtilo and Sorrell (1986) described as the "intricate web of professional–personal roles" (p. 23), complicate professional boundary issues. Overlapping relationships are difficult to avoid in rural and other small communities, in which community involvement lessens suspicion and increases approachability and in which "denying help to a potential client because of a preexisting relationship could mean that the person gets no help at all" (D. Smith & Fitzpatrick, 1995, p. 502).

The uniqueness and complexity of each professional interaction, combined with a need to be cognizant of relevant laws and standards, is especially present in small-community psychological practice. As Rich (1990) stated, "Informal expectations and formal rules are more likely to come into conflict with each other in rural practice than they are in urban settings" (p. 33). Yet these urban–rural differences and conflicts are not adequately addressed in professional codes of ethics, and these professional codes and guidelines frequently "tend to place the rural practitioner in opposition to prevailing rural community standards" (Rich, 1990, p. 17). Rich's words ring true for many other small communities, even those that have sprung up within a larger urban area, such as a deaf community or an ethnic immigrant community.

In these and other small communities, the urban standard of a psychologist intentionally living separate from clients would likely lead to distrust of the psychologist. Members of small communities often seek out treatment from an individual psychologist precisely because they *do* know the person, know others who are being treated by the psychologist, or have seen and interacted with the psychologist at community events. As Fisher (2003) stated, "in some instances the best interests of the affected person and maximal compliance with other standards in the Ethics Code may require psychologists to remain in the multiple roles" (p. 68).

Psychologists enter into a professional fiduciary relationship with clients, who place trust into that relationship. Psychologists have knowledge and expertise that can be of help to clients. This power must not be used in ways that exploit clients and must always be used in the clients' best interests. Clients may lack the sophistication to evaluate services rendered and must be able to trust professionals to provide the best and most appropriate treatment (Kutchins, 1991). For a practitioner who is one of only a few psychologists in a small community, the responsibility looms large to provide competent and ethical services. Most clients perceive mental health professionals as powerful, and this "imbalance of power exists regardless of what transpires in the future between the counselor and the client" (Chapman, 1997, p. 75).

Psychologists are likely to encounter difficulty in applying their traditional, urban-based skills to small-community settings. Until recently, most psychologists have received little, if any, training in graduate school on the ethical issues inherent to small-community practice.

Increased Visibility and Concern About Potential Harm

A lack of privacy and anonymity is the price paid for being well known and well liked in a small community. The work of small-community psychologists is often seen as an extension of themselves (Heyman & VandenBos, 1989; Klopfer, 1990), and professional roles are often defined by personal interactions (Kofoed & Cutler, 1982). This high visibility can be a disadvantage, because opinions in the small community can affect one's professional reputation more profoundly than in a traditional urban setting, where one's personal and professional lives are more separate (Catalano, 1997; Dunbar, 1982). Psychologists in small communities may feel like they are continually on display and that actions, values, and behaviors in their personal lives can have a major impact on their professional reputation. As Catalano (1997) indicated, "For the therapist who lives and practices in the same community, the anonymity which facilitates boundary delineation does not exist" (p. 24).

Concept of Treatment Boundaries

Treatment boundaries are more than just a set of rules for disciplining errant psychologists and enforcing distance and remoteness between psychologist and client (Gutheil & Gabbard, 1998). Clear boundaries serve a higher purpose in "maintaining the integrity of the therapy process" (Schank, Slater, Banerjee-Stevens, & Skovholt, 2003, p. 191) while protecting both clients and the therapeutic frame to "create an atmosphere of safety and predictability within which the treatment can thrive" (Gutheil & Gabbard, 1998, p. 410).

Therapeutic Frame With a Defined Set of Roles for Participants

The safety of the clearly delineated roles and functions of traditional psychologists is not available to their small-community colleagues. To be accepted in the community, small-community psychologists must balance conflicts between personal and professional roles. They must also work within the existing community system; establish support networks; and use a systems approach to understand politics, power structure, and informal communication networks (M. J. Jeffrey & Reeve, 1978; Sobel, 1984).

Psychologists who practice in more traditional settings face some of these same challenges within their work settings, but they have the luxury of much more clearly defined demands. Their work usually begins and ends in the office. However, offering services only in the office does not meet the needs of many small communities. Hargrove's (1982) description of the dilemmas faced by rural psychologists will sound familiar to other small-community psychologists. He stated that they must cope with a "multitude of involvements and levels of involvement" (p. 22) and with "multiple levels of relationships" (p. 23). These psychologists are "subject to a wide range of demands at any given time" (p. 23). Their response affects how they and their agency are seen by the community and increases the importance of their sensitivity to community needs.

Underlying Principles

In accordance with the General Principles of the APA Ethics Code (2002a), psychologists should be guided by and aspire to uphold beneficence and nonmaleficence, fidelity and responsibility, integrity, justice, and respect for people's rights and dignity. Such principles require that psychologists interact with former clients in ways that reflect adherence to these principles and avoidance of harm (Anderson & Kitchener, 1998).

Although these principles may be difficult to define or apply in some situations, they are a vital foundation for practitioners in psychology and other helping professions. Without such principles, the moral foundation of the profession would be open to question and susceptible to corruption.

Quality of the Therapeutic Alliance

The relationship between clients and psychologists differs from most other involvements between people. The necessity for psychologists to maintain objectivity and not pursue their own needs at the expense of their clients is a central tenet of the profession (Borys, 1992).

This alliance is essential to the success of therapy, for without a sound relationship the best therapy techniques fail miserably (Bachelor & Horvath, 1999). The importance of the therapeutic alliance cannot be overestimated and must be at the forefront of concern for psychologists striving to practice ethically and successfully.

Rationale for Maintaining Treatment Boundaries

A traditional model of ethical psychological practice holds professionals responsible for maintaining distance from clients outside of the therapy session. According to Pope (1985), psychologists must place the client's best interest first in return for the special status that is accorded mental health professionals. Psychologists are powerful "by virtue of the client's need for professional services and the structure of the relationship itself" (Pope, 1985, p. 5). Clients may be vulnerable and lack "the objectivity and ability to exercise genuinely free choice" (Pope, 1985, p. 5). This power continues even after the therapy relationship ends. Treatment boundaries must be imposed to provide "a therapeutic frame which defines a set of roles for the participants in the therapeutic process" (D. Smith & Fitzpatrick, 1995, p. 499).

Boundaries may also serve "as a metaphor for the internal structure of the patient's emotional life" (Borys, 1994, p. 270) and may be necessary for the progress of clients in therapy. Clients whose internal structure is chaotic and unpredictable need the structure and stability provided by clear and consistent boundaries, with the hope that they will eventually internalize "the calming and organizing experience of this structure as a model for a more organized inner life" (Borys, 1994, p. 270).

A *fiduciary relationship* occurs when confidence and trust are placed in professionals on whose advice and judgment the client has come to rely. Professionals have special power through their ability to influence clients and the clients' best interests, and thus they are bound to act in the best interest of the client and not promote their own interests at the client's expense (Kutchins, 1991).

Kitchener (1988) identified conflicts between professional and personal/business/political obligations as conflicts of interest. Psychologists must put the needs of others above their own and are obliged to use their own professional knowledge in the best interest of consumers, rather than themselves. Kitchener pointed out that psychologists cannot sacrifice objectivity and must exercise due care with potential role conflicts. If such conflicts do occur, the psychologist has a responsibility to minimize the impact.

In their book on ethics in psychotherapy, Pope and Vasquez (1998) stated that "dual relationships can jeopardize professional judgment, clients' welfare, and the process of therapy itself" (p. 193). The blurring of professional roles "erodes and distorts the professional nature of the therapeutic relationship, which is

secured within a reliable set of boundaries upon which both therapist and patient can depend" (Pope & Vasquez, 1998, p. 115). The
fiduciary nature of such a relationship means that clients cannot
be on equal footing with therapists. Dual relationships create conflicts of interest that compromise the professional distance and
judgment that are necessary to best serve clients. Clients may al-
ter their own behavior in therapy if there is a possibility of a relationship outside of therapy. Psychologists need to avoid such dual
relationships to be able to render objective information regarding clients.

Psychologists are also advised to avoid personal and social relationships with clients. Such relationships are inherently influ-
enced by the power differential between the parties and may negatively affect the therapy, friendship, or both. Psychologists may
not be as confrontational, may lose objectivity, and may struggle
with the need to be liked by clients with whom they have an
outside-of-therapy relationship (Corey, Corey, & Callanan, 1998).
Butler (1990) emphasized that

> A key question to ask is whether or not the dual relationship
> will in any way inhibit the client's actions and choices in other
> areas of their [sic] life, and if there are ways in which the client
> will feel that he or she cannot disagree with the therapist be-
> cause of outside demands of any sort. (p. 23)

We are describing a major dilemma. However, although these
questions may be helpful in examining potentially prohibited dual
relationships in the practice of good psychotherapy in traditional
urban settings, they may not be applicable in many small communities. To win the trust that is essential to successful small-
community practice, psychologists must be viewed as active members of their communities. They must maintain their own
professional and personal boundaries but in a manner somewhat
different from their traditional urban counterparts (Schank &
Skovholt, 1997). This is the dilemma.

The example that follows, and the examples that we use
throughout this chapter, are taken from our own work: Schank
(1994) and Schank and Skovholt (1997). The psychologists quoted
are from small towns, but the examples are also valid and common for other small or contained communities. One small-town

psychologist provided this example of out-of-therapy contact with clients:

> I think one of the areas that I can think of is church. Because it is such a small community, you don't have a choice of a lot of denominations. . . . all of a sudden in walks a client who didn't know that I was [a member there]. Well, I can't ask them to leave. I don't want to, and I shouldn't have to. . . . I just try to let the client or the former client make the first move toward me. I don't make a point of going up to them. If that appears not so warm and cordial, that may be a little difficult for them. Once they do come up to me, I say, "I'm glad that you came over." . . . Usually my clients or former clients are very warm and friendly and do come over and want to say hi. The children, particularly, come up; and again, you get into that little gray area. I have several kids [as clients] that I have seen before they came to church. Now they come to church, they see me, and they run up and put their arms around me and hug me. Of course, in the therapeutic setting that would be totally out of line. But it is at church, there are lots of people, and the kids are very warm and open. I make sure that their parents are there. . . . At first, I was kind of at a loss. Then I decided that I had to leave my setting behind. I can't carry my setting with me every place I go in a small town. I think church is one place that I've noticed that you can't cut it off and just go to another church. You can't avoid people all your life in a small town. (Schank, 1994, p. 45)

Another psychologist offered a different example:

> I belong to a couple of conservation organizations, and paths cross. I think, in general, that the philosophy and intention to try and say that therapy can only be in this room is probably a distortion. It probably is really an inaccuracy in that if I am secure in my work, I should be just as able to walk out at a local event and say hello and not make a big deal out of it and go on with my life. (Schank, 1994, p. 46)

Sexual Dual Relationships

Sexual dual relationships with current clients are never appropriate, even in small communities. The prohibition of sexual intimacy with clients "is the clearest prohibition in all mental health ethics codes and practice laws and one of the oldest ethical mandates in the health care professions" (Vasquez, 2003, p. 564). This was outlined 2,500 years ago in the Hippocratic Oath and is the basis of current standards outlawing such relationships. However, Brodsky (1989) indicated that it was addressed even earlier in the ancient code of Nigerian healing arts. Although laws differ from state to state in regard to the length of time that is necessary after termination of therapy before psychologists can engage in sexual relationships with former clients (or whether such relationships can ever be considered acceptable), none allow sexual relationships between psychologists and current clients. As Pope and Vasquez (1998) pointed out, "That this prohibition has remained constant over so long a time and throughout so many diverse cultures reflects to some extent the recognition that such intimacies place the patient at risk for exceptional harm" (p. 161).

All professional ethics codes forbid sexual contact between therapists and current clients, but they vary in how they deal with posttherapy relationships (Schoener & Luepker, 1996). Complications of such sexual contact include "abuse of power, exploitation of trust, potential harm to the client, and the undermining of the therapy itself" (Schoener & Luepker, 1996, p. 392). Schoener and Luepker (1996) expanded the discussion by applying it to the difficulties of sexual contact with therapy group members. They identified further complications of betraying the trust of other group members, creating confusing group dynamics, and breaking the overall injunction against sexual contact between group members.

Schoener (1986) offered a list of nine particularly useful factors to weigh when considering the risks of posttermination relationships: (a) the length and level of therapeutic involvement; (b) the degree of transference, dependency, or power inequity that remains after termination; (c) personality variables and therapy style; (d) whether there has been therapeutic deception; (e) whether there was an actual termination; (f) who initiated the posttermination contact; (g) whether the pros and cons of such a relationship have been discussed; (h) whether the psychologist has sought consultation; and (i) consideration of the legal context, professional setting, and local standards.

These factors illustrate the complexities and ambiguity contained in any discussion of a posttermination sexual relationship, and they are even more complicated within certain cultural or other small-community settings. Psychologists can never be really sure that their own assessments of such situations are completely objective or that clients will not claim later that such posttermination sexual relationships were coercive or damaging, especially if the relationship ends badly. Such relationships must be considered high risk, and the potential for harm is significant.

Psychologists should remember that it will be their responsibility to prove that a former client has not been exploited through a posttherapy sexual relationship, should a complaint be lodged. As Vasquez (1991) cautioned, "To rationalize the acceptability of sex after termination, one must demonstrate that transference no longer exists, and we know of no good research that demonstrates that the transference is usually resolved" (p. 51). In addition to "interrupting the post-therapy integration process" (Vasquez, 1991, p. 52), clients no longer have the option of returning to therapy with a psychologist with whom they had or are having a sexual posttherapy relationship.

Taking a different angle, while attending to the overlapping roles in small communities, Gonsiorek and Brown (1986) included possible complications of applying prohibitions against posttermination sexual relationships. They suggested that such a ban makes sense at first glance, especially in ensuring that client welfare is primary. However, they contended that a simple ban on such relationships needs to be reexamined under a broader context of dual-relationship complexities, both sexual and nonsexual, that includes discussion of small-community issues.

Gabbard (1994a) presented a contrasting argument in an article that addressed concerns over whether sexual posttherapy relationships should ever be permitted. He identified five concerns: (a) transference, (b) internalization of the therapist by the client, (c) continuing professional responsibilities, (d) unequal power, and (e) harm to patients and the therapeutic process. Gabbard (1994a) outlined nine arguments used by those who favor allowing posttherapy sexual involvement: (a) constitutional arguments, (b) passage of time, (c) lack of conclusive proof of harm, (d) instances of apparent harmlessness, (e) use of atypical possibilities, (f) well-known therapists who have engaged in sexual relationships with clients, (g) therapists not being able to control with whom they fall in love, (h) marriage as justification, and (i) the reality that sexual relationships with former patients cannot ever be totally eliminated.

Gabbard (1994a) suggested that an honest and complete examination of the issue is clouded by several factors, including the tendency to blame the victim (even though maintenance of boundaries is always the therapist's responsibility), the prospective financial burden of prosecuting violators under a more rigorous standard, the difficulty of confronting colleagues who are involved in sexual relationships with former clients, and the confusion and guilt often felt by therapists who are attracted to clients but do not act on that attraction.

The power differential between client and therapist "can and does continue beyond termination," and "it is the therapist's responsibility to prove that no such power differential exists before pursuing a sexual relationship with a former client" (Shopland & VandeCreek, 1991, pp. 40–41). The debate over this issue is ongoing and sometimes contentious, and it is important that the voices of small-community psychologists be included in the discussions, however difficult or trying those discussions might be.

Nonsexual Dual or Overlapping Relationships

Nonsexual overlapping relationships and posttherapy relationships with clients provide additional sources of confusion, especially for psychologists in small communities. There are differences of opinion within the profession and in the literature. However, these opinions and discussions are more than theoretical or abstract for small-community psychologists who face the confusion of these dilemmas in their professional and personal lives.

Lack of Consensus in the Literature

Some psychologists feel strongly that nonsexual posttherapy relationships with clients are always unethical under any circumstances, whereas others believe that termination ends the therapeutic relationship as long as concurrent roles are also compartmentalized. In the middle of this continuum lie psychologists who think that some of these relationships can be unethical or at least awkward (Anderson, 1993).

Anderson and Kitchener (1996) studied nonromantic, nonsexual posttherapy relationships between psychologists and former clients and found that length of time since termination and the natural evolution and discussion of issues related to the new relationship were factors in justifying social relationships. Situations in which psychologists and former clients worked together were identified as more problematic. Their study also made the distinction between circumstantial contact and intentional contact, although psychologists are still ethically responsible for either type. There was little consensus among the participants regarding whether nonromantic, nonsexual relationships were ethical. In contrast, in a study conducted by Borys and Pope (1989), a majority of respondents indicated that such relationships were rarely or never ethical.

The 2002 APA Ethics Code does not contain an absolute prohibition against nonsexual posttherapy relationships. However, as Fisher (2003) explained, these relationships "are prohibited if the posttermination relationship was promised during the course of the original relationship or if the individual was exploited or harmed by the intent to have the posttermination relationship" (p. 66). Kitchener and Anderson (2000) suggested that the greater the risk of a negative consequence, the greater the need to avoid entering into the nonsexual posttherapy relationship.

Problems

Dual or overlapping relationships in small-community psychology may result from treating friends' children; treating close friends and family members of clients or former clients; and treating acquaintances from school, neighborhood, and church activities. The following example describes such overlap:

> Like at a social gathering, what do I do when ten percent of them are previous or current clients—run? I had a psychia-

trist in the Twin Cities call me a few years ago [to confront
me] because of the adolescent [client] she was seeing. [This
former client's] sister was in daycare with my daughter, I oc-
casionally spoke to the mother, and the little girl came over to
birthday parties. I said, "Look, you come on up to a community of 8,000 people and tell me that is not going to happen."
(Schank, 1994, p. 47)

Sobel (1984) posited that therapists in rural areas have a responsibility for educating the community through involvement
in community groups and professional or social organizations.
Yet, within strict dual-relationship criteria, small-community psychologists may have to decline social invitations that would compromise the boundaries of professional relationships.

Sobel (1984) reminded readers that clients may share information about each other with a therapist. Because of a lack of privacy, small-community therapists' personal lives may become a
part of therapeutic relationships. Riddle (1982) described a similar dilemma as living in a "glass bowl" and used as an example
the notion that getting angry in a local store can have immediate
repercussions and can result in negative labeling of the mental
health professional. However, small-community psychologists
need to interact humanly, as well as professionally, as it is not
appropriate or even possible to maintain the traditional distance
between psychologist and client in many small communities.

Riddle (1982) suggested additional examples of dilemmas:
home visits, clients offering small gifts and food, and mental
health professionals giving opinions on local issues as a few of
the compromises that rural and (other small-community) psychologists may indeed face.

Small-community psychologists are likely to have out-of-
session contact with clients and know clients in a variety of ways.
However, that outside contact is not the criterion for harm in dual
relationships. Instead, of most importance is that the client and
psychologist stay in appropriate roles.

> The critical issue is just being very careful to keep them sepa-
> rated. I have some clients who—one, in particular, was aware
> of that issue. She felt very strongly that when our paths crossed,
> she wanted to be treated like anyone else in the community.

She expressed it as, "I don't want to be treated any differently by you than I would by my dentist, my doctor, or my accountant." (Schank, 1994, p. 48)

Confusion of client and therapist roles is avoided by controlling the kind, rather than amount, of outside contact (Horst, 1989). However, kind of contact can also be difficult to control.

Informal conversations with people in the community are viewed as a common form of mental health education and may in fact be more useful than formal presentations (Heyman & VandenBos, 1989). However, rural and other small-community psychologists face ongoing challenges in maintaining professional boundaries, such as receiving services from clients and responding to the need to treat people with whom psychologists have had personal relationships. At the same time, rural and other small-community psychologists' work in prevention requires that they step outside their traditional role; become involved in the community; and intervene in nontraditional, nonpsychological ways (Kenkel, 1986).

Although there are clear restraints against posttherapy sexual relationships with clients, "with the exception of confidentiality and record keeping, there appears to be almost no ethical constraint on the behavior of psychologists with regard to nonsexual relationships with former clients" (Pipes, 1999, p. 255). Even though such relationships are more difficult to define and to evaluate in regard to the potential for harm, further discussion on limits and other related issues would be beneficial (Pipes, 1999).

Strategies of Justification

It is difficult for small-community psychologists to avoid blending multiple or overlapping roles without isolating themselves from the community (Kitchener, 1988; Rich, 1990). This is much different from a traditional urban setting, with its "discrete, compartmentalized relationships" (Rich, 1990, p. 22). Because these small-world hazards (Koocher & Keith-Spiegel, 1998) may exist on multiple levels, small-community psychologists cannot isolate themselves from client contacts outside of the therapy session:

> I have children who are adults, and my daughter has a friend
> that is a former client. So, she brings [the former client] over to
> my home. She is a lovely person, and it is not a problem. But
> she carries it off well, and I carry it off well. It would breach
> her confidentiality for me to say, "Listen, you can't have her
> as a friend in my home." So it means that it's an ethical di-
> lemma. . . . You totally breach confidentiality if you start lim-
> iting your family's friends and your family's social life because
> of what you do. (Schank, 1994, p. 54)

There is a need to keep asking when such contact constitutes
impaired objectivity in the professional relationship, especially
because it is very difficult to avoid seeing clients in a variety of
roles and settings. When combined with incidental contact, it is
likely that small-community psychologists will know clients in
other contexts and sometimes be less likely to have referral resources available.

> I see a lot of business owners and a lot of people in the profes-
> sional fields [as clients]—doctors, nurses, psychologists, that
> kind of thing. There is no way to avoid [dual relationships], so
> it's the kind of thing we talk about when they first call. If I'm
> in their shop and I buy a lawn mower—oh, well. I guess as far
> as I'm concerned, if there is no exploitation of that, then that is
> the way it has to be. . . . We can't even hire a builder. . . .
> Sometimes we discuss if it would be okay if my husband called
> and hired them. I don't know, so we have to bypass that. I've
> been here seven years—ten more years and we may not have
> a lot of bypassing advantage to some of this. There is nothing
> that I do in my daily or my professional life that I don't have
> to consider those issues. (Schank, 1994, pp. 51–52)

St. Germaine (1993) asserted that dual relationships are not
necessarily problematic if the client's welfare is of most importance. These situations can even become opportunities for effective role modeling by psychologists in small communities, especially when psychologists are sought out by clients precisely
because of their familiarity. Clients may want to know that their
therapist has children in the same schools or is involved in similar community activities; these perceived similarities may enhance

the clients' motivation and trust (Catalano, 1997). A more extreme example is that of the small world of an aircraft carrier. Johnson et al. (2005) wrote:

> [On an aircraft carrier] It is typical for clients to be those with whom a psychologist has daily contact. A client may be the person who takes the trash out of one's stateroom, serves food in the officer's cafeteria, cuts one's hair, cleans one's teeth, or exchanges social pleasantries during the myriad chance meetings in the passageways, bathrooms, exercise facilities, and social-gathering areas within the ship. (p. 77)

However, clients may not understand the concepts surrounding multiple relationships. Psychologists must take the time and make the effort to explain the inherent difficulties to clients who seek them out because their lives do overlap in some way (Catalano, 1997).

Flax, Wagenfeld, Ivens, and Weiss (1979) examined the need for rural mental health professionals to maintain a balance between professional and community identification. Because of the lack of anonymity, rural and other small-community psychologists are inherently active participants in the community. They have a more holistic view of clients and must balance the accepted role of an urban setting versus the complexity of simultaneous relationships in a small-community setting. Because it is impossible to isolate themselves from clients and former clients, psychologists must be able to compartmentalize relationships according to the needs of the moment.

Psychologists need to find ways to be accepted into small communities and trusted by the people who form the complex web of rural social stratification. This community acceptance and trust are established through involvement in the community (Horst, 1989). The resultant visibility, along with role flexibility, leaves rural and other small-community psychologists vulnerable to conflicts between personal and professional roles. These psychologists cannot just offer traditional urban-based services; instead, they "need to function in a variety of community-oriented roles" (Murray & Keller, 1991, p. 227).

Other Areas of Ethical Concern

Overlapping relationships are the most obvious areas of ethical concern in small community psychology. But there are other, equally important ethical conflicts that occur. These include limited resources and limits of competence; community expectations and values differences; interagency issues in working with other community agencies, groups, and professionals; professional isolation and burnout; accepting gifts from clients; and bartering.

Limited Resources and Limits of Competence

Although it is sometimes difficult to define competence, Haas and Malouf (1989) suggested that "a competent clinician is one who has the requisite *knowledge* to understand and conceptualize a particular clinical issue, the necessary *skills* to apply this knowledge in effective ways, and the *judgment* to use such knowledge and skills" (p. 16; italics in original). There are great demands for the competent services of rural and other small-community psychologists, and sometimes few alternatives are available in providing services. In addition to the geographical distance between clients and rural mental health centers, professionals may be far away from one another. Specialized services and educational opportunities may also be at a prohibitive distance for both clients and professionals.

The needs of clients in small communities may require cultural or other professional competencies and knowledge to provide ethical services. The 2002 APA Ethics Code provides an entire section on competence. Relevant subsections from the standard include the following:

> 2.01 Boundaries of Competence
>
> (a) Psychologists provide services, teach, and conduct research with populations and in areas only within the boundaries of their competence, based on their education, training, supervised experience, consultation, study, or professional experience.
>
> (b) Where scientific or professional knowledge in the discipline of psychology establishes that an understanding of factors associated with age, gender, gender identity, race, ethnicity, culture, national origin, religion, sexual orientation,

disability, language, or socioeconomic status is essential for effective implementation of their services or research, psychologists have or obtain the training, experience, consultation or supervision necessary to ensure the competence of their services, or they make appropriate referrals, except as provided in Standard 2.02, Providing Services in Emergencies.

(c) Psychologists planning to provide services, teach, or conduct research involving populations, areas, techniques, or technologies new to them undertake relevant education, training, supervised experience, consultation, or study.

(d) When psychologists are asked to provide services to individuals for whom appropriate mental health services are not available and for which psychologists have not obtained the competence necessary, psychologists with closely related prior training or experience may provide such services in order to ensure that services are not denied if they make a reasonable effort to obtain the competence required by using relevant research, training, consultation, or study.

(e) In those emerging areas in which generally recognized standards for preparatory training do not yet exist, psychologists nevertheless take reasonable steps to ensure the competence of their work and to protect clients/patients, students, supervisees, research participants, organizational clients, and others from harm.

2.02 Providing Services in Emergencies

In emergencies, when psychologists provide services to individuals for whom other mental health services are not available and for which psychologists have not obtained the necessary training, psychologists may provide such services in order to ensure that services are not denied. The services are discontinued as soon as the emergency has ended or appropriate services are available.

2.03 Maintaining Competence

Psychologists undertake ongoing efforts to develop and maintain their competence.

2.04 Bases for Scientific and Professional Judgments

Psychologists' work is based upon established scientific and professional knowledge of the discipline. (APA, 2002a, pp. 1063–1064)

The Office of Ethnic Minority Affairs of APA (1993) provided guidelines for psychologists who are working with ethnic, linguistic, and culturally diverse populations. In August 2002 the APA Council of Representatives approved as APA policy *Guidelines on Multicultural Education, Training, Research, Practice, and Organizational Change for Psychologists* (APA, 2002b). This document, which was developed over a span of 22 years, reflected the joint efforts of APA Divisions 17 (Society of Counseling Psychology) and 45 (Society for the Psychological Study of Ethnic Minority Issues). Both sets of guidelines outlined the importance of understanding the role in clients' lives of culture, ethnicity, sociocultural identification, and socioeconomic and political factors.

One limitation of the general literature regarding multiple relationships in psychotherapy is that it falls short when applied to culturally diverse clients and therapists (Kessler & Waehler, 2005, p. 67). Professional organizations "have been slow in developing new policies, practices, and structures to accommodate the diversity of our society" (Sue, Bingham, Porche-Burke, & Vasquez, 1999, p. 1062). In addition, "traditional psychological concepts and theories derived from research were developed in a predominantly Euro-American context and may be limited in their applicability to the increasingly racially and culturally diverse population in the United States" (Sue et al., 1999, p. 1062). An extrapolation of these factors to the work that psychologists do in other small communities is important, both in direct service and in referral to other psychologists and resources.

Sobel's (1984) article on psychotherapy in small communities stressed the need for rural mental health practitioners to be generalists and the importance of continuing education for knowledge and competency in a broad generalist practice. However, it may be difficult for rural practitioners to travel to educational institutions or conferences and to arrange coverage by other professionals while out of town. Other small-community psychologists with specialized expertise (e.g., a deaf psychologist working with deaf clients) may also have difficulty finding a competent replacement if he or she takes time off for continuing education or vacation.

There are other logistical problems that arise from having few or no other professionals nearby to treat family members of current clients or to provide specialty service. Rural or small-community psychologists must decide whether to cover the needs themselves, refuse treatment, provide service that may not be the treatment of choice, or provide service outside their areas of competence (Sobel, 1984). If psychologists refuse to treat all the people with whom they have overlapping relationships, many potential clients may not receive treatment. As one small-community psychologist indicated,

> If there is no [other] resource, my feeling is that we [should] do the best we can. We can be up front with the client on our level of expertise and experience. I was also working in a system where I have to see them, or no one else would take them. It wasn't even a matter of referring. (Schank, 1994, p. 63)

Psychologists are likely to see rejected clients in social situations and around the community, making it difficult to say no (Purtilo & Sorrell, 1986).

Community Expectations and Values Differences

Any approach to mental health service delivery in rural areas must be multifaceted, taking into account the needs of both the client and the community (Sladen & Mozdzierz, 1989). Traditional therapy approaches directed toward building self-esteem and toward personal fulfillment may not be appropriate or accepted in rural areas and other small communities when there are other, more pressing needs (F. T. Miller, 1981). This is evident in the following example from Schank (1994):

> The wonderful thing about people in rural areas is that they tend to be hard workers, very individualistic. Whereas they may be often willing to help people, a lot of times they still will not go for help themselves. They have to wait until the saddest time in their life. (Schank, 1994, p. 70)

Keller, Murray, Hargrove, and Dengerink (1983) proposed that clinical training for rural (and other small-community) psychologists should include cultural differences because psychologists need to be knowledgeable, sensitive, and responsible. To be successful, rural (and other small-community) psychologists may have to adapt to the community and deal with prevailing attitudes toward mental health (Elkin & Boyer, 1987).

Residents in rural areas and small communities may be more interested in concrete problem solutions and relief of symptoms rather than self-actualization. They may also expect help in the shortest time possible (Flax et al., 1979). Although these expectations are certainly not unique to small communities, they represent a more evident pressure on psychologists, whose definitions of "good mental health" probably include more than prompt abatement of negative symptoms. The more visible nature of small-community practice makes such expectations for quick results all the more difficult.

Small communities have role expectations for psychologists to effectively practice there. Thus, psychologists may need to consider a compromise between professional and community standards (Sobel, 1984). Practice takes on unique characteristics of the community as psychologists become familiar with "all the formal and informal political, social, economic, and professional networks in the community" (Sobel, 1984, p. 111). To really know and meet the needs of the community, community participation is essential in the decision-making process of psychological service providers (Perlman, 1977).

As new residents in a small-community setting, psychologists may be met with curiosity, mistrust, or hostility (Solomon, 1980). They are on "community display" and may be judged by image rather than by professional ability. According to Solomon (1980), there is often an expectation that psychologists will actively participate in the community. They may receive many invitations to join or get involved in community groups and events, and they will need to weigh each one carefully, because they will be judged by the way they handle such invitations.

The active, informal communication network in rural areas and small communities means that "word travels about the psychologist personally, as well as professionally, very rapidly and this can be a double-edged sword" (Mann & Stein, 1993, p. 4). People make assumptions, based on what they have heard from others, before meeting small-community psychologists. This active communication network can add stress for psychologists, who may worry about how others see them and who may worry that they cannot act truly like themselves in some situations (Nigro, 2004).

Rural and other small-community psychologists need to get to know people with power and leadership positions in the community and develop good relationships with them (Bagarozzi, 1982). Building these and other positive relationships within the community can make it easier to negotiate official and unofficial channels, when necessary, to advocate for clients (Heyman, 1982; Sladen & Mozdzierz, 1989).

Gaining the trust of the members of a small community may take some time, but personal trust may be the most important variable in the success of small-community practice (Solomon, Hiesberger, & Winer, 1981). To gain this trust, rural or other small-community psychologists must be adaptable, flexible, and sensitive to community standards (Solomon, 1980). Those standards and values may differ in myriad ways from those of the psychologist. As Libertoff (1980) noted, "Distances cannot be simply measured in terms of miles but in the attitudes, habits, and traditions of local residents" (p. 9).

One major challenge comes from small-community attitudes toward client confidentiality. Community members may expect that information will be shared freely (Hargrove, 1986; Mann & Stein, 1993), and psychologists who refuse to do so may be seen as lacking concern for the client's welfare. People in small communities are often concerned about friends, neighbors, and relatives, and they may ask the psychologist for information. These concerned others often get angry when told that the information is confidential and interpret the rejection as the psychologist believing that others cannot be trusted with the information (Phillips & Baker, 1983). There is further frustration about professional procedures, for example, mandated reporting of issues of suspected child abuse and other times when the psychologist must break client confidentiality (Zipple, Langle, Spaniol, & Fisher, 1990). Informed consent and release of information forms may be seen by clients as barriers to service (Solomon et al., 1981). Although it may be harder to adhere to standards of confidentiality in rural areas and other small communities, these standards should still be maintained, even if handled more informally (Sobel, 1984).

Interagency Issues in Working With Other Community Agencies, Groups, and Professionals

Effective rural and small-community psychologists need to have good relationships with community agencies and local schools. Effectiveness as a team player means finding ways to cope with pressure from other agencies and the legal system to not "make waves" (Sobel, 1984). Often, people in rural areas and other small communities fear being stigmatized for using mental health services and may turn first to physicians or other professionals (Kenkel, 1986). Sundet and Mermelstein (1984) indicated that it is important to work closely with other health care providers regarding methods, goals, and length of involvement to maintain common ground. They stated that when authority figures give conflicting advice or directions, a client will become even more confused and upset.

Psychologists need to have access to a variety of resources. If new to a small community, psychologists may be viewed with mistrust by other professionals, who may fear that their roles and the work they have done will not be appreciated. There may also be old skeletons in the closet or conflicts within or between agencies about which the new psychologist is naive (Solomon, 1980).

Contact between agencies may be more informal in rural areas and small communities (Kofoed & Cutler, 1982). According to Solomon et al. (1981), a new psychologist who is unaware of local norms regarding confidentiality or who does not take them into account may quickly become professionally isolated and ostracized. There is a need to be flexible within professional ethical limitations while still recognizing that interagency confidentiality may put small-community psychologists in a difficult position. Schools, social services, spiritual leaders, and physicians may expect that information will be shared more freely than the psychologist is able to do. Not complying with their requests may cause conflicts between professionals and agencies, who may view sharing of confidential information as different from sharing information with the general public. Solomon et al. also noted that agency staff people are sometimes born and raised in the small community. These staff members may already have informal professional information networks established and may view confidentiality issues differently than would a rural or small-community psychologist who was trained in another geographic area.

Rural people and residents of other small communities may turn first to family, friends, or spiritual leaders and initiate contact with psychologists and other professional helpers as a last resort. Because many members of small communities have been a part of those communities for generations, it is more acceptable to seek out informal assistance (P. J. Miller, 1994).

Psychologists need to be flexible yet still maintain boundaries, a concept that may not be easily understood by others in the small-community context. Maintaining these boundaries, along with adhering to confidentiality and other ethical practices, may eventually be viewed as a positive, safe thing by clients and other professionals (Solomon et al., 1981).

Some small communities provide natural helpers. These helpers, who are often part of informal, natural support networks, can be an important part of successful treatment and may be of special value to family members who are not in therapy (Bagarozzi, 1982; Dunbar, 1982). Kenkel (1986) indicated that rural residents often turn to clergy, family, and other natural helpers rather than face the stigma of mental health services. Psychologists in rural areas and other small-community settings can both work with the helpers and train these natural helpers to build on their own skills.

Increasing available support is one of the most effective interventions in small communities, and this network of support often needs to be established within the client's own subculture (Kenkel, 1986). A network of community resources can provide helpful support (self-help groups, people in other agencies, churches, and other organizations). Small-community psychologists may need to move outside a traditional clinical framework in collaborating with support resources. Geographical distance and lack of psychologist colleagues may make this collaboration with others even more important (F. T. Miller, 1981). Because clients may be likely to first seek out informal helpers, psychologists need to find out who these helpers are and whether they plan to stay involved (Sundet & Mermelstein, 1984).

If small-community psychological practice is to be successful, it is essential to build coalitions and recognize the vital role these natural helpers play. Natural helpers may be reluctant to give up their helping roles (Solomon, 1980), and psychologists must be careful about disrupting natural support systems. If overlooked or diminished, natural helpers may think that psychologists are invading their domain and may resist collaborating with mental health professionals (Solomon et al., 1981). Instead, psychologists can promote greater linkage within a system to increase the density of the network and promote less reliance on specific individuals (Kenkel, 1986). If the existing networks are not helpful, psychologists will need to find ways to intervene or redirect the efforts of both clients and natural helpers. It will also be important to establish and educate involved others about appropriate professional boundaries (Dunbar, 1982).

Professional Isolation and Burnout

Several authors (DeStefano, Clark, & Potter, 2005; Kenkel, 1986; Libertoff, 1980; Mann & Stein, 1993; F. T. Miller, 1981) have addressed the isolation experienced by many rural (and other small-community) psychologists. The isolation can be geographical, cultural, professional, educational, or medical. This isolation produces personal and professional pressure, which is compounded by the need for psychologists to function as generalists and by the lack of specialists available for referrals. Mann and Stein (1993) expanded on the sources of professional isolation to include fewer opportunities for intellectual stimulation, collegial support, and sharing of ideas.

DeStefano et al. (2005) interviewed 827 rural mental health workers in Arizona and found that they experienced greater levels of burnout and exhaustion compared with a national norm sample. The lack of available resources, the need to be a generalist and to practice at the outside limits of competency areas, the isolation from clinical supervision, and the stress of overlapping roles within a small community were all identified as factors contributing to feeling emotionally overwhelmed. In spite of these pressures, the rural mental health workers experienced high levels of personal achievement and empathy for their clients. However, DeStefano et al. cautioned that if this sense of personal accomplishments diminishes, rural mental health workers may be vulnerable to "lowered levels of productivity, depersonalization of clients, and staff attrition" (p. 22). Case managers, therapists, and medical providers in their study seemed more likely to have experienced significant burnout.

A psychologist interviewed by Schank (1994) gave the following example:

> We had a loosely formed, go-get-'em [coalition] of rural mental health practitioners, although now we have kind of disbanded. We had to because we had no one to speak for us. It is all metropolitan-based, all metro driven. When I joined the [state psychological] association, I asked to get on two or three of their committees and did. I would get my notice on Monday for the meeting at noon on Wednesday. Sure, I'll just jet right on down and give you my wonderful words of wisdom. Then they can't understand why there is suspicion and antagonism. (pp. 90–91)

The lack of attention to small-community dilemmas by the profession of psychology has provided the freedom to develop and apply models in a more flexible way to fit a specific community (Heyman, 1982). However, along with this freedom comes the danger of professional isolation and a lack of outside professional input. A small-community psychologist may come to think of him- or herself as the sole arbiter of ethical decision making. Thus, there is a responsibility to remain connected with existing professional standards while also modifying what Heyman and VandenBos (1989) identified as the small-community approach to treatment.

An open discussion of ethical dilemmas regarding traditional–small community differences seems to be missing from most professional meetings and conferences. Urban psychologists may not stop to consider the issues that are a part of daily practice for their small-community colleagues. Small-community psychologists may worry about being misunderstood by their traditional counterparts, and so the discussion is avoided.

The work of the practitioner, regardless of setting, is usually very demanding. Emotional depletion and compassion fatigue are often just around the corner. The demand for attuning to the needs of the client; to be energetic for the client; and to listen carefully to the often-present fear, despair, and defiance requires active resiliency efforts on the part of the practitioner (Baker, 2003; Skovholt, 2001).

The difficulty of the work and the need for resiliency-building is important in the small community setting. Solomon (1980) identified the lack of privacy and personal space for psychologists in rural areas and other small communities as contributing to burnout, along with professional isolation, loneliness, fatigue, frustration, work overload, and few opportunities for collegiality.

The lack of privacy can be constricting when psychologists feel they are always "on" when within the small community. They must be aware of their personal behavior, such as the use of alcohol, and realize that they can receive inquiries at any time about the behavior of certain individuals or mental health topics (Mann & Stein, 1993).

Pope and Vasquez (1998) examined general issues of stress and dysfunction in ways that are applicable to burnout in small-community settings. They cited surveys that indicate that substance abuse, grief and loss, depression, physical illness, marital problems, and other relationship problems are major contributors to the professional burnout of small-community psychologists.

Mental health professionals may not seek therapy because of concerns regarding confidentiality, fear of professional consequences, and lack of resources—issues that are especially pertinent to those practicing in small communities. Pope and Vasquez (1998) pointed out that the mental health profession itself is stressful, and they underscored the importance of peer support and review. Personal problems do not excuse unethical behavior, so psychologists must constantly monitor themselves, especially if limited or no peer support and review are available. A concept from a study of master therapists—*boundaried generosity*—can be of use to small-community practitioners who do not have the natural boundaries of practice in a large urban area (Skovholt & Jennings, 2004).

Accepting Gifts From Clients

Clients may bring gifts to psychologists for a variety of reasons. They may believe that gifts will ensure that they will receive better service or attain special status, that gifts will keep the psychologist interested in them, that gifts can be used as bribes toward a positive report or special favor, or that gifts are a token of appreciation or remembrance after termination (Welfel, 1998). Gift giving can also be part of a strong cultural tradition, as in Asian and other cultures, where gifts are given to respected leaders, such as teachers and doctors. These factors are important considerations in deciding whether to accept gifts from clients. In addition to possible motivations, psychologists need to consider the monetary worth of gifts and the impact that accepting or not accepting certain gifts can have on the therapy relationship and on the client.

There are some situations in which it is not unethical to accept a gift from a client—and may even be countertherapeutic or inappropriate to refuse (Haas & Malouf, 1989). Professional codes offer little guidance on this issue. It is easy to see why the acceptance of gifts as a means of bribing or manipulating a psychologist is contraindicated. However, token gifts offered as a way of thanking a psychologist for having a special impact on the life of a client may be different. A client who sincerely offers such a gift may be genuinely hurt and confused if such a gift is rejected, particularly within some cultural contexts, and progress made in therapy may be damaged. Occasional gifts may serve a useful function, particularly when the counseling relationship is terminated. Clients may want to show their appreciation or to leave behind a reminder of themselves with a psychologist who has been important to them.

Welfel (1998) offered the following criteria for deciding whether the acceptance of a particular gift is ethical:

- ☐ It promotes rather than endangers the client's welfare.
- ☐ It does not compromise the therapist's objectivity or capacity to provide competent service in the future.
- ☐ It is a token of appreciation consistent with the client's cultural norms and with a small monetary value.
- ☐ It is a rare event in counseling rather than a recurrent practice. (p. 178)

Discomfort about the issue of gift giving can be addressed in the informed consent that is reviewed with clients at the beginning of therapy. Although this may prevent later misunderstandings, it has the potential to be awkward and burdensome as part of an already-lengthy list of topics to be addressed prior to the beginning of therapy. In some cultural contexts, such a policy would also be vulnerable to misinterpretation and misunderstanding (Welfel, 1998).

Bartering

The 1992 Ethics Code provided a specific position on bartering and acknowledged that it can be acceptable under certain conditions, if not exploitive or clinically contraindicated. The 2002 Ethics Code, in Standard 6.05, Barter With Clients/Patients, continues these same conditions and includes a more specific definition of bartering:

> 6.05 Barter With Clients/Patients
> Barter is the acceptance of goods, services, or other nonmonetary remuneration from clients/patients in return for psychological services. Psychologists may barter only if (1) it is not clinically contraindicated, and (2) the resulting arrangement is not exploitative. (APA, 2002a, p. 1068)

Bartering is most likely to be viewed as ethical in small-community situations, where the prohibition of bartering means that a client would not be able to receive services, conflicts with local practices, or is viewed as a lack of respect for a client's dignity (Fisher & Younggren, 1997).

As outlined by Welfel (1998) and others (Corey et al., 1998; Herlihy & Corey, 1992; Koocher & Keith-Spiegel, 1998), bartering for services provided by the client sets up a dual relationship in which the psychologist is, for all intents and purposes, the employer of the client. The client may have limited power to disagree with working conditions or other problems in the arrangement, and the psychologist may be vulnerable to impaired objectivity regarding the service provided by the client. If the client improves and no longer needs therapy before a specific job is completed (e.g., carpentry work on a psychologist's house), the psychologist may be held liable if there is the appearance of therapy being continued until the bartered work is completed.

There is also the possibility of disagreement between the psychologist and client as to the actual worth of or satisfaction with goods or services provided. If either party to the bartering were dissatisfied with the services, the process of therapy would be threatened. In a worst-case scenario, confidentiality could be compromised by any civil proceedings.

It may also be difficult at the outset to estimate the length or duration of therapy. Conflict may arise if therapy ends earlier than expected, meaning that the client may have "overpaid" through the bartering arrangement. The converse may also occur (Borys, 1992). Any disagreement, however objective, has the potential to damage the therapeutic relationship or the gains that may have been made in therapy.

In some small communities, bartering is a common form of exchange. Not being able to barter for services may mean that potential clients in small communities would not be able to access psychological help. It is also a way for people with no insurance coverage or monetary resources to be able to offer something of value in exchange for therapy, ensuring their investment in the process or sense of pride in being able to contribute. R. H. Woody (1998) offered a valuable consideration in reminding readers that "if bartering is used, prudence holds that it should be the option of last resort" (p. 176). He also suggested that "it would be less risky to provide gratis services than to credit the value of a gift to the client's account" (R. H. Woody, 1998, p. 176).

Before entering into a relationship in which services are bartered, both parties should come to a clear agreement and understanding of the exchange. It would also be helpful to talk about how possible disagreements would be handled and what alternatives might be available. Psychologists need to exercise their own good judgment and consider the cultural context within which a bartering arrangement may be offered (Corey et al., 1998).

R. H. Woody (1998) suggested the following guidelines when considering a bartering arrangement:

☐ Any exchange should be as close to established professional practices as possible.
☐ The rationale for such an arrangement should be documented in case notes.

- [ ] The agreement and subsequent discussions should be detailed and in writing.
- [ ] There should be a preference for goods, rather than services.
- [ ] The value of what is bartered should be "verified by an objective source" (p. 177).
- [ ] Both parties should reach a written agreement.
- [ ] Any new comments or considerations should be included in the client's records.
- [ ] The agreement should include "a provision for how valuations were determined and how any subsequent conflicts will be resolved" (p. 177).
- [ ] Any misunderstanding that may develop should be dealt with by a mediator, rather that the client and psychologist.
- [ ] If any negative effects from bartering are evident as treatment progresses, "it should be remedied or appropriate termination of the treatment relationship should occur" (p. 177).

Summary

The exploration of multiple relationships and other ethical issues in this chapter was wide and varied. We defined these relationships and addressed how they can sometimes be problematic and unethical. We considered many contextual factors in small-community practice that are instrumental in how practice is constructed in these settings. Separate consideration was given to sexual and nonsexual dual relationships in these settings. Most important, we discussed how small-community practice can be enhanced through deliberate, highly nuanced, and culturally sensitive ethical practice.

Chapter

4

Rural Practice: Illuminating Dilemmas in One Kind of Small Community

In a study of the myths and realities of rural practice, Rich (1990) noted that in urban practice both clients and professionals expect a separation between the personal and the professional. Rich went on to say that in rural practice personal and professional roles can easily become unintentionally blurred. In these rural settings, prevailing standards in codes of ethics cannot be applied in automatic ways, especially when the multiple relationships in rural settings have a significant effect on which services are provided and how those services are provided (Brownlee, 1996).

As we have seen from the discussion in chapter 3, out-of-therapy contacts between rural psychologists and clients are commonplace. Thus, forming any relationships with others in the community may mean that psychologists may be "in the position of limiting the delivery of already scarce psychological services to a small number of inhabitants" (Faulkner & Faulkner, 1997, pp. 226–227). Faulkner and Faulkner (1997) suggested that "Cultural, social, and local norms in a small, rural community tend to produce an ambience where 'everybody knows everybody' and if they do not, they soon will" (p. 229).

Simon and Williams (1999) emphasized that rural mental health providers "may have met or may personally know a number of the community's residents, especially if [the provider] was raised there" (p. 1443). This range of contact may be greatly enlarged if the provider is married or has children. Simon and Williams also suggested that it is likely that providers "will also encounter and interact with former patients" (p. 1443).

People in rural areas tend to see psychologists as outsiders and tend to be resistant to help, especially from these outsiders (Solomon, Hiesberger, & Winer, 1981). The negative stigma about mental health services, coupled with a perception that providers do not understand the issues of rural and agricultural people, may deter some rural people from getting the services that they need (Gamm, Hutchinson, Dabney, & Dorsey, 2003).

Psychologists need to find ways to be accepted into the community and trusted by the people who form the complex web of rural social stratification. This community acceptance and trust is established through involvement in the community (Horst, 1989). The resultant visibility, along with role flexibility, leaves the rural psychologist "vulnerable to political and community conflict" (Murray & Keller, 1991, p. 227) and to a conflict between personal and professional roles. Psychologists cannot offer solely traditional services; instead, they "need to function in a variety of community-oriented roles" (Murray & Keller, 1991, p. 227).

Most psychological training, both theoretical and practical, does not adequately prepare mental health professionals for the flexibility and adaptations that are necessary to live and work successfully in rural areas (Catalano, 1997). Their training usually occurs in urban areas with access to many services and is based on an urban model of psychology (Helbok, 2003; Human & Wasem, 1991).

Once they have been accepted into the community, rural psychologists are seen as experts and are imbued with the special power of their professional role. This is also true in urban settings, but it may be particularly pronounced in rural areas, where there may be few mental health professionals and sometimes only one psychologist. The power lies with the professional, so clients cannot be expected to objectively evaluate what the professional advises and then reject it if it is not in their best interest (Kitchener, 1988).

The resulting pressure and need to be a generalist require the ability to work with diverse problems and cope with a relative lack of other resources in the community (Heyman & VandenBos, 1989; Sobel, 1984). Dunbar (1982) identified an additional and related conflict for rural psychologists: Part of the psychologist's role as a generalist may involve advocacy, public relations, grant and proposal writing, participation in community organizations, and other roles outside of direct treatment that put the psychologist into a variety of contexts within the community.

Some of the difficulties encountered by psychologists in small-community practice are not experienced, or are experienced to a lesser degree, by psychologists in urban areas. These may include values differences, religious issues, and mistrust and stereotyping of psychologists. Although not always ethical in nature, these issues, along with incidental out-of-therapy contact with clients, can be troublesome and stress producing for both psychologists and clients.

However, even though overlapping relationships are frequent in rural areas, psychologists cannot relax their ethical standards (Helbok, 2003). Although psychologists may encounter clients in the community and interact with them in a variety of ways, they cannot engage in behavior with clients that can easily be avoided. In fact, rural psychologists may need to be even more vigilant than their urban counterparts to examine their relationships and avoid overlapping involvement whenever possible. Helbok (2003) stated that this vigilance may include "making these relationship issues clear to clients, defining and explaining role boundaries clearly, and making extra efforts to minimize any role confusion" (p. 374).

Dilemmas Involving Professional Boundaries

Nonsexual overlapping relationships are not a matter of "if" as much as "when" in small community practice (Barnett & Yutrzenka, 1995). For example, psychologists in rural areas and other small communities frequently live in the communities in which they practice; thus, "social or other nonprofessional contacts outside a primary professional relationship are not only inevitable but imminent" (Faulkner & Faulkner, 1997, p. 225), and "the anonymity which facilitates boundary delineation does not exist" (Catalano, 1997, p. 24). Professional contacts, such as patronizing local businesses, may occur between psychologists and current, past, or potential clients. Rural psychologists are also faced with the fact that sometimes "denying help to a potential client because of a preexisting relationship could mean that the person gets no help at all" (D. Smith & Fitzpatrick, 1995, p. 502), especially as there may be few local resources and options for referral to other clinicians (Catalano, 1997; Perkins, Hudson, Gray, & Steward, 1998).

This out-of-therapy contact with clients may not actually be as uncomfortable for current and former clients as it is for psychologists, especially because rural residents are used to running into doctors and other professionals during daily life in a small community (Dittmann, 2003). However, there is a difference between running into clients in stores or serving together on committees and being involved in a more personal way (Helbok, 2003). "When a psychologist has a relationship with a client outside of the therapeutic milieu, both the psychologist and client must change roles" (Helbok, 2003, p. 371). This can be confusing to both parties and can affect the psychologist's objectivity, even in chance encounters. Thus, it is the potential for harm, rather than the overlapping relationship in and of itself, that may be problematic (Helbok, 2003). The issue is further complicated by the expectation by most rural residents that participation in community life "is not only normal but expected" (Perkins et al., 1998).

In a qualitative research study, 16 rural and small-community psychologists in Minnesota and Wisconsin (Schank, 1994, 1998; Schank & Skovholt, 1997) described boundary dilemmas they faced in daily practice, how various relevant factors are weighed in dealing with dilemmas, and how decisions are made when providing psychological services to clients in small communities. Their responses, along with an extensive review of the literature, identified several areas of concern that are described by the following eight themes: (a) the reality of overlapping social relationships; (b) the reality of overlapping business or professional relationships; (c) the effects of overlapping relationships on members of the psychologist's own family; (d) seeing more than one family member, or seeing people who have friendships with each other as individual clients; (e) getting unsolicited out-of-therapy information about clients; (f) high visibility and lack of privacy; (g) collecting unpaid bills from clients; and (h) bartering.

The Reality of Overlapping Social Relationships

Simultaneous or overlapping social relationships occurred in a variety of settings that were identified by all 16 of the psychologists who were interviewed: church, parties and social gatherings, eating out in local restaurants, cultural activities, school events, and volunteer activities. The following are quotations from psychologists in the research study:

> One of the things we have done in our church for the last six years is that we have taken a group of kids to Colorado skiing as part of the youth program. I feel some kind of tension about that sometimes. For example, one of my clients happened to be on the ski trip three or four years ago. Well, I thought, "Okay, we don't do anything socially with this family." But I don't think those pressures are so unusual. It's just that you have to keep those dual relationships clear in your mind. (Schank, 1994, p. 45)

> I am single. One of my big fears is that I'll meet someone [that I want to date], and they'll say, "You don't remember, but nine years ago I came with my husband for one interview." (p. 45)

> In a small community you see the people that you treat all the time. And there is no way to avoid that. I see different clergy [as clients], and if you go to their church you see them there. You can't avoid it. (p. 45)

> I went to a wedding of my next-door neighbor, and a client of mine was at the wedding. I said hi, and that was fine. We got to the reception (my husband had no idea who these people were), and we ended up sitting with them. My husband is really a wonderful man, but he kids me sometimes about talking to crazy people and doesn't really mean it. He really is very sympathetic to the kinds of things that we deal with. But we were sitting there, talking about socializing, and my husband said, "Well, we don't do a lot of it because I have a busy job, and my wife is busy talking to crazy people all day." It just sort of came out. I looked at her (she was sitting right across from me), and she looked at me, and I looked at him, and he just shut up. Then her husband said, "What do you do?" The three of us just sort of changed the conversation, and we spent the whole evening with them. (p. 46)

Psychologists face dilemmas in terms of boundary issues in deciding whom to see as clients, and they seem to make these decisions on the basis of three different criteria. Some make the decision on the basis of their own comfort level as to whether they can successfully manage overlapping relationships with particular clients. Others involve prospective clients in the decision-making process. Some psychologists use type and severity of clients' presenting problems as indicators of whether they would enter into overlapping relationships. For example, when there is even a potential for a dual relationship, some are more likely to see clients for advice-giving or problem-solving situations, but they are unlikely to take on a client with a possible personality disorder. An often-mentioned situation involves seeing children as clients who are in school or other activities with a psychologist's own children, a situation that cannot always be predicted or avoided. Some psychologists talk about how their spouse, as a minister, attorney, or physician, has professional contact with people. These contacts affect decisions about taking those people on as clients. Others find that duality is unavoidable. Psychologists in supervisory roles have an additional constriction: Besides coping with dual contexts with their own clients, they also have to manage knowing about the clients of the psychologists they supervise.

Rural psychologists and their clients need to be prepared for meeting each other in the community. Many psychologists choose to talk directly with clients about the likelihood of encountering each other outside of therapy. They make it clear to clients that they will respect client privacy by waiting to see if clients want to acknowledge or greet them. This open discussion helps to clarify the overlapping relationship and the importance of clients and psychologists staying in appropriate roles:

> It is always establishing boundaries. I live on a very busy street in town and was doing some landscaping and working out in the front yard. One of my clients must have seen me and later said, "Oh, is that where you live? I saw you." I said yes, and she said, "Well, I noticed that the house next to you is for sale. Wouldn't that be cool? You know, my parents are thinking of helping me buy a house." I said, "No, that would not be cool

because you are my client—you are not a friend. If you moved in next door to me, it would be extremely uncomfortable. I know what you are saying—I listen to you, I care about you—but friends know about one another. You don't come in, and I sit and tell you about my problems and my life. I don't call you when I am hurting or need a friend for support." She said, "Oh, yeah. I didn't even think about that." And so it's continually having to establish boundaries with a number of clients. (Schank, 1994, p. 49)

The Reality of Overlapping Business or Professional Relationships

In a small community, it is likely that psychologists will encounter their clients in business situations. In fact, in many small communities, psychologists may be seen even more as outsiders if they choose to take all of their trade to businesses located outside of town. It appears that degree of involvement is the primary factor to consider in such overlapping relationships. For example, it may be nearly impossible to avoid business interactions with clients in local stores, but it would be very unwise to enter into a business partnership with a client or a client's family:

> There is kind of a conflict. When you live in a small town, you want to patronize the stores here because they really struggle against places like Wal-Mart. You want to go to these downtown businesses, but you know everybody. So you can't avoid entering into business relationships. (Schank, 1994, p. 51)

> I have clients who are locksmiths or electricians that have come to my house, with me not knowing that I was calling the company that they work for. It is hard to make small talk with someone who the day before was in your office talking about really powerful things. Sometimes clients will joke about it, which is kind of nice. They will break the ice. (p. 50)

Some decisions appear to be more complex. When alternatives are available, some psychologists avoid contact with clients by shopping and trading exclusively outside of their own communities. Others try to deal with the ambiguity and confusion that come with overlapping business and therapeutic contacts:

If something went wrong with a piece of equipment, I just wouldn't make an issue of it. If it was just a general return policy, then that is what I would follow. If it was something that would create an argument or something, I just wouldn't do it. Maybe you make it up as you go, but what I have always tried to do is put those boundary pieces in terms of my clients' needs absolutely foremost. (Schank, 1994, p. 51)

I don't want to have to deal with it. If my hairdresser called and requested me and then I was the intake, I would probably call her and say, "I appreciate you requesting me and that you enjoy my company. But I'm concerned and would really rather have you see a different therapist. I can give you the names of a couple of therapists that would probably be helpful to you. I would just feel uncomfortable." (p. 51)

When you do have business dealings with someone, I find it really hard. I won't bargain with them. Recently someone [who was a former client] worked on my car, and I thought the price was a little high. I trust the guy, but I felt awkward in asking him what the charges were for. If it were someone else, I would have had no problem asking. (p. 51)

Psychologists also may have overlapping professional roles with medical providers and referral resources:

We have a nice, isolated building here in a beautiful, quiet place. So professionals many times will come here. Now, I have seen a lot of professionals in town [as clients], either for personal counseling or for their children. Then I refer [clients] to [those same professionals] because there is no one else. If you read the rules about dual relationships, that is not allowed. (Schank, 1994, p. 52)

The most difficult situations may be those in which psychologists provide therapy to colleagues or to family members of colleagues. Those who choose to do so may acknowledge the discomfort and potential liabilities of such overlapping relationships but believe that, in protecting a client's confidentiality or acting in the client's best interest, one ethical choice overrides another ethical choice:

I do consulting at a fair number of group homes. Sometimes I'm in that dilemma where there is someone [working there] that I've seen as a client. In fact, I can think of two instances where I currently was seeing people as clients and subsequently discovered that they had obtained employment at one of the group homes. So I was dealing with them as clients, as well as in a professional relationship in terms of some of the consulting. (Schank, 1994, p. 52)

Effects of Overlapping Relationships on Members of the Psychologist's Own Family

Although identified only once in the literature on dual relationships (Jennings, 1992) before our 1997 article (Schank & Skovholt, 1997), rural and small-community psychologists talked about the significant impact that their professional practice has on their families. This issue seems especially significant. It resulted in much questioning and searching for ethical balances on the part of most of the psychologists interviewed for the study. Rural psychologists may have to discuss the potential interaction between their families and the families of their clients, balancing what Catalano (1997) described as "the need for independence and autonomy of [the] children and [the] family's relationship in the community in which they reside, and any real or potential risks to confidentiality" (p. 27).

Psychologists who are parents face having clients or former clients as friends of their own children. Psychologists have to weigh which of two competing ethical stances best serves their clients' interest. Do they have to accept having clients in their homes as guests of their children, or do they break confidentiality by setting limits on whom their children can have as friends? How, when, and where do they limit their children's social lives and involvement in activities?

> I think there are a lot of variables. If I can avoid a situation, I will. Let's say it is a function like a hockey party. My kids are on the hockey team. The kids want to go, and they want the parents to go. So you are at this function [with clients]. You're not going to say to the kids, "Gee, I can't go to the hockey banquet." So you just go. . . . Sometimes you just kind of live with it. My older kids have friends who have been my patients in the past. I prefer that they not come over to our house,

but you can't say to your kids, "Don't invite so-and-so."
(Schank, 1994, p. 54)

Young people that I've seen are becoming friends with my
daughter through the school system. I was so surprised—one
night I came home from work to discover that one of my clients was a good friend of my daughter's through school and
was staying overnight with her. (p. 54)

Some psychologists in small communities face a troubling dilemma when their adolescent children end up dating clients or
former clients. They resist compromising their clients' confidentiality but experience the unease and worry that come with knowing things about the former client or the former client's family:

I think that the more difficult situation is interaction that my
daughter has had. She is now away at college, but when she
was here she would end up dating clients—only to find out
and just be absolutely horrified and angry. That is probably
the most difficult circumstance that we have been in. The confidentiality piece is really difficult because she would confront
me with, "Is so and so your client?" She is real glad to be done
with that. (Schank, 1994, p. 56)

I had a [client] who had problems and just came in a couple of
times. He was extremely bright and very talented, but inside
he wasn't feeling so bright. I don't think he ever really dealt
with too much. I suppose about six months later he took out
my daughter. . . . My daughter now [has stopped seeing him].
I'm glad she figured it out—it was kind of a relief. . . . If they
are having a rough time in the relationship, they will hope-
fully tell you why they are having a rough time so you can
focus on that. I could see it being an issue where you don't
know the individual but do know the family, the cousins, uncle,
or something like that. (p. 56)

The volunteer or professional activities of spouses sometimes
create a dilemma for psychologists in deciding whether they
should set boundaries in social situations:

My husband met another [colleague's] wife who wanted to
socialize, and I had to say that I can't go to their house for
dinner. . . . He was understanding but was still feeling cur-

tailed by my practice because we couldn't socialize with people that he would have enjoyed because they had come to me for family counseling. (Schank, 1994, pp. 56–57)

Seeing More Than One Family Member or Seeing People Who Have Friendships With Each Other as Individual Clients

Limited therapy resources within rural areas make it highly likely that psychologists will see clients who have connections to other clients. Although some psychologists practice in settings in which new clients can be referred to other therapists, others do not have such options. When other referral options are not available, psychologists find themselves forced to make difficult decisions about how to balance the intersections of relationships. Sometimes psychologists know in advance that their clients' lives overlap; other times, they discover the overlap in the course of therapy. Not only are such previously unknown overlaps difficult for a psychologist; they may also become difficult for clients who may feel deceived on discovering that their psychologist knew of the overlap but did not inform the respective clients (Tribbensee & Claiborn, 2003). Consultation and evaluation requests are another source of such overlap:

> [A client's] daughter is also a client of mine. Her daughter is getting married. After quite awhile, it came to me that the people who are going to be her daughter's in-laws are also clients. That would be okay if it would be just information. But one of this woman's presenting concerns is issues she has with her daughter's future mother-in-law, who is a very [disturbed] person. (Schank, 1994, p. 57)

> It is very bizarre because I have clients [who] seem to know each other and talk about their therapy with each other. I have even had cases where two people who are friends who were in therapy with me separately—one will call and say, "I can't make it, but my friend wants my spot. We talked about it, and is it okay if he comes in at 10:00?" (pp. 57–58)

> As a matter of fact, one time I had—I did not know this—I had two new clients starting. They didn't know that the other one

was coming here, and they were having affairs with each other's mates. Well, I had to make a choice of whom I was going to see. In that particular case, it worked out fine. But just to let you know—there is tremendous overlapping. (p. 58)

Who is related to whom or who knows whom is always an interesting kind of question to be sensitive to. I've had that experience, at times, to discover without knowing it that I was seeing three generations of the same family. Unless I take the time to do a detailed family history with all the names, I just don't know that. (p. 58)

Getting Unsolicited Out-of-Therapy Information About Clients

Rural psychologists face the dilemma of getting unsolicited information about clients from other clients, the local grapevine, or community news. Although sometimes it is helpful to have a more complete picture of clients' lives, psychologists may have little control over when and what they hear. They struggle with what to do with this out-of-therapy information while trying to best meet the needs of clients. Psychologists choose different methods of managing what one person referred to as the "information that I need to withhold from myself!" This quotation captures the essence of the struggle that rural and small-community psychologists face as they try to respect and protect clients' confidentiality and privacy. Psychologists have to be ever vigilant and actively aware of where and from whom some of their client knowledge comes. They are frequently on the spot in making instantaneous decisions about what they can and cannot reveal or acknowledge, both with clients and with nonclients:

I know so many people. People come in here and talk about other people in the community, and I know those people— but I never indicate that I know them. Or they will say, "I'm a sister of so and so," and then I'll think, "Maybe that's how they got a referral here." But I hardly acknowledge that I even know that other person. (Schank, 1994, p. 59)

You know what you know. The way I usually deal with some of the stuff is to always be straight. Where it gets to be a problem is when it comes from another client. Many of my clients, because they know each other or refer one another, know I'm seeing so and so. They will come and say, "Well, such and such happened." But it is confidential, and so I can't share that I know it. What I often do in that case is ask the client who shared it to either share with the person if they have shared it with me or give me permission to share it. That usually works out fairly well, but that happens all too often. . . . There are cross-connections—an aunt of this client is also the stepmother of that client's boyfriend—so I get all this other information coming from other sources. . . . Eventually the client is going to find out I knew, and then they feel betrayed that I didn't share. So that is always the case. I think the ethical guidelines don't really allow for what is actually in the client's best interest. (pp. 59–60)

High Visibility and Lack of Privacy

Their own lack of privacy is an issue for the psychologists themselves, both in their professional lives and in day-to-day living, as members of rural areas and small communities:

> Running into patients out in the community, depending on what the setting is, can be real uncomfortable. There is almost this feeling that you have to kind of make sure you shave every day and take a bath. You can't go out looking kind of grungy because you might run into somebody. . . . For some clients who have real severe problems, I don't necessarily feel comfortable having them know who my kids or my family are. I remember a client once who was probably pretty close to being psychotic—having a lot of bizarre hallucinations. My wife and kids and I went to [local store] one day. There was this little guy dressed up in a costume for some kind of promotion, and my kid ran up to him. This guy was talking to him, and I thought, "That voice sounds familiar." He picks up my kid and is hugging him, and suddenly I realized that it is this client. Because of the knowledge that I had about this guy, I did not want him hugging my son or anything like that. So you always have to be on guard. (Schank, 1994, p. 60)

There is the gossip about outcomes of particular cases having to do with custody or divorces or things, where people are angry with you because you are seen as the promoter of such-

and-such an outcome. I have had situations—although this is not true today with our little community being much more sophisticated—where people would actually confront me directly on the street with that. I have had people walk up to me and ask me if I was analyzing everybody as I was just walking down the street and out of the hardware store. I had never lived in a small town, and it took quite a bit of adjustment. (pp. 60–61)

Collecting Unpaid Bills From Clients

Payment for psychological services is more personal in rural areas and small communities. Some psychologists have no qualms about turning clients' unpaid bills over to a collection service or using the court system, even if it means that the transaction will be published in the local newspaper:

> We will take a dollar a week, or if they can't pay for a year—you wouldn't believe my accounts receivable. But if I know they can [pay] and they weren't honest with me, then we send them to collection. Everything is up front when they walk in the door, and they know exactly what everything costs. We do a pretty active business with the collections people, and we have taken people to small-claims court. I figure I'm just like a retail person, you know. I do provide the service. If they think that something is wrong with me, I don't think they'd come back. If someone calls me up and says, "I've lost my job," I never tell anyone that I'll treat them for nothing, particularly around here—they think that's insulting. I tell them I'm going to bill them just like everybody else, but we'll take teeny payments or whatever. It works out fine. (Schank, 1994, p. 61)

Others agonize over collecting unpaid fees or gratefully rely on the larger organization by which they are employed:

> You can't send a collector after your neighbor or after the person in your church or service organization or whatever. So it is very tough. I have the advantage somewhat of working for this [corporation]. They do all that, and I can remove myself from that whole process and say, "If you have a financial prob-

lem, take it up with the clinic." That is a pleasure that I wouldn't have if I were in private practice. (p. 61)

Bartering

Some small-community psychologists speak openly of bartering for services. The 1992 American Psychological Association (APA) Ethics Code (APA, 1992), in which psychologists were advised to ordinarily refrain from bartering, was thought to have "unnecessarily tainted bartering relationships which are common among some cultural groups" (Knapp & VandeCreek, 2003, p. 112).

The 2002 Ethics Code clarified the issue of bartering:

> 6.05 Barter With Clients/Patients
>
> Barter is the acceptance of goods, services, or other non-monetary remuneration from clients/patients in return for psychological services. Psychologists may barter only if (1) it is not clinically contraindicated, and (2) the resulting arrangement is not exploitative. (APA, 2002a, p. 1068)

Although still ethically acceptable only under certain conditions, bartering is more engrained and acceptable in rural than in urban economic systems. It represents a way to maintain pride and enhance self-esteem in rural and small-community clients:

> I would take chickens—if that is what they could afford and it makes them feel good, that's what I would take. (Schank, 1994, p. 62)

> Bartering—I don't do a lot of that. I was real nervous about that. But an awful lot of people will come in here and say, "I cannot pay you, and I don't have insurance. But I own a green-house. Can we swap?" . . . There is an issue of self-esteem here. . . . One woman came in, and she had some needlework that she does. It was probably worth $500, and I said, "No, I would rather just see you for free." That didn't feel good to her. I did not take the cloth. But more often than not, it would be better for them to be able to give me something, to be able to come and take charge or do something. That really has not felt good. People will wind up giving me gifts, which we are not supposed to take either. But yes, a lot of people barter. It is

just that everyone is so afraid of getting nailed by the [State] Board of Psychology for it that they don't bring it up. . . . Nobody talks about it. (p. 62)

Knapp and VandeCreek (2003) indicated that bartering goods is less risky than bartering services, because goods can be examined and evaluated before being used as payment, or they can be returned if defective. They suggested that psychologists and clients come to a written agreement as to the worth of goods being bartered to guard against any potential disagreement and resultant negative feelings.

Limited Resources and Limits of Competence

Although some psychologists have been trained as generalists through their internships and work experience, none can be equally competent in all of the problems that clients present. Psychologists practicing in rural settings may be faced with competing dilemmas—should they attempt to meet the needs of all clients or should they turn away potential clients who may not have other psychological resources available?

Limits of the Psychologist's Own Competency or Expertise

The 2002 APA Ethics Code states the following:

2.01 Boundaries of Competence
   (a) Psychologists provide services, teach, and conduct research with populations and in areas only within the boundaries of their competence, based on their education, training, supervised experience, consultation, study, or professional experience.
   (b) Where scientific or professional knowledge in the discipline of psychology establishes that an understanding of factors associated with age, gender, gender identity, race, ethnicity, culture, national origin, religion, sexual orientation, disability, language, or socioeconomic status is essential for effective implementation of their services or research, psychologists have or obtain the training, experience, consulta-

tion, or supervision necessary to ensure the competence of their services, or they make appropriate referrals, except as provided in Standard 2.02, Providing Services in Emergencies.

(c) Psychologists planning to provide services, teach, or conduct research involving populations, areas, techniques, or technologies new to them undertake relevant education, training, supervised experience, consultation, or study.

(d) When psychologists are asked to provide services to individuals for whom appropriate mental health services are not available and for which psychologists have not obtained the competence necessary, psychologists with closely related prior training or experience may provide such services in order to ensure that services are not denied if they make a reasonable effort to obtain the competence required by using relevant research, training, consultation, or study. (APA, 2002a, pp. 1063–1064)

Rural psychologists are sometimes put in a position of deciding how far they can stretch their own levels of competence in attempting to best meet the needs of their clients and yet still practice within the ethical and legal guidelines of the profession. Many may practice in areas in which continuing education opportunities are only available at some geographical distance. Others may have adequate background as a generalist but limited experience with specific problems. Although some psychologists work in agencies that employ staff with a range of competencies and interests, others find themselves searching for ways to extrapolate from their own backgrounds or quickly learn more about a specific client's own presenting problem. This is evident in the following quote from one psychologist who participated in Schank's (1994) study:

> I have practiced outside the scope of my license a million times since I have been here because I sometimes feel like something is better than nothing. You know, it is tough to kind of say that and to be up front with that. But there is so little available in communities like this that whatever you may know is helpful. (p. 63)

The "decreased numbers of providers and long distances for obtaining diagnostic and other evaluative services" (Coyle, 1999, p. 203) leave rural psychologists caught between the needs of their communities and the realities of their own background and experience. Psychologists talk of the pressures, both from within themselves and from their communities, to try to be everything to everyone to meet what sometimes seem like overwhelming, diverse needs. Some deal with the pressure to address client needs that may be outside their own competencies by doing telephone screening intakes with prospective clients. This lessens the chance that they will be put in a position of trying to respond to the emotional pull of individuals whose needs might be better served elsewhere. They can then offer other resources to people whom they are not willing to accept as clients.

Some rural psychologists talk about quickly educating themselves by reading books and journal articles in an attempt to learn along the way. Because "opportunities for continuing education and consultation/collaboration are often limited" (Coyle, 1999, p. 206), distance learning and electronic resources (including Web searches, Webcasting, and video teleconferencing) are proving invaluable to rural psychologists. Other psychologists inform clients from the beginning that their presenting problems are on the edge of the psychologists' areas of expertise. They may suggest that they try working together, with the understanding that the clients will be referred if it later seems more appropriate. These psychologists focus on general skills that they would use with any client as they learn more about a specific problem while also trying to recognize their own limitations.

However, some psychologists talk about the increase in available mental health resources within the past few years and their resultant relief in being able to refer clients to other mental health practitioners. They talk about being able to consult with local colleagues when practicing at the edge of their areas of competency and of realizing that some clients are willing to drive to larger cities, if necessary, to get the most appropriate treatment. Technological advances also make it easier for psychologists to develop expertise quickly and in response to the immediate needs of particular clients (Schopp, Johnstone, & Reid-Arndt, 2005).

Geographical Distance

Geographical distance can sometimes be an issue, both for clients and for psychologists (Gamm et al., 2003). Distance, along with lack of resources and the high cost of transportation (Crawford, 2003), can have a major impact on how and where a client receives services:

> I don't think people who don't live in small towns understand that a lot of people don't even have telephones. A great many of them don't have cars, and there is no public transportation. They often will schedule appointments around a dozen other things that they are doing in town, like shopping, dentist, and visiting Aunt Mary, because they don't have gas to get here or they don't have a car and they have to piggyback with somebody who is coming in. If you say, "I want you to go see one of my colleagues out in _____" or wherever, that might as well be Africa because they can't get there. (Schank, 1994, p. 65)

Other psychologists talk about the hardship that clients face in having to drive many miles to get to psychological resources, particularly if the clients are low income and assigned to a specific mental health center or hospital for services. A related issue involves those who live close to the state border in having to help clients go outside the state to the closest hospital. Insurance and Medical Assistance benefits can be difficult, if not impossible, to negotiate across state lines, even if the nearest in-state facility is 2 or 3 hours away. Referrals across county lines may even be problematic.

Psychologists struggle with geographical distance as they try to maintain consultation groups and collegial relationships across many miles:

> We have hired another psychologist, which has been just a wonderful addition. Up until then, it was a tremendous problem. In the couple of years that I practiced here by myself, I would call colleagues—people I went to school with. I have a friend in Washington, DC, who is an expert on the Rorschach and another one in Boston who is an expert on working with elderly folks. I would call them, and I would talk to them and ask them for supervision. There was a time for about a year when about six therapists who practice in a tri-county region here had loosely affiliated into kind of a therapist support group. We were meeting for a time once a month . . . kind of rotating the site. We would either talk about difficult cases, or

somebody would be assigned a topic and they would do a literature review. It is unfortunate that it didn't work out, primarily because of competing [demands] for time or whatever. It was pretty neat how we would network with each other. Networking with somebody 60 miles away is real different for me than networking with someone in the next building. But we would send patients to each other, and we would bring difficult cases. We met once a month for probably six months to a year before it fell apart because of the distance and driving in the winter. So that, plus probably doing literature reviews as much as I could, although at times I am so busy that there wasn't any time to read the articles—I guess that's the way you make it. You develop some sort of close or distant support group with other clinicians. (Schank, 1994, pp. 65–66)

Recent technological advances have made it easier for psychologists to educate themselves on the Internet and through telehealth opportunities. However, this is only a partial substitute for important face-to-face interactions with other mental health professionals.

Limited Educational Opportunities

Although some psychologists welcome trips to larger cities or other areas for educational opportunities, the distance and time involved pose a hardship for others. It may be difficult to arrange coverage for clients while the psychologist is out of town, along with the added stress of taking time off to travel for educational purposes:

It's selecting the right kind of workshop, and sometimes it's a financial issue. If I take a day off, it's a whole day. Somebody has to pay for the office and the secretary. It you are in Minneapolis, you jump in the car, and you're there in half an hour. But for me it's usually a whole afternoon minimum, most likely the day really, to get it in. So when I do select a workshop, it tends to be an all-day or two-day kind of thing. (Schank, 1994, p. 66)

Many rural and small-community psychologists make a real effort to educate themselves through their own professional reading:

I think if you are going to practice in a rural area, you should be prepared to practice in a rural area. Part of it is using the library and reading journals. If people aren't around, you should be willing to read, look stuff up, and tap into the computer system. If you are not prepared, you are up a creek. (Schank, 1994, p. 66)

Limited Access to Specialized Services

The lack of specialists and specialized services can be an issue for rural psychologists. The general push toward specialization within the profession of psychology as a whole can also be a source of ambivalence:

> There is an interesting conflict in my mind. Professional psychology is moving toward this idea of having a national college, having stated competencies, and passing tests in certain areas. There seems to be an American Psychological Association movement toward specialization in the way it's competing with other disciplines. But you cannot afford to be a specialist in a rural community. We really are the Lone Rangers, and you have to do everything. You have to know something about everything because there is no one else to refer to. (Schank, 1994, p. 67)

Specialization often comes about in response to client needs, rather than from a proactive stance:

> Because we are a smaller agency, we don't have all the special services. Most of us are generalists, and we do a little bit of everything. Some people handle more kinds of things than another, but it is not like in the cities where you have people that can focus on one area. (p. 67)

Natural talent or interest on the part of specific psychologists can be another route for specialized services:

> We really don't have a therapist on staff who has specific training and only works in one area. But we have some therapists who kind of take to [some more specialized areas] more naturally and kind of learn as they go. But in terms of being able to

point to some specific training in it, really there is no one here
that can say that. (p. 67)

Community Expectations and
Values Differences

Because psychologists are trained almost exclusively in urban
areas, there may be significant problems between the values of
many mental health providers and the residents of small communities and rural areas. As examples, Kersting (2003a) identified possible rural–urban attitude differences regarding racial issues, binge drinking, and domestic violence, along with some
rural resentment toward highly educated people. Some rural
residents may experience it as an intrusion when a more highly
educated professional "comes into a relatively closed community wishing to educate and liberalize the population" (Coyle,
1999, p. 203). Some rural and small-community psychologists
do identify issues that are problematic for them, especially values differences, but they also talk about positive aspects and
areas of agreement.

Values Differences

One psychologist's description seems particularly representative
of most rural psychologists:

> My values are different than the stereotypic values of the ru-
> ral community, but I'm not alone in that. Most of us who have
> had the blessings and the opportunity of higher education have
> more of a broad-based, metaphoric, poetic way of looking at
> our lives and the lives of others and are at odds with sort of a
> self-righteous, rigid, good/bad type of mindset. (Schank, 1994,
> p. 68)

Abortion is an issue that some psychologists raise in response
to questions regarding values differences. Some choose to keep
their views private to avoid generating consequences or making
clients uncomfortable. Others are more open about their views

on abortion, expecting that clients or prospective clients will have to make choices as to whether they want to see a psychologist who is pro-abortion or anti-abortion. The following excerpt is an example of one person's learning experience:

> I made a big mistake once, which I needed to do as part of my learning process. I was at a Rotary meeting with 80 people or so. One of the local priests was giving a presentation about abortion. His particular speech was that [abortion] was not a good thing and that women who have abortions suffer forever emotionally. Then there was time for questions and answers. I raised my hand and said, "I just want to add that researchers have done a lot of studies looking at post-abortion syndrome, and they found that it is temporary and that it is not a lifelong process for the majority of women." Ohhh, I might as well have said that I'm a Communist! I realized that was not a smart move. It may not have been the right way to do it. In a city it might have been okay, but here there is a more conservative approach. I think I turned off some people with that. I wasn't necessarily trying to present my personal opinion but that this is factual information. But it wasn't the right thing to do. (Schank, 1994, p. 69)

Some small-community psychologists find values differences between themselves and the community related to sexual orientation, as well as physical punishment. In some rural communities, physical punishment and abuse may be more accepted:

> The one that comes to mind first is what I would call very traditional, you might call sexist, values. As a matter of fact, it kind of blew my mind. I have a fair number of women I see who are in battered situations, marital rape situations—very abusive—who come to me with absolute conviction handed down from their mothers that "I owe this to my husband." To try to get them to see that as abuse is really complex. I know that's true everywhere, but here it is the culture that feels that way and not just within a given dysfunctional family. One really blew my mind this week—a mother took it the next step and told her daughter, who had not wanted to be sexual until she gets married next fall, "You are unreasonable. He has needs, and you have to oblige." (Schank, 1994, pp. 69–70)

Clients in rural communities may tend to come to therapy only for very specific problems, often postponing any sort of therapeutic contact until or unless the problem is very serious in nature:

> I think there is much less of wanting to do it to enhance your life. In rural areas you don't have that much of a leisure class, so most people aren't into personal growth. When I first moved here, I talked with a psychologist down in _____, and he made a comment that has always stayed with me. He thinks that people in this area—and I think this would be true of any rural area—have a real high tolerance for pain. They really have to be in crisis or they have to really have hit bottom before they come in. (Schank, 1994, p. 70)

Community denial is sometimes raised as a values difference in rural communities. It is a value with vast power:

> You will hear from the town if you don't keep your grass cut, but if I were having a knock-down, drag-out fight with my husband, I would be very surprised if anyone would call and complain. It's like what goes on inside is fine as long as the outside of your house looks nice and is painted. . . . It's a great place to raise kids, it's a great place to live, but it wouldn't be a great place to have a problem. In a lot of ways, of course, we believe we don't have any problems. (Schank, 1994, p. 70)

Informal Communication Network

The informal communication network in small towns carries information on psychologists' personal and professional behavior, especially if it diverges from community norms and expectations:

> We would go to the local steak house, and I would have a beer or something. I would hear from patients that "Oh, so-and-so saw you with a beer." You might lose some patients because of that. (Schank, 1994, p. 71)

Successes and failures are more visible, and pressure to react in certain ways may come into play:

> Not everybody that comes in works with you real well and follows through. That is a problem that will occur on occa-

sion. . . . I have people that have wanted me to lock somebody up. Any time I get that pressure, I just slow down and work even slower until I get to the bottom of where the pressure comes. People who know me know I don't fold. They are better off just to be quiet than to try to influence me. It just won't work. (p. 71)

This other psychologist we hired has only been here for three months. This is the first time he has ever lived in a small town. . . . The first thing that happened when he got here is that he had a real sticky child abuse case that involved a local dignitary. He had no desire to start off on the wrong foot with somebody who was in a position of power in the community. He ended up, after a lot of discussion, referring that person out of town because he felt it would be just too difficult. . . . Things that you do with clients spread like wildfire. Everybody knows everybody. If you did something naughty, then it is going to hurt; if you do a good job, they will be knocking down your doors; if you do something wrong, you're in trouble. (p. 71)

Religious Issues

A related issue has to do with religious values in some small towns. One psychologist speaks of trying to bridge the distance between her profession as a psychologist and the charismatic Christian beliefs of some of her clients:

We seem to have what I consider pretty extreme fundamentalism. It can be sticky because people will often throw up a roadblock. We don't talk about that, especially not here in a small town. . . . I have a client who is an incest survivor, and she is a charismatic Christian. One of the things that really worried me was that her [religious] community deemed it necessary to cast the demons out. That was going to cure her, and she must forgive. What I try to do is translate my psychology talk into Christian terms so that I am talking in her terminology. (Schank, 1994, p. 72)

Expectations for Community Participation

Requests for participation in community events, organizations, committees, task forces, and educational activities may lead some psychologists to feel overwhelmed or burned out:

Everybody wants you to do something—be part of their club, serve on the board of directors. They want me to give talks all the time. That's just separate from the actual job-related things—the emergencies and the crises you have to attend to. . . . There are a lot of demands that are separate from actually providing services. You kind of have to balance. . . . My wife and I have had a lot of discussions about trying to find that line. . . . So I try to weigh every request with the potential value of it—could someone else do it, would this be a new source of referral or something that could continue the patient load? But it does seem like you just can't hide. (Schank, 1994, p. 72)

I can remember during the farm crisis going to a meeting that I was asked to participate and be involved in. I can remember this one being just terrible because around here there were farms that were going to go and were in the process of going—you could see the writing on the wall. I was really torn by that. It felt like a never-ending thing for me—like I was eaten alive in there—and yet I wanted to help. I ended up being emotionally and physically drained and thought, "I can't get immersed in this any more; I have to draw back a little." I did return to that about three years later. Then it was time limited, and there were some boundaries on it, whereas the other one was a bottomless pit and you would sink right down into it. (p. 72–73)

Mistrust and Stereotyping of Psychologists

Lack of exposure to the profession in some small, conservative communities seems to produce mistrust and stereotypes of psychologists:

Because people haven't been exposed to it, it still is not acceptable to come for therapy. I don't know how people feel about using therapy in the cities. I would guess that the percentage of people that use counseling or therapy is much, much higher in the cities. (Schank, 1994, p. 73)

A minister came up to me and said, "After you have been here for seven years, we may begin to think you are okay." That is true. In small towns they are very worried about people coming and going and don't like the idea of people moving around.

Ministers aren't supposed to leave their parish until after ten years or so. I can see where they have some concerns about agencies that bring folks in for a year or two, and then they move on again. There are some real disruptions with that. (p. 73)

A psychologist gave an example from her community, where "psychologists are often viewed as weird":

especially among older people. [Here in this small town] just two weeks ago [someone] was introducing me to this very nice lady, and she slipped and said, "Oh, you're that . . ." and I said, "The head shrinker . . ." She laughed and said, "We need people like you here, too." But I could tell that wasn't really what she thinks. I guess that is probably true in the cities as well, but it is just absorbed as part of the community. You are not really targeted like you are here. (p. 73)

Another psychologist spoke of "going to a social gathering—you tell people that you are a psychologist, and they usually put about 40 feet between you and them" (p. 73).

Confidentiality

Paradoxically, maintaining confidentiality contributes to some of the mistrust. Residents of rural areas and small communities are used to knowing about and sharing information regarding the health and well-being of others. In addition, rural psychologists are faced with the aftereffects of times when they are mandated to break confidentiality in ways that their less visible urban colleagues are not (Helbok, 2003).

Concerned others in the community, including family members, may expect that psychologists will disclose information about clients (Simon & Williams, 1999). Rural residents, including clients, may need education around issues of confidentiality, a standard that is usually more automatically assumed by their urban counterparts (Coyle, 1999).

A number of years in a very typical small town, I was seeing a woman who was about 70 years old. She was at a point in her life where she had lost her job, had major health problems, and was in a real transition stage in her life. Her brother called and wondered how she was doing, and I couldn't tell him anything. I think that is very typical. Here is somebody really well intended, yet I could not share anything with him. He was very put off by it. Interestingly, I think the standard for confidentiality in small-town medical clinics is very different. If somebody has cancer, people will know about that. In general, people open up more about what is happening if it is a medical problem. . . . It is very much a healthy sort of thing—"What can we do to help?" But that does play into times where confidentiality gets pushed. (Schank, 1994, p. 74)

Interagency Issues: Working With Other Community Agencies, Groups, and Professionals

Issues around working relationships with other professionals in rural areas illustrate both the pros and cons of working in small communities. Although many psychologists in these settings talk about the positive aspects of working with other agencies and related professions, there are also difficulties. Information may be shared more casually among agencies in rural areas, and psychologists may be expected to provide information on clients without appropriate informed consent (Helbok, 2003). It is essential to address these difficulties, especially when many clients may need wraparound or other services from a range of providers within the small community.

Other professionals may be guided by codes that differ from those of psychologists or that have been "shaped by practice on the frontier" (Kersting, 2003a, p. 68)—a far cry from what psychologists may learn in an urban academic setting.

One of the most common concerns is the competence of other professionals, particularly mental health professionals. Referrals to and from other agencies and professionals also surface as problematic, especially when there may be few other service providers available.

Questioning the Competence of Other Professionals

Visibility and the local grapevine make it hard for psychologists to openly challenge other professionals. Some express concern over the lack of other qualified professionals and the dilemma of hearing about poor-quality, but not blatantly unethical, practice. Many rural psychologists choose to handle these situations by helping clients make informed choices as to plans of treatment, talking directly to practitioners if they have concerns, and not referring clients to questionable mental health practitioners. However, in small communities, confronting other professionals and pushing for adherence to ethical standards can have lasting implications:

> I sent a letter stating that I thought that was very unprofessional. That is all I can do. You know, the other part in a rural area is that you don't want to be known as someone who reports every little thing that happens because we all blow it [at times]. Because there is so much that happens, I never try to judge anyone that has done a bad job because, you know, personalities are different. I'm certainly not going to work well with everybody else. But I don't know what can be done about that—it is scary. (Schank, 1994, p. 77)

Some rural psychologists talk about dilemmas over clearer ethical violations by other mental health practitioners: misrepresentation, practicing outside areas of stated competency, failure to report, and misuse and misinterpretation of psychological tests.

> I wrote a rather explicit complaint to the [State] Board of Psychology about reporting on this issue. An older adolescent was abusing a young adolescent very clearly and repeatedly. His parents had told his therapist, and the therapist took no action. He reported it to no one and saw this kid every other week for an ice cream. This is not acceptable. (Schank, 1994, p. 78)

> The only conflicts I've had with anybody have been over ethics—well, misrepresenting themselves. The thing that really drives me up a wall is taking tests to do at home. There is one character around who sends tests home all the time. I've run

into at least three people who couldn't read, and they were sent home with a test. I confronted [him] about that and got a lot of bad feelings. . . . I think it is probably easier here to get away with unethical behavior. I see it in stuff like testing and misrepresentation. (p. 78)

Questions of competence also come up around dealing with social service agencies, particularly their responses to abuse issues and systemic concerns around who defines and responds to client needs:

[Clients] will come to me and talk about or complain about someone else in the community, who is only trying to do [his or her] job. But my clients don't think it is done properly. It is difficult. I can't side with them, of course. But sometimes I think I have information in the back of my mind, and sometimes they are right. I just try to give them someone else to help them or some other way to go. (p. 78)

Local schools may be the focus of some concerns regarding competence of other professionals:

People look to the school system as the "have all" and "be all." I see them as poorly situated to be of much help, so I don't ask them to do much, and I don't include them. I haven't seen their level of expertise and their commitment to the psychological [issues] to be there. . . . I find it kind of a drain. You know, we move as slow as the slowest person, so we have to educate the teacher before we get the child served. We're going to have to bypass it or find a way to work with the existing system. (p. 78)

The behavior of physicians leads some psychologists to seriously question the physicians' competence. The conflicts remain out of the public eye, for the most part, because of the possible consequences of openly challenging the prestigious reputation of the small-town doctor:

Many people, when I first see them, will say, "I have panic disorder. My general practitioner has been prescribing for me for five years, and it is really not working." I get real irritated when people come and tell me that, but it happens a lot. They will often have prescription medications—sleeping pills, anxiety-reduction pills. They will come in and say, "Well, my doctor tells me I have a problem with nerves." What century are we living in?! We have a local psychiatrist, who shall remain nameless, but I will not refer to this person. He gave a presentation a couple years back that "Valium is your friend." Unfortunately, he is the most close by for many people and often more available—but I think I know why that is! I've had people come and say, "I have been seeing Doctor So-and-So." I just kind of grit my teeth. If it seems like what is going on is helpful, I keep my mouth shut. That gets to be kind of tricky, too. (Schank, 1994, p. 79)

Concerns about the behavior of police are raised, including the concerns of one psychologist who tells of an incident where the police brought a violent, intoxicated, suicidal client to her home in the middle of the night. The psychologist was concerned about her own and her family's immediate and long-term safety:

This was a person who had been multiply-hospitalized, like 17 times, and he wasn't even 30 years old. He is arguing, rather articulately for a person who is drunk and violent, that, "You know darn well if they put me in the hospital, that it isn't going to make me any better." I said, "No, it probably won't. But it is going to keep you from being dead or someone else from being dead. At this point, that's what my goal is." So he was threatening to do away with me as they cuffed him and dragged him out of my house, but I thought, "Fine." (Schank, 1994, p. 80)

Referral Dilemmas

Referrals from social services, community mental health centers, and schools are significant issues for psychologists. Long-standing political and financial connections affect the range of client choices. Some psychologists in private practice and in clinic or hospital settings report poor relationships with local community mental health centers. They talk about making overtures or attempting to network, sometimes to no avail. One person who worked in an outpatient hospital setting described the problem:

> The county, for instance, gives all of the block grants to the community agency, which really narrows down the selection for the client. I have had numerous clients who have wanted a specific kind of emphasis, say on the spiritual or the holistic, but couldn't go [where that was offered] because the funding was . . . over at the competitors. That is really inappropriate for the community. The money [should] go to the client, not the client to where the money is. (Schank, 1994, p. 80)

Another person in private practice told of more direct attacks:

> When I started, that mental health center went after me. They had people go to meetings and not only do and say unethical things about me, but they told me that they would give me six months and I would be gone. They told me that, and they tried really, really, really, hard. (p. 81)

Local schools can prove problematic in terms of referrals, as described by one psychologist who practices in a community mental health center:

> The conflict that we have been having is with the schools. . . . My good friend who is a counselor in the elementary school was told that she could not make a formal referral to the mental health center because the school would be liable to pay for those services. (Schank, 1994, p. 81)

Uninformed physicians are described by one psychologist as a source of inappropriate referrals:

> The dynamics of that relationship between a physician and a psychologist have been real interesting for me to try to understand—what they see my role as being, what I see my role as being, and trying to educate the physicians about what I can and cannot do. I find that they either have a much, much higher expectation of what we can do than what we really can do or it is much, much lower. . . . They will send me somebody who may be totally inappropriate. . . . Or they call and want to

walk me through what they want me to do, as though I have no credentials whatsoever. It's because they have never had any contact with us. (Schank, 1994, p. 81)

Maintaining Confidentiality and Appropriate Boundaries

Maintaining confidentiality and appropriate boundaries presents a challenge for some small-community psychologists who interact with the court system (attorneys, judges, social workers, probation officers) and the schools:

> What I had to get used to was basically making sure that there were the boundaries with attorneys. That was always something I had to fight with. They would once in awhile try to sabotage a custody evaluation or press for information from a report before the report was done. I have to be very careful not to get into an adversarial role. What I found worked for me is if I maintained my practitioner's role and explained that to them. . . . Schools—the biggest thing there is communication back and forth. It is surprising, but they have trouble with understanding confidentiality in therapy. They want to know what is going on, so it is almost an insult to them as a professional. . . . But, ultimately, the clients' [needs] have to come first. (Schank, 1994, pp. 81–82)

More general issues revolved around competing demands:

> I have really felt that there was always tension between the Department of Social Services and us [at the community mental health center]—different goals, different purposes. If they're antagonistic, they're not going to follow through for whatever reason. (Schank, 1994, p. 82)

Peer Helpers and Other Alternatives to Traditional Treatment Methods

It is important for rural psychologists to work with peer helpers within their communities, especially because the "scarcity of qualified professional service providers in rural areas [necessitates] the training and utilization of informal networks of support" (Gamm et al., 2003, p. 1). These peer helpers may be clergy, nurses, county extension agents, attorneys, veterinarians, and others to whom rural residents turn for advice and assistance. However, conflicts may arise between rural peer helpers and more formally trained mental health professionals regarding differences in beliefs and concerns about boundary issues:

> There have been some that would have resisted anybody. I don't see that as being me personally. For example, I had patients come in that I was trying to do some pain management with. I was using some hypnotic techniques. They were told by their priest or minister that "you shouldn't do that because it allows the devil to come in." One client said, "I can't do this anymore." I said, "Why? It will help." "No, my minister said this is not good." So I don't think it is me personally, but I think it is some of the things that I represent. Others who are a bit more progressive have been real pleased and happy to coordinate services. (Schank, 1994, p. 85)

Burnout

An overwhelming workload, along with difficulty setting limits in a rural community in which everyone knows each other, may affect rural psychologists' ability to function professionally and personally. Although community mental health centers, crisis centers, hospitals, and other colleagues may provide or share after-hours emergency coverage, rural psychologists themselves must educate clients and others in the community to know about available resources and psychologists' boundaries. Some rural psychologists struggle to find a balance that is respectful to themselves, their clients, and their communities:

> The physicians from the group man the emergency room at the hospital. Because there is no psychiatric triage system in this community, mental health emergencies end up at the emergency room. If it is a mental health problem the physicians will call me, not because I have signed up but because

I'm *it*. I have privileges at the hospital, and so does my business partner. But no other mental health professional in the area does. It ends up like being on call. We carry beepers, and it is intrusive. But I don't know any other way for it to be handled. . . . No one has ever said you have to be here to answer every crisis, but I don't know how you can come here and be in the profession without some compulsiveness already to be the helper. (Schank, 1994, p. 87)

I usually have a hard time recognizing my burnout level until I'm in it. I look at my schedule, and I have three weeks booked in advance. Then my codependency kicks in, and I know I can't cancel this client. They give me *&#! when I take a vacation—"Well, you already had one this year!" Then they come to my house when I take time off. (p. 87)

Work Overload

Work overload that comes from having to be a generalist in rural psychology practice affects the stress level of many practitioners. Although some welcome the variety, it can also be problematic:

I think part of the burnout issue is you can't really carve out a neat little niche. . . . I have a heck of a time moving from a session with a child to a session with an adult. To me, it is just a whole different mindset. I tried saying [that] I'm not going to work with kids, even though I had the training. It's too hard. There's no one to work with kids, and then that guilt thing— that is real stressful to me. It's always having to switch gears. (Schank, 1994, p. 88)

Responding to the needs of the community adds to the stress of working with individual clients. Requests to be on committees and task forces leave rural psychologists with the dilemma of how to help provide resources and education while still maintaining the energy needed to work with individual clients. Rural psychologists who are already overbooked talk about the additional stress of requests from prospective clients:

The overload comes more from the fact that we turn away approximately seven new calls a week—we have been keeping track. It is real hard on me. If I answer the phone, it is real hard for me to do. The secretary is much better at it. (Schank, 1994, p. 88)

I think that is really the number one ethical dilemma—that waiting period and how quickly we are to respond. There was one time I had a woman call this spring, and I was not taking any new referrals. She said that the earliest she could get in even at the mental health center was six weeks. . . . One of the ethical dilemmas is that you are supposed to be able to make sure that you provide services within a [reasonable] length of time. My waiting list right now is three months. (p. 95)

Blurring of Roles and Lack of Privacy

Blurring of roles and lack of privacy, as contributors to burnout, are illustrated by the comments of the following rural psychologist:

It is more the intensity of never being done. I can't go out of my house. It never fails that if I am in the middle of a project and am wearing my grubbiest clothes and just want to run and get a can of paint, five clients are there. And it's just like, "Leave me alone!" (Schank, 1994, p. 88)

Isolation

Rural psychologists frequently raise the issue of isolation, primarily professional but also personal, of practicing in a small, rural community. This isolation has been lessened in recent years through the Internet and through telehealth, both of which provide important connections (Sawyer & Beeson, 1998). However, it is still easy for rural psychologists to become isolated, because Internet and telephone connections cannot "replace the day-to-day learning and growing through daily interactions with peers" (Helbok, 2003, p. 378). As one psychologist described earlier, they may try to arrange to get together periodically with other psychologists in their part of the state to discuss cases and stimulate professional growth, but bad weather and heavy caseloads may make such a plan difficult:

One thing is not having as many colleagues around. I think there could be a possibility, anyway, of a lack of professional

stimulation—not just the support but the stimulation. I sometimes feel like there are people in cities that are doing things
that I don't even know about, and I'm just kind of down here
trying to keep my head above water. When I worked in the
city, I would really keep track of what the hot issues were and
the current trends. (Schank, 1994, p. 90)

Some rural psychologists find it difficult to get involved in state-
wide professional organizations, and others feel misunderstood
or disempowered:

[The state psychological association] sent out a survey wanting to know how they could get more rural involvement. I
wrote on the survey that my workload, my caseload, my stress
level are so raised that to take time [for that is too much]. Even
though it would be interesting, it would feel like work. . . . I
think with the professional organizations being focused in the
cities that not a lot of attention is paid and issues aren't raised
from the rural community. (Schank, 1994, p. 90)

It is difficult to find the time, and sometimes the money, to travel
to cities for professional training and development: "It is the lack
of or difficulty getting to places where you can do some professional growing. You know, here we have to go someplace, where
in the cities you have something right around the corner or whatever" (p. 91).

Personal and cultural isolation also can be at issue. A sense of
isolation from the community, due to the need to maintain appropriate professional boundaries, adds to the isolation of having few available colleagues. Community attitudes toward psychology sometimes contribute to the isolation: "I think there is
that sense of isolation. Probably a psychologist in rural America
still faces an uphill battle in terms of where they stand in the big
picture in the community because people are still suspect"
(Schank, 1994, p. 91).

Lack of Privacy for Clients

Another issue of importance is the lack of privacy for clients, especially because of the stigma surrounding the use of mental

health services in many rural areas. Rural clients are reluctant to participate in group therapy because confidentiality cannot be guaranteed and because group members' lives may frequently overlap outside of the group therapy session. They may also encounter support staff who are their acquaintances or relatives.

Psychologists in rural private practice choose their locations carefully, either in less traveled parts of the community or in places (e.g., medical settings or small malls) where clients can blend in with other patients or consumers. Rural psychologists talk of clients' fears of running into other people in the waiting area and of setting up their practice space with different entrances and exits available for clients. Office staff may know clients, which can prove uncomfortable for both parties. Sometimes the contacts are unavoidable:

> It is very hard to hide in a small town . . . there seem to be crossovers between the clients. If we have a client waiting in the waiting room, another client will walk in and they know each other. So we can't always protect confidentiality. There have been times when that has been kind of difficult—like when we have some real high profile clients who are known to the whole community. One patient will walk out, and then they see this person. It's like, "What are you doing here? Guess what, I'm here too." There is nothing that we can do to stop that, short of shuffling people out the back door. We have had some real funny little things that go on out there; and I'm not sure what to do, if anything, about that. (Schank, 1994, p. 92)

> [Privacy] is a big problem. . . . [Clients] may see each other in the waiting room. They have their cars parked out in front, and people know their cars . . . at times, people will park a couple of blocks away so that they won't be identified. (p. 92)

The lack of privacy also makes attempts at group treatment problematic in rural settings, especially because psychologists cannot ensure that all clients will maintain the confidentiality of other group members. Even if confidentiality prevails, clients may not be comfortable sharing personal information with other group members whom they are likely to encounter within their community.

Constrictions/Visibility of the Psychologist's Personal Life

Personal anonymity may be largely nonexistent in rural and other small communities in which everyone knows everyone else's business (Coyle, 1999; Helbok, 2003; Simon & Williams, 1999). Limitations in and visibility of rural psychologists' personal lives add to their stress in maintaining ethical practice. They talked about the difficulty of having a social life or doing volunteer work while trying to avoid contact with clients and about the visibility of a psychologist in a rural community:

> I grew up in [large Midwestern city], and mentally I still assume, at times anyhow, that I'm invisible—nobody knows me. A lot of times I am shocked that they know everything about me. Particularly as a professional, you are more noticeable. If I go through a divorce, everyone knows. It's like your personal life is under scrutiny. . . . About six months ago I had my two wine coolers. A patient came in on Monday and said, "Well, you know, you had two wine coolers" . . . I think being single in a small town, if you are a professional, is—you just can't meet anybody. (Schank, 1994, p. 92)

> The other issue for rural practice is that everyone knows my name. There are lots and lots of things that are attributed to me, things I've said. . . . That absolutely blows me away. Because I'm a known commodity in town—people tend to use whatever experts they can to fight with their husbands or whatever. My name comes up, and I will get calls—"You said this to my wife". . . . That is really tough. I don't know how often that happens down in the urban area. My guess is very little. . . . It gets to be a little difficult because a lot of things can get attributed to me. I have no control over that. (pp. 92–93)

Finding therapy for themselves or for family members usually involves driving some distance or crossing boundaries to rely on local colleagues:

> My son, for awhile, was a little confused. I kind of felt like he should go to someone whom I didn't know. I did talk to a couple of therapists here, and they said that they would see him. But he never ended up going. (Schank, 1994, p. 93)

Because the potential number of close friends may already be limited just by being in a small community, psychologists may feel somewhat lonely and isolated (Coyle, 1999; Dittmann, 2003). Despite the best of intentions, problems can occur in posttherapy friendships or business dealings with former clients. Posttherapy friendships with former clients are complicated by the potential for damaging therapeutic gains and the removal of the options for the client to return to therapy at a later date if needed. It can also prove difficult if the psychologist wants to be friends with some former clients and not with others (Coyle, 1999).

Changes in Health Care Delivery

Increased pressure from managed care, including pressure to affiliate or to be included on provider panels, is worrisome to rural private practitioners, especially when that means covering a large geographic area:

> I think the health care reform and going to the limited networks is cutting out all of the seasoned people, particularly in the rural areas. (Schank, 1994, p. 93)

> I think in a small-town practice, or at least in a solo practice, my survival depends on spreading myself out in a number of different areas. I had the experience about three years ago now with the employee state health plan of suddenly losing some of my clientele. So survival in a setting like this depends on being very diversified. I do court evaluations, I do Social Security evaluations, I do consulting with group homes, I do some consulting for Lutheran Social Services, plus seeing a number of clients here in the private practice. My survival depends on being sufficiently diverse in what I do that, regardless what changes come through, it is going to have some effect on me. But I am not totally dependent on one source for my practice. (p. 94)

There are also problems in rural areas related to a shortage of adequate resources for hospitalizing clients:

> Enormous problems—particularly with so many Medical Assistance [MA] clients. My understanding is that you cannot

commit an MA client to a hospital outside of your state, and we usually use a hospital just across the state line that has an adult psychiatry unit. Other than that, the only place to send them is to the state hospital, and nobody wants to go there. There is a real stigma to going there, and I know from people who have been there that they don't get a lot of help. With children it is just a nightmare because we don't have anything in this area. They have to go across the state line to get hospitalized. There is a child and adolescent unit there. If a kid has to be committed, you can't send them there if they have MA. It is real tough. Plus, hospitals that are money-making institutions don't want to admit an MA client, and they don't get a lot of help at the state hospitals. So it is a problem being on the border because you may have someone who is a specialist in some things across the state line an hour away, but clients may just have to go [many miles away to] the city to get the same thing because it is in the same state. (Schank, 1994, pp. 94–95)

A related issue is one of finding competent mental health professionals to practice in rural areas, especially when reimbursement rates may be lower than in urban settings.

Summary

Throughout this chapter, we have discussed a number of issues that are integrally involved in ethical practice for psychologists in rural areas. These include boundary issues in overlapping social and professional relationships, limited resources available to rural psychologists and limits of the psychologists' own competence, expectations of other members of the rural community, working with other professionals in the community, working with alternative and peer helpers, burnout and isolation, lack of privacy for both clients and psychologists, and changes in health care delivery. In the next chapter, we look at several other small communities in which psychologists share many similarities with their rural colleagues as they strive to practice ethically and sensitively in meeting the needs of their clients.

5

Other Small Communities

The issues of rural psychologists, which we addressed in the previous chapter, bear a striking resemblance to issues raised by psychologists who practice in other small communities. Small colleges; communities of color; gay, lesbian, bisexual, transgender (GLBT) communities; the chemical health/chemical dependency community; and communities based on religious affiliation, feminism, the military, law enforcement/criminal justice/corrections, suburbs, disability, deafness, and therapists who see other therapists as clients are some of the examples of small communities in which psychologists face a range of dilemmas. Yet the difficulties of practicing within a small community receive little attention in most training programs, textbooks, and professional presentations.

Similarities Across Communities

Many psychologists in these small communities face the same dilemmas as their rural colleagues: professional boundaries and overlapping relationships, limited resources and limits of competence, community expectations, interagency issues, working with peer and alternative helpers, maintaining confidentiality, and lack of privacy for clients and practitioners. Like their rural colleagues, they frequently live and socialize within the communities they serve. It is important that they be known and trusted, and clients frequently seek them out because they *are* visible and involved.

Such interdependence leads to both expected and unexpected overlap, even in small communities within larger, urban areas. If managed ethically, these overlapping relationships may enhance the therapeutic relationships and validate clients' experience. Seeing a psychologist at community events may help to normalize the profession of psychology and the psychologist as an individual. Members of the community may be more willing to seek out psychologists whom they have seen at community events or whom they know through family, friends, or other contexts.

It is important for psychologists to examine possible conflicts, potential consequences, and their own motives prior to entering into a therapeutic relationship with another member of a small community. They may be able to offer services within the community that are more effective and far reaching than efforts of psychologists who are outside of the community and who have little overlap but less knowledge of issues specific to that community. Situations that test such boundaries are not always clear or easily anticipated, and "guidelines regarding how to identify and respond to such situations are not routinely available" (Lamb & Catanzaro, 1998, p. 498).

Broader mainstream approaches to psychology are probably most useful when combined with local knowledge of "situationally or culturally specific sets of beliefs and values" (C. E. Hill & Fraser, 1995, p. 554). There may be commonalities that bind residents of small communities together in ways not identifiable to people outside of the community. Some small communities have individuals who are identifiable as local healers, with whom collaboration increases the effectiveness of therapy for clients and leads to more integrated mental health services (C. E. Hill & Fraser, 1995). Although it has not been addressed in the literature on small-community psychology, such collaboration may also provide support to psychologists and lessen their sense of isolation and stress. As we discussed in chapter 4, this collaboration is one of the advantages of practicing in a small community.

Small Colleges

Psychologists who practice in small colleges must quickly learn the nuances of the community and of their role. Overlapping relationships can occur with clients and with other college personnel. As Spooner (1992) suggested, "The key is not to avoid [overlapping relationships] at all costs but to be aware of the issues and conflicts that can arise and be prepared to deal with them as ethically and professionally as possible" (p. 159). Some overlapping relationships are circumstantial or coincidental, like being waited on by a client in a store. They can usually be managed with a discussion about the likelihood of interaction and the importance of not confusing roles. Other conflicts can be eased through changes in organizational structure or personal and professional roles (Pearson & Piazza, 1997).

Dilemmas Involving Professional Boundaries

Unplanned meetings outside of therapy, or what Sharkin and Birky (1992) referred to as *incidental encounters*, present dilemmas for psychologists within small-college settings, who may find it problematic to preserve clients' confidentiality when encountering clients on campus or in the surrounding community. In Sharkin and Birky's survey of college counseling staff, 87% of therapists felt uncertainty, and 83% felt discomfort, during incidental encounters with clients. Sixty percent were concerned about maintaining clients' confidentiality, and 73% were concerned about violating therapeutic boundaries. The fact that the therapists had little control over the contacts or what might be revealed during the incidental encounters added to their feelings that boundaries were threatened. Most significant may have been Sharkin and Birky's finding that "63% of the respondents had little or no training experience dealing with incidental encounters with clients" (p. 328).

Small-community dilemmas can be compounded in small colleges within small towns. For example, an African American psychologist in a college within a small town has another layer of complexity with which to deal in being simultaneously a part of three small communities.

Social relationships with clients can be naturally limited by age differences if the vast majority of students are much younger than the psychologist. However, the numbers of older adults who seek out higher education mean that psychologists in a small college may indeed be in social situations with clients. Social relationships within a small-college community may be particularly difficult for a young psychologist, whose peer group outside of work may include friends and family members of clients.

There may be an overlap between in-therapy and out-of-therapy contact for both the client or former client and psychologist. Many psychologists in small colleges have such contact when serving on college committees with students, attending discussions and other campus events, and interacting with student workers. Although many students come to college with previous individual therapy experience, others do not. It is important for psychologists in small colleges to talk with clients at the beginning of therapy about the high likelihood of out-of-therapy contact. Together, they need to devise a respectful method of managing out-of-therapy contact.

Communities of color, athletes, fine arts students, musicians, international students, students with disabilities, and GLBT students are among the important small communities within small colleges. Like their rural counterparts, psychologists in many small colleges are viewed as more accessible and trustworthy if they are known to constituencies and to individuals. This may mean attending public events in which clients are in attendance or are in positions of leadership. Such interactions can enhance the visibility of the college's counseling center and can signal to students that psychologists are interested in knowing more about the complexities of their lives. For example, a psychologist who is at an event sponsored by international students may be remembered and sought out later if an international student needs help. This familiarity can be particularly helpful in bridging the gap between the work of psychologists and cultures in which psychology is relatively unknown and problems are kept within the extended family.

One small-college dilemma that may be especially difficult to manage involves getting unsolicited out-of-therapy information, both about clients and about other members of the college community. Clients "may or may not be aware of the fact that people they talk about in therapy are also clients of their own therapist" (Sharkin, 1995, p. 185) or at least known to the psychologist from other campus contacts. Psychologists themselves may not know that there are overlaps until they are far into therapeutic relationships with both parties. It is likely that psychologists will have to deal with knowing things about their clients through information from other clients, students, faculty, staff, and administration. Often, the person sharing the information has no idea that the psychologist is seeing the individual as a client, and the psychologist is then in the difficult position of knowing information that he or she may have to keep from a client.

Psychologists may also hear things from clients about other people on campus. Imagine the dilemma of a psychologist who hears from clients who are being sexually harassed by an administrator or faculty member with whom the psychologist works closely. In such cases, consultation is essential, especially in situations in which referral options are limited and in which psychologists must be especially vigilant about maintaining objectivity and preserving confidentiality.

Psychologists must also be prepared to not acknowledge during a therapy session any relationships with clients who might know each other. They may need to talk about potential problems or refer one of the parties off campus, and they must be scrupulous about sources of information so that they will not accidentally reveal information about one client to another (Sharkin, 1995). The importance of maintaining objectivity and confidentiality is illustrated by Sharkin's (1995) example of learning something about one client from another client and wondering why the first client had not trusted the psychologist enough to share that information in therapy.

Overlapping and entangled relationships are also likely to emerge in therapy groups. Sharkin (1995) suggested pregroup screenings and direct discussion when such relationships are discovered at the first group meeting.

High visibility and lack of privacy within a small-college setting means that psychologists need to be constantly aware of how their behavior can affect their clients as well as the willingness of their colleagues to consult with them on difficult issues. Statements at public forums, choices in personal friendships and relationships, and use of alcohol at public events are but a few of the possible situations where psychologists open themselves to public scrutiny.

McGuinness (1987) stressed the importance of role in college counseling work, as most counseling centers "perform multiple functions and . . . assume multiple roles" (p. 37). He used the example of a psychologist who consults with an administrator about a troubled student. That student may also serve on a committee with both the psychologist and the administrator and be a former client of the psychologist. These demands are everyday occurrences for college counseling psychologists and must be managed seamlessly and professionally.

Confidentiality

Confidentiality is one of the most challenging issues in college counseling. Maintaining confidentiality is a difficult and complex matter that is further complicated by the systems dynamics of the larger institution (McGuinness, 1987). Psychologists who practice within colleges are often pressured to share confidential information about students' use of counseling services (Birky, Sharkin, Marin, & Scappaticci, 1998; Malley, Gallagher, & Brown, 1992; Sharkin, Scappaticci, & Birky, 1995). Staff, professors, administrators, and parents may ask for information about student clients. For example, psychologists must learn how to deal with the anxieties of parents, who are often geographically far away, while simultaneously maintaining client confidentiality and informing clients about communication with parents (Sharkin, 1995).

Stone and Lucas (1990) suggested that "The ethical issue concerns the different perspectives on the need to know" (p. 443). Although the concerns of others on campus may be well founded and driven by their own roles, psychologists must protect the confidentiality of therapy relationships. Requests for information usually "come from involved and caring persons who are instrumental in referring students for therapy or psychological evaluation" (Birky et al., 1998, p. 179). This often results in what Sharkin (1995) described as one of the biggest dilemmas faced by college therapists: By preserving confidentiality, the therapist "protects" the client but may anger or alienate concerned others. . . . By withholding information, then, therapists risk being perceived as arrogant, aloof, evasive, secretive, uncooperative, or unhelpful. Such perceptions can strain relations with other members of the campus community and may contribute to a sense of isolation. (p. 186)

Small-college psychologists often face the good intentions, anxiety, and even hostility of others on campus who ask for information that they believe might help them when working with students. However, because of the overall lack of privacy in small colleges, student clients often have heightened concerns about how and with whom psychologists communicate. It is important to explain to college counseling clients the limits of confidentiality and then to scrupulously adhere to written releases of information so that clients know that they are in control of what information is shared in nonemergency, nonmandated situations.

It is vital to educate others on campus regarding information they may or may not expect to receive about students whom they have referred for counseling (Birky et al., 1998; Sharkin, 1995; Spooner, 1992). One option that may satisfy all parties is to ask students to give written consent. The psychologist can then communicate with the referral source to let that person know that the student kept the initial appointment (Birky et al., 1998; Sharkin, 1995).

May (1994) cited a survey of 355 counseling center directors in North America that highlighted the clash in expectations. Whereas 30% of the directors indicated that their supervisors wanted feedback on the progress of students whom they had referred for counseling, only 4% of directors indicated that they would provide it. Sixty percent of the directors reported that administrators believed that counseling centers should report whether a student has been seen for counseling (even if the student had not given permission), whereas only 16% of counseling center directors would do so. Eighty percent of administrators believed that they should be told whether a student whom they referred to the counseling center kept an appointment (even if the student had not given permission), whereas only 35% of directors agreed.

Similar beliefs and differences occurred in regard to a variety of other campus issues: vandalism, harassment, voluntary mental health hospitalizations, and sexual assault. Most administrators believed that their right to receive such information "is the decent, collaborative thing to do, part of our all working together in the student's best interest" (May, 1994, p. 12). May (1994) went on to say that psychologists who uphold their own ethical and legal obligations are, at best, viewed as uncooperative and, at worst, likely to anger administrators and invite negative projections because of "the quality of hiddenness about what we do" (p. 13).

Sharkin et al. (1995) looked at both expectations and preferences regarding confidentiality of people who refer students to counseling. They found that 68% of resident hall assistants, 65% of student affairs professionals, and 57% of faculty expected that confidential information about students whom they had referred would be shared with them. Even more (88% of resident assistants, 84% of student affairs professionals, and 89% of faculty) believed that they *should* have access to such confidential information. These results highlight the difficulties that college counseling center staff face when protecting confidentiality (Sharkin et al., 1995; Sherry, Teschendorf, Anderson, & Guzman, 1991). Sharkin et al. suggested the need to educate the wider campus community regarding confidentiality and client consent for release of information, possibly through pamphlets or other written information to be distributed to faculty, staff, and administrators.

Community Expectations and Values Differences

Psychologists who practice in colleges need to be sensitive to the needs of both the individual clients and the wider campus community (Sharkin, 1995). Psychological services exist within a duality: "the font of instantaneous solutions and remedies" (Amada, 1996, p. 47) and "an insidious, capriciously clandestine, and even rather renegade organizational entity" (Amada, 1996, p. 47). The 2002 American Psychological Association (APA) Ethics Code (APA, 2002a) states in Ethical Standard 1.03, Conflicts Between Ethics and Organizational Demands, the following:

> If the demands of an organization with which psychologists are affiliated or for whom they are working conflict with this Ethics Code, psychologists clarify the nature of the conflict, make known their commitment to the Ethics Code, and to the extent feasible, resolve the conflict in a way that permits adherence to the Ethics Code. (p. 1063)

However, other members of the college administration and community may be unable or unwilling to understand the necessity for psychologists to uphold these standards and relevant state laws and codes.

The confidential nature of the services adds to the distrust and negativity, and psychologists who protect confidentiality may come to be viewed by administrators, staff, and faculty as uncooperative and elitist at best and subversive and deleterious to campus life at worst (Amada, 1996). Amada (1996) told of psychologists who had been accused by colleagues of being self-serving and even of covering up professional misconduct by maintaining confidentiality. He provided a frightening example, one that will sound familiar to many in college counseling: An administrator demanded information about whether a particular student was using the services of the counseling center. Despite reassurance from the psychologist that the administrator would be informed if a duty-to-warn or duty-to-protect situation arose, the psychologist was accused of insubordination, pressured and intimidated by the administrator to justify his unwillingness to provide confidential information, and threatened with termination—in spite of advice to the contrary by the college's legal counsel.

A common challenge for psychologists on college campuses involves students who have an adverse impact on other individuals or the campus by their unusual behavior (Sharkin, 1995). Psychologists may be placed in the position of trying to maintain a trusting, therapeutic relationship with the student client "while also trying to manage anxieties within the campus community" (Sharkin, 1995, p. 187).

College counseling centers serve a valuable purpose in supporting the overall missions of academic excellence, increasing student retention and satisfaction, consulting with staff and faculty, providing on-campus programming, and handling crisis situations. Yet, as Amada (1996) pointed out, "A certain degree of wariness, skepticism, and even outright hostility toward college mental health services is expectable, commonplace, and multiformed on most campuses" (p. 46). Amada (1996) indicated that this might be evidenced by the unwillingness of some faculty or staff to make referrals to the counseling center and by negative comments to the larger community about counseling services. Administrators may contribute to the difficulty by attempting to implement policies that undermine the counseling program or by failing to provide adequate funding and staffing.

The general stigma around seeking counseling that is so prevalent in U.S. society is also present on college campuses. Campus officials are reluctant to recognize or even admit that students may have mental health problems or issues. There is profound ambivalence about publicizing counseling services that are available on campus. To do so would burst the bubble of the idyllic public-relations picture that colleges present to prospective students and their parents.

Other college personnel may see the counseling staff as rivals, fear that the staff are privy to private and damaging information, or see the counseling center as a luxury and a drain on already-scarce resources. They may view the mental health service as a symbol that there are problems that interfere with the public image of perfection or consider them complicit in maintaining problem students on campus (Amada, 1996). Amada (1996) illustrated the difficulty in the following quote from a college counseling center director:

> Our very existence . . . punctures the illusion that all the students are healthy and doing well. We then come to stand for such unpleasant realities as anxiety, defect, or craziness, and then we are marginalized in the institution as a way of trying to fend off those issues. (p. 62)

Those doubters would no doubt be surprised to learn that many student leaders are among counseling center clients. However, the protection afforded clients by confidentiality also means that counseling center staff cannot share specific information that might invalidate negative perceptions and criticisms.

Communities of Color and Cultural–Ethnic Communities

Psychologists who practice within communities of color and cultural–ethnic communities face dilemmas similar to their rural and small-college counterparts: the potential for harmful overlapping relationships, limited competence or training, differences between community expectations and values, and working with other agencies and providers within the community. However, there is a more fundamental conflict. Ethical guidelines, which are based on majority-culture practice and values, have historically failed to address differences basic to various other cultures. Sue, Arredondo, and McDavis (1995) stated that "Too often, lip service is given to multicultural concerns, without the commitment to translate them into ethical standards" (p. 630). According to the APA *Guidelines on Multicultural Education, Training, Research, Practice, and Organizational Change for Psychologists*, "racial/ethnic minority students are underrepresented at all levels of psychology, but most particularly at the doctoral level, the primary entry point to be a psychologist . . . [and] racial representation within the profession of psychology is similarly small" (APA, 2002b, pp. 7–8). Nagayama Hall, Iwamasa, and Smith (2003) contended that people

> from ethnic minority groups that are directly affected by the actions and inactions of the governing bodies of psychology should have a voice and may be in a better position than persons who are not ethnic minorities to determine what is ethically appropriate. (p. 314)

If psychologists have not been sufficiently trained in issues of diverse populations, they may "also lack the skills to deal with ethical issues presented by clients with multicultural backgrounds" (Sadeghi, Fischer, & House, 2003, p. 179) or lack information on culturally different symptom manifestations (Lefley, 2002). Textbooks, research, and theories are likely to contain culture-specific assumptions and have, until recently, been based on utilitarian, Kantian, and individualist philosophical principles (Sadeghi et al., 2003).

Until about 30 years ago, diverse populations "were almost absent from the psychological literature [until] ethnic minority and international psychologists began questioning what APA meant about *human* and to whom the vast body of psychological knowledge applied" (Trimble, 2003, p. 15; italics in original). Trimble (2003) went on to say the following:

> The changing demographic context calls into question the relevance of a psychology that historically has not been inclusive of ethnic and racial groups and that fostered a research agenda that is ethnocentric and bound by time and place. How well prepared will practitioners be in the delivery of quality mental health services to ethnic and language minorities . . . (p. 15)

if the unique, distinctive cultural "values, attitudes, beliefs, languages, and corresponding behaviors" (p. 16) of diverse populations are not a part of that preparation? Trimble (2003) also reminded us that the theories and practices of psychology seem to be applicable to people from cultures "who valued talking about their problems with professionals with the hope that the problems could be solved or cured" (Trimble, 2003, p. 30).

Sue, Bingham, Porche-Burke, and Vasquez (1999) warned that "traditional psychological concepts and theories were developed from a predominantly Euro-American context and may be limited in their applicability to the emerging racially and culturally diverse population in the United States" (p. 1063). Parham (1997), too, questioned whether such ethical standards were "sensitive to different cultural groups whose values and worldview . . . are markedly different from those of European American psychologists and counselors" (p. 110). Ethical practice for all psychologists "requires a multicultural orientation" (Ivey, Ivey, & Simek-Morgan, 1997, p. 18) because they base their work on the core responsibility to do no harm. As Pedersen (1995) posited, "Ethical principles generated in one cultural context cannot be applied to other substantially different cultural contexts without modification" (p. 34).

Even well-intentioned psychologists may consider cultural differences as secondary and fail to provide empathy based on awareness of both client and culture (Ivey, 1987). It appears that codes of ethics do the same. Individual versus relativistic values, extended family relationships, and involvement of indigenous healers are just a few of the values in which cultural–ethnic communities may differ between themselves and from the majority culture. If these cultural differences are not recognized, then it is unlikely that competent service—that is, service that requires "an integrated, embedded understanding of a cultural perspective" (Rolland & Hughes, 2004, p. 20)—will be provided.

Derald Wing Sue, in the address he gave after receiving the Award for Distinguished Career Contributions to Education and Training in Psychology during the 2004 Annual Convention of the American Psychological Association, highlighted the power of one group "to impose its reality and beliefs upon another group" (Sue, 2004). Sue directly addressed this issue within the ethical codes and standards of practice that govern the field of psychology. He pointed out several features of Western mental health that reflect its ethnocentric viewpoint: admonishments to generally avoid self-disclosure, giving advice, entering into overlapping relationships, accepting gifts from clients, and bartering for services. Although these features are anchored within the well-intentioned avoidance of client dependence, conflicts of interest, and loss of objectivity, Sue (2004) asked a question of great significance: "What if other culturally diverse groups consider these behaviors or alternative roles to be qualities of the helping relationship?" (p. 765).

Sue (2004) concluded that "It appears that the group who 'owns' history also controls the gateway to knowledge construction, truth and falsity, problem definition, what constitutes normality and abnormality, and ultimately, the nature of reality" (p. 766). He quoted the 4th-century Chinese sage Chang-Tsu, who said "How we view the world is not only about what we see, but about what we do not see" (Sue, 2004, p. 766)—a reminder that the reality on which ethics codes are based is only one of many other realities.

Ridley (1995) proposed that current ethical guidelines are ineffective, biased toward the values of European-based cultures and standards, and "fail to reflect the state of knowledge regarding diversity" (p. 27). He went on to suggest that because therapy and counseling theories are derived from Eurocentric assumptions and ideologies, they may be of questionable relevance to clients of color. In addition, the knowledge derived from traditional research models tends to view people of color from a deficit-based model rather than a strength-based model (Arredondo, 1999; Ridley, 1995). This, along with what Arredondo (1999) described as the monocultural nature of psychologist and counselor training, is likely to result in "unethical and potentially harmful behavior" (p. 102) by psychologists who apply this limited training to clients from different cultures. Psychology ethics based on this knowledge and training may as a result be infused with content and values that perpetuate this harm. In addition, "although the codes of ethics address the importance of culturally sensitive counseling, they are often vague when it comes to assisting counselors in dealing with real dilemmas that arise in multicultural counseling situations" (Sadeghi et al., 2003, p. 190).

Pedersen (1997a) stated that existing ethical guidelines were culturally biased, and he called for a "more situational and relational alternative" (p. 277) to address the importance of cultural context. He stressed that "Not only do ethical guidelines need to be interpreted in each situation, but they also must be interpreted for and within each cultural context" (Pedersen, 1997b, p. 23). He went on to suggest that biases that exist within current ethics codes are discrepant with the many cultural contexts in which codes are applied (Pedersen, 1997b). For example, there is an implicit valuing of individualism over collectivism in the code of the American Counseling Association and codes of other helping professions:

> A comprehensive code of ethics needs to respect the values of both individualistic and collectivistic cultural contexts (Pedersen, 1995). If that is not possible, the code of ethics at least needs to make its dependence on individualistic values explicit for the benefit of those who do not share their assumptions about the importance of the individual over the group. (Pedersen, 1997b, p. 24)

Current codes of ethics are "so deeply rooted in values of the dominant culture that it would be difficult to separate those values from the practice of counseling" (Pedersen, 1997b, p. 26). This poses a particularly burdensome challenge to psychologists within cultural–ethnic communities, who already struggle with the more standard small-community issues of overlapping relationships, community expectations, alternative helpers, and so on. For example, psychologists within the Native American community are part of an extended family system that helps to define who they are, to whom they are related, and their role within that community. Separating themselves from their community may lead to distrust and would limit their ability to build the relationships necessary to practice effectively within their community. Native psychologists may also join with traditional healers and other family members to provide culturally competent therapy.

Psychologists within many communities of color and cultural–ethnic communities must constantly balance the culture of their community with, for example, communal–collectivist values and the culture of psychology with its more individualistic values. The small numbers of mental health professionals within many cultural–ethnic communities may mean that it is difficult for these professionals to take the time to support each other, especially when trying to respond to overwhelming needs of the populations that they serve. Thus, Pedersen (1997b) suggested that ethical guidelines go beyond safe, proscribed options and instead provide assistance in dealing "with the moral dilemma of contrasting cultures" (p. 27).

The APA's *Guidelines for Providers of Psychological Services to Ethnic, Linguistic, and Culturally Diverse Populations* (APA, Office of Ethnic Minority Affairs, 1993) contains several principles that are potentially relevant in addressing the need to include a wider range of viewpoints into the ethical standards of the profession. The pertinent guidelines include the following:

> 3.b. Psychologists' practice incorporates an understanding of the client's ethnic and cultural background. This includes the client's familiarity and comfort with the majority culture as well as ways in which the client's culture may add to or improve various aspects of the majority culture and/or of society at large.
>
> 4. Psychologists respect the roles of family members and community structure, hierarchies, values, and beliefs within the client's culture.

> 5. Psychologists respect clients' religious and/or spiritual beliefs and values, including attributions and taboos, since they affect worldview, psychosocial functioning, and expressions of distress.
>
> 8. Psychologists attend to as well as work to eliminate biases, prejudices, and discriminatory practices. (pp. 4–5)

If these guidelines and principles are vital to the provision of services to ethnic, linguistic, and culturally diverse populations, then they should also be an integral part of the ethical guidelines that underlie such practice.

The following principle is part of the foundation for the recent APA *Guidelines on Multicultural Education, Training, Research, Practice, and Organizational Change for Psychologists* (APA, 2002b) and is relevant to the quest for more inclusive standards of ethics:

> Ethical conduct of psychologists is enhanced by knowledge of differences in beliefs and practices that emerge from socialization through racial and ethnic group affiliation and membership and how those beliefs and practices will necessarily affect the education, training, research and practice of psychology (p. 20).

Although not explicitly mentioned, this enhanced conduct is an integral part of the worldview of racially–ethnically diverse psychologists and clients (APA, 2002b) and should be included in the foundation of the ethics code governing the profession.

Significant efforts were made by APA in response to the historical and cultural issues raised earlier in this section. An Ethics Code Task Force was formed by the APA Ethics Committee with group members that included representation from many diverse groups—communities of color and ethnic communities, members from the GLBT community, and a member representing psychologists who work within the military and law enforcement agencies.

The 2002 APA Ethics Code (APA, 2002a) makes a concerted effort to address long-standing and historical omissions on racial–ethnic differences in several areas. Principle E, Respect for People's Rights and Dignity, states the following:

> Psychologists respect the dignity and worth of all people. . . .
> Psychologists are aware of and respect cultural, individual,
> and role differences, including those based on . . . race,
> ethnicity, culture, national origin . . . language, and socioeco-
> nomic status, and consider these factors when working with
> members of such groups. Psychologists try to eliminate the
> effect on their work of biases based on those factors, and they
> do not knowingly participate in or condone activities of oth-
> ers based upon such prejudices. (p. 1062)

The 2002 APA Ethics Code highlights the necessity for psychologists to "acquire the necessary competence when dealing
with certain populations, such as cultural or linguistic minorities
. . . (2.01b) [and not to] . . . engage in unfair discrimination (3.01)"
(Knapp & VandeCreek, 2003, p. 177). The Ethics Code also af-
fords protection by requiring that psychologists who work with
diverse populations use tests and assessments appropriate to that
population and interpret the results of other assessments with
caution and with appropriate reservations (Standard 9.02b). Psychologists "make their interpretations with consideration for the
situational, personal, linguistic, and cultural differences that may
affect the results (9.06) . . . and, when using interpreters . . . obtain
consent and ensure the confidentiality of information obtained
(9.03c)" (Knapp & VandeCreek, 2003, p. 177). These changes and
inclusions are important steps on the part of APA to address the
issues of populations who have been traditionally underrepresented in the field of psychology and as consumers of psychological services. Although it is too early to know whether these
changes will effectively address problems identified in the literature, attention to these changes may both increase understanding of the new requirements for psychologists who work with
special populations and provide guidance in facing related ethical dilemmas.

The APA's *Guidelines on Multicultural Education, Training, Research, Practice, and Organizational Change for Psychologists* (APA,
2002b) has also been adopted as APA policy. Although these
guidelines constitute recommendations and suggestions for professional practice, they are not mandatory standards. They are
not definitive but are intended to facilitate the continued system-

atic development of the profession and to help assure a high level of professional practice by psychologists. The guidelines call for psychologists to do the following:

- ☐ Recognize that they may hold attitudes and beliefs that can detrimentally influence their perceptions of and interactions with individuals who are ethnically and racially different from themselves.
- ☐ Recognize the importance of multicultural sensitivity, knowledge, and understanding about ethnically and racially different individuals.
- ☐ Use the constructs of multiculturalism and diversity in psychological education.
- ☐ Recognize the importance of conducting culture-centered and ethical psychological research among people from ethnic, linguistic, and racial minority backgrounds.
- ☐ Apply culturally appropriate skills in clinical and other applied psychological practices.
- ☐ Support culturally informed policies and practices in all facets of society, from the private sector to government. (Martin, 2002)

Dilemmas Involving Professional Boundaries

Collectivist cultures, as opposed to the individualistic culture in which the traditional ethical stances of psychology are grounded, may find it difficult to exclude overlapping relationships. In fact, in collectivist cultures such overlap can be "desirable or even essential to appropriate caregiving" (Pedersen, 1997a, p. 243). Psychologists who are members of and practice within communities of color or other cultural communities have lives that overlap with their clients. In fact, clients may seek them out for therapy precisely because of that overlap, seeing the psychologist as a role model, wanting to support the work of others within their community, and believing that the psychologist will better understand their culture and empathize with their experiences of racism or discrimination (Gonsiorek & Brown, 1986; Parham, 1997).

Sue (1997) discussed taking cultural differences into consideration when evaluating the potential of help versus harm resulting from overlapping relationships. He suggested that within many Asian cultures it is forbidden to discuss personal matters outside of the family and that clients from these cultures may benefit from having a more personal interaction with a counselor. Alexander and Sussman (1995) challenged the profession of psychology to consider ethically appropriate practice "within the cultural context in which it occurs" (p. 377) and to expand traditional roles and boundaries to create more effective interventions.

McGoldrick (1982) raised a similar issue with her recommendation that therapists within communities of color be willing to broaden their definition of therapy and their role within it. Pedersen (1997b) supported this viewpoint with his reminder that overlapping relationships "by themselves are neither absolutely wrong nor absolutely right in all cultural contexts" (p. 25). He pointed out that "a dual relationship of reciprocal trust and 'connectedness' may be required" (Pedersen, 1997b, p. 25), especially within cultural contexts where outsiders are not customary sources of help and advice. Role diffusion is unavoidable for most psychologists who work within such cultures. Psychologists need to step outside of their traditional, culturally encapsulated perspective to "reframe these multiple roles in a way that is complementary and faithful to the intention of the guideline" (Pedersen, 1997b, p. 26).

In a study of African Americans' perceptions of psychotherapy and psychotherapists, Sanders Thompson, Bazile, and Akbar (2004) found that approximately one half of their 201 participants shared the perception that "psychologists, unlike social workers and counselors, failed to participate in community education, prevention, and outreach" (p. 23). These participants also expressed a reluctance to trust professionals who were not active in the community or in activities that would contribute to the well-being of the community.

As a specific example, Sue (1997) highlighted the importance of gift-giving within many Asian communities as a way to express thanks and respect. To refuse the gift by standing behind traditional boundaries would be an insult to the client. While acknowledging that such traditional boundaries serve a purpose in many settings, Sue (1997) urged psychologists to avoid rigidly applying them to all situations and to take into consideration community characteristics, values, and perceptions. Although his focus was on Asian communities, his suggestion may also be applicable to other cultural–ethnic communities.

Many psychologists of color may seek out graduate training and education with the express purpose of returning to serve their often-underserved communities. They may patronize retailers and other professionals from their community as a way to support and strengthen the community itself. Within their communities, psychologists may often attend social, cultural, or religious events with current or former clients or serve with them on boards, advisory committees, or community service organizations (Gonsiorek & Brown, 1986). Gonsiorek and Brown (1986) suggested that

> it is both naïve and insensitive to respond to the complicated boundary situations that often result in a dictum that minority . . . counselors simply should absent themselves from these activities. The idea is tantamount to suggesting that such psychotherapists avoid participating in the life of the community. To do so often will be seen as a disparagement of the community. (p. 297)

Some clients want to be acknowledged in out-of-therapy contacts, and others do not. An African American therapist described herself in the following way:

> Most of the time, how I appear to be in a social setting or in the community is possibly real opposite for me, because I tend not to approach clients—I will not speak first. I wait for them to speak first, so I appear to be more introverted, and that's the last thing that I am! I'm very social, and so that's very, very awkward for me. It troubles me, in that, I'm not often sure how the client wants the response . . . depending on what's going on with them. . . . The longer I've worked in this business I think the better I got at trying to do something about this. I've started asking in sessions, "If sometime we see each other, how do you want me to respond?" . . . Sometimes they want me to say hello to them, sometimes they don't. (Adams, 1994, p. 47)

Overlapping business or professional relationships can also be problematic, even after therapy has ended. An African American therapist in Adams's (1994) study gave the example of relating to former clients, including one who wanted to pursue a friendship:

> I've had a number of former clients who I do have a kind of a friendship relationship . . . but we encounter each other in the community, and we have worked on task forces together . . . it's a friendly relationship. I think this one was different because there probably was some sexual attraction there. That felt awkward. . . . The awkward part is that you're trying to explain that you don't want to have a relationship with somebody because you like them . . . and you don't know how they're going to take that. (p. 41)

As in other small communities, psychologists within cultural communities struggle with having in-therapy information about others in the community. Adams (1994) quoted an African American therapist as saying that there are times when "[I know] unsavory things about prominent people in the community, and it's hard not to act on that knowledge due to confidentiality" (p. 33).

Adams (1994) included another example of an African American therapist who was shopping and encountered a former client—a well-known, married businessman in the community who was with a woman who was not his wife:

> They were at the counter all hugged-up, and he was buying her a piece of jewelry. . . . Right before Christmas he called me up and wanted to come in. Of course I couldn't see him because I was too booked. But, I have seen him since, and he came in with an explanation for me. And I told him, "You really don't owe me an explanation. But, obviously you felt some guilt about it." I struggle with keeping the personal and professional piece in balance. . . . The personal side of me could take over in those particular types of situations, and I don't have the right to judge—I need to keep it professional. (p. 40)

Psychologists within communities of color or other cultural communities may also have to contend with their own high visibility and lack of privacy, as illustrated in the following example:

> They know where I live, or know somebody that I know. Clients will often come up to you and say, "I know somebody

that you know" so it's like they're saying to you: "I've been checking up on you. I've been asking my friends about you, my friend knows you, and they're telling me whether or not you're a straight shooter." (Adams, 1994, p. 38)

As with their rural colleagues, the issues surrounding overlapping relationships are further complicated by the psychologist's family involvement within the community. For example, a psychologist may find that her son brings home a schoolmate, who is a client or the sibling of a client, to play computer games or stay for dinner. Or, a teenage daughter might be excited about meeting a new boy at the mall, who turns out to be a former client of her psychologist parent. Or, a spouse may have accepted an invitation to another couple's home for dinner, not knowing that the psychologist just had an intensely emotionally counseling session that afternoon with the husband. A male therapist in Adams's (1994) study of awkward posttermination contacts talked about running into clients when he was with his family:

> Initially, my wife would say, "Who is that?" and I'd say, "Oh, just somebody I know"—because I didn't think it was right to identify them as clients. That was kind of awkward, trying to explain to my wife how I know this person. She was always real curious about who I knew, particularly if they were women. . . . There was something awkward about that . . . I think she kind of learned over time that I know a lot of people . . . and I've also seen a lot of clients, clients who have some prominence in the community. (p. 42)

Earlier ethical guidelines discouraged bartering under most circumstances in an attempt to avoid overlapping roles and client exploitation. However, within some cultures bartering is a positive exchange. The assumption about the negativity of bartering, based on a belief that money is the most fair economy across all cultures, was unfair to many cultural communities and a barrier to receiving needed psychological assistance (Pedersen, 1997b). The 2002 APA Ethics Code took these cultural values into account with its updated stance regarding the practice of bartering:

6.05 Barter With Clients/Patients

Barter is the acceptance of goods, services, or other non-monetary remuneration from clients/patients in return for psychological services. Psychologists may barter only if (1) it is not clinically contraindicated, and (2) the resulting arrangement is not exploitative. (APA, 2002a, p. 1068)

Limited Resources and Limits of Competence

In cultural–ethnic communities that are isolated by geography or language, psychologists often feel enormous pressure to provide services that are outside their realm of competency or experience. As their rural counterparts discussed in chapter 4, there are many issues to balance. They must inform clients of limitations. Then, if they and the client choose to proceed with therapy, psychologists must take the steps necessary to gain the knowledge and supervision needed to provide essential services.

Community Expectations and Values Differences

The knowledge necessary to work within communities of color and other culturally based communities is a combination of traditional training and culture-specific beliefs and values (C. E. Hill & Fraser, 1995). Clients within these communities may explain problem causes and solutions in ways that are very different from those of traditional psychology. Psychologists from these communities may be challenged to synthesize cultural values and behaviors with those in which they were trained. It is also important to learn about community values, behaviors, and expectations to "better assess the client, or the client system, within a situational, environmental, and cultural context" (Rolland & Hughes, 2004, p. 21). Gone (2004) cautioned that

> awareness of one's own deeply embedded cultural assumptions is often quite elusive unless or until one encounters others whose shared (i.e., collective, as opposed to idiosyncratic) sense of what is true, good, right, proper, and beautiful collides with one's own. (p. 15)

Sadeghi et al. (2003) identified "fundamental cultural tension between traditional counseling culture and the cultures of some multicultural clients regarding the values of independence versus interdependence" (p. 187). The traditional Western value of clients taking "responsibility and ownership for their lives . . . is not always shared by clients coming from collectivist cultures" (p. 187). The authors went on to stress the importance of mental health professionals' being "aware of how their own values, beliefs, attitudes, and personality styles may influence how they behave with clients from more collectivistic cultures" (Sadeghi et al., 2003, p. 187).

When ethical guidelines "continue to support the perspective of a dominant culture" (Pedersen, 1997a, p. 265), psychologists within other communities may have to practice what Pedersen (1997a) termed *responsible disobedience* to arrive at ethical consciousness. Rather than taking an absolute position that all cultures must adhere to the same traditional ethical outlook, as if reality is defined the same in all cultures, it is important to understand that other cultures have a complex set of beliefs whereby familiar psychological processes may manifest themselves differently (Ibrahim, 1996).

As an example, within many Native American communities, clients may be most comfortable integrating traditional Native American and conventional psychological approaches. LaFromboise (1988) pointed out that "new solutions to problems or new ways to see old problems become possible through interconnectedness with the community" (p. 392). Psychologists within Native American communities need to search for ways to avoid imposing the biases of the field on clients or attempting to shape "the behavior of the client in a direction that conflicts with Indian cultural lifestyle orientations and preferences" (LaFromboise, 1988, p. 392).

The following suggestions may serve psychologists well in working successfully within the Native American community: linking to traditional Native American community approaches to healing, connecting to traditional community and kinship support systems, knowing about specific tribal societies and how they influence the individual and family (Gurnoe & Nelson, 1990), understanding holistic viewpoints and alternative explanations for being out of balance with the natural world (Heinrich, Corbine, & Thomas, 1990; Thomason, 1991), learning about experiences within specific Native American cultures, respecting extended family relationships, and acknowledging belief in the strength of a collective rather than individualistic orientation (LaFromboise, 1988).

Collectivist cultures that prize family and kinship bonds, rather than individuality, may view confidentiality and personal privacy "as selfish or self-centered in ways that are destructive to the welfare of the community" (Pedersen, 1997b, p. 25). These cultures may focus less on individual rights and attainments than on group rights or goals (Ibrahim, 1996). This poses a dilemma for a psychologist who is trying to balance ethical and legal mandates for confidentiality with community needs and requests for information on members.

Lefley (2002) discussed the importance of knowing about the support system available to clients within their communities. Clients from diverse cultures may be more willing to have their families involved in their treatment, and families may also expect to be informed—raising a dilemma around confidentiality and information-sharing. This is especially salient because confidentiality is seen as intrinsic to the basic premise of therapy in Western individualistic cultures, along with an expectation that independence from one's family of origin should be encouraged as a part of therapeutic progress.

Family versus individualistic cultural differences may be especially salient in African American, Native American, Hispanic, and Asian families. Lefley (2002) gave the example of a Chinese therapist who was caught between individualistic professional ethics and the collectivist cultural needs of a family in which individuals are expected to make sacrifices for the good of others within the family group. Individual personal sacrifice for the good of the family or extended cultural group is common in many cultures and flies in the face of traditional Western psychological principles of self-actualization and individual rights to self-determination.

Different expectations may also occur around gift-giving. To refuse a gift in some cultures would be insulting—demeaning the gift and devaluing the donor (Lefley, 2002). Gifts are symbols of gratitude in many cultures, but gift-giving creates a double bind for psychologists who strive to combine their cultural knowledge with ethical guidelines.

Another value difference may stem from touch. Ethical guidelines prohibiting most touch have been developed to protect clients, but adherence to this paradigm may cause discomfort in clients from cultures that view touch differently. Refusal of touch may seriously disrupt the therapeutic alliance and result in clients' discontinuing therapy (Lefley, 2002).

Ongoing consultation with community members is essential and is the basis for true collaboration. Instead of treating clients only as individuals, this kind of collaboration would include "the interface between the clinic and the community to maximize the relevance, efficiency, and utility of the services" (Gone, 2004, p. 16). This genuine, respectful connection can strengthen the individual client, the participating psychologist, and the community as a whole.

Interagency Issues: Working With Other Community Agencies, Groups, and Professionals

Psychologists working within cultural–ethnic communities may need to rely on other professionals within the community to assist their clients with services outside the realm of psychology. Agencies often compete with each other for funding. They may also be the outgrowth of competing political and social agendas. The situation can be further complicated by legal and language issues—for example, services provided for Spanish speakers only. Because word travels quickly within small cultural–ethnic communities, psychologists need to manage these dilemmas and foster positive working relationships with other agencies or groups that can help their clients.

Psychologists and other mental health professionals within cultural–ethnic communities may find themselves in conflicting roles as they try to contribute their expertise and support to other agencies. They may find themselves serving on boards of other agencies, working with agencies that employ their relatives, or dealing with historical antagonisms between agencies. The dilemma becomes one of how or where to become involved in giving back to the community and deciding when those overlapping relationships have the potential to harm clients or impair the psychologist's objectivity.

Peer Helpers and Other Alternatives to Traditional Treatment Methods

As C. E. Hill and Fraser (1995) pointed out, "Every community has individual(s) who are regarded as 'local healers'"(p. 561) and who try to restore physical, spiritual, emotional, and social balance to others. Members of cultural communities and communities of color may view these religious and spiritual leaders as important sources of help. Psychologists who want to practice ethically and successfully within these communities need to respect these leaders and seek them out as valuable sources of collaboration and knowledge. Medical providers, teachers, school counselors, wise elders, and a host of others may also be sources of help to clients and to psychologists within the community. These people are important allies and can sometimes provide a path by which clients access psychological help. This is especially true for people who fear stigma or shame for themselves and for their larger family group if they admit to difficulties or ask for psychological assistance. Rather than viewing these beliefs, values, and alternative providers as barriers to service, they can be important resources in an integrative delivery of psychological services (C. E. Hill & Fraser, 1995). In fact, this "lay referral network strengthens the ties of professionals to communities and channels knowledge to and from the community to the appropriate resources" (C. E. Hill & Fraser, 1995, p. 566).

Elders are community members who are recognized by others within their community as "holders of knowledge, tradition, wisdom and who possess multiple skills and talents and have a commitment to serve and support the community" (Rolland & Hughes, 2004). They can prove invaluable to psychologists as problem-solving partners and bridge-builders (Rolland & Hughes, 2004). Connections with elders may be of utmost importance in working effectively with culturally based communities.

Gone's (2004) work regarding mental health services for Native Americans in the 21st century urged close collaboration with important members of the community, including medicine persons and spiritual leaders. By stepping outside a traditional model of psychological service delivery and respecting the spiritual context of Native American views on disorders and healing, Gone advocated building this collaboration as a way of gaining insight into what the community views as culturally relevant interventions. Although Gone addressed the needs of Native American people, his words carry wisdom appropriate for a range of cultural–ethnic communities. Not only will the members of the community gain through a collaboration of traditional and conventional Western intervention, psychologists working within cultural communities will also be enriched by opening themselves to other ways of seeing and doing.

Gay, Lesbian, Bisexual, Transgender Communities

Gay, lesbian, bisexual, transgender psychologists constitute another small community that faces multiple challenges to ethical practice. As they try to balance professional and personal lives, GLBT psychologists may find themselves being pulled between the needs of their clients, the political and social issues of the GLBT community, and their own needs for privacy and personal space.

Dilemmas Involving Professional Boundaries

Like colleagues in other small communities, psychologists within GLBT communities must sort out myriad overlaps between their personal and professional lives. Unless they choose, often painfully, to forgo the social and political support of their community, GLBT psychologists encounter clients at community events, social settings, political action committees, and a range of other settings. As in other small communities, clients may seek out GLBT psychologists primarily because of their membership within the community. These potential clients expect that another GLBT person will have a greater understanding of and empathy for their life events and will provide a therapeutic atmosphere free of antigay prejudice.

The prohibition against sexual relationships with clients is clear. In other situations, GLBT psychologists must make difficult decisions, often on the spot, on how best to maintain professional boundaries and how to keep the best interests of the client paramount. Kessler and Waehler (2005) suggested that GLBT therapists should behave ethically but must also maintain some flexibility when considering an overlapping relationship between client and therapist. Gonsiorek and Brown (1986) pointed out the following:

> For such therapists, social distance from clients may be impossible and, in some cases, undesirable to attain. They must constantly negotiate issues of overlapping professional and personal boundaries, often in public, and with little prior warning or time to reflect on the best course of action. (p. 295)

Shernoff (2001) described the issue as "finding a balance between the right of the therapist to have a private life and ensuring that the therapist not behave in a manner that negatively impacts the treatment of his patients" (p. 86). He stressed that a satisfying personal life is essential to being a good therapist but also recognized the difficulty of being surprised at encountering clients on arrival at dinners or an overnight house party. Such unexpected proximity affects how comfortable or open GLBT therapists might be in similar settings. Shernoff also pointed out the difficulty posed by personal Internet interactions, in which clients might find their therapist cruising in a chat room or in which client and therapist make initial anonymous personal connections that later result in awkward face-to-face meetings.

As Shernoff (2001) stressed, the responsibility lies with the therapist to ensure that an out-of-therapy interaction does not damage the therapy relationship. It is up to the therapist to use supervision and peer consultation and to make informed decisions about personal choices that may possibly have negative professional effects.

Gartrell (1992) gave an example from her own practice as a lesbian therapist who actively participates in the lesbian community, in which she encounters clients in out-of-therapy situations. She tells clients at the beginning of the therapeutic relationship that she will just say "hi" to them if either she or the client is with someone else, unless the client prefers not to be acknowledged.

Gartrell further protects her privacy and that of her clients by telling clients that she will not stop to be introduced to anyone who may be with them, nor will she introduce clients to someone who is with her. Gartrell tells clients ahead of time when there is the possibility that they will be attending the same event. She is friendly with former clients but avoids friendships with them because of the inherent imbalance in their relationship and her one-sided knowledge about the details of clients' lives. Because it is difficult to change the expectations, roles, and patterns of interaction that have already been established in the therapeutic relationship, Gartrell does not advocate posttermination friendships within the GLBT community. Not only would it be difficult to explain and justify friendships with some former clients and not others, clients tend to continue to view the therapist as their therapist, even if their therapeutic work together has terminated. In advocating "a style that allows *friendliness, but not friendship*" (Gartrell, 1992, p. 46; italics in original), the door is still open for a former client to return for therapy if needed.

The complication of possible overlapping involvements with families and partners of clients adds to the stress of living and participating within the community while maintaining appropriate boundaries. In addition, many members of the GLBT community may choose to patronize gay-owned businesses, which can lead to difficulties similar to those described by the rural psychologists quoted in chapter 4, especially when the services or products provided are substandard or unsatisfactory.

Because many GLBT psychologists, like their colleagues in ethnic–cultural communities, may have chosen to enter the field to serve their own community, they are often viewed as role models. Being a role model means increased power and the possibility of harming clients (Gonsiorek & Brown, 1986). These psychologists struggle to balance that obligation with a need to meet their own needs for support and socialization within the community. Gartrell (1992) provided the following thoughts:

> I would prefer to have a personal life that is so separate from that of my clients that I never encounter them outside the office. Such a set-up would certainly allow very clear boundaries. Not only is that unrealistic if I choose to participate in

the lesbian community, but it also appears unrealistic to hope for privacy with some clients even in non-community activities. To know that despite my best efforts to the contrary, I may be observed as I head out to a job, walk to a park with visiting nieces and nephews, or drive home from the hospital, is fairly unsettling. . . . One way around this dilemma has been to take frequent weekend trips out of town; traveling gives me a nice opportunity to be anonymous . . . In sum, I do not want to be a recluse, rigid, uptight or paranoid, but I have been working in the lesbian community long enough to understand that privacy outside the office is hard to come by. . . . But it is strange to realize that the private, quiet life I had envisioned for myself as a lesbian psychiatrist may be unrealistic. And that privacy can be a costly commodity. (pp. 44–45)

Lyn (1990) referred to the "small town" dynamics for GLBT therapists, especially because she suggested that GLBT people tend to see therapy as socially acceptable and may use mental health services more frequently than heterosexuals. As if overlapping relationships with current clients are not problematic enough, Adams (1994) reminded us that nonsexual, posttherapy relationships present additional ethical quandaries for therapists who live and work within the GLBT community. Given the strong possibility of such encounters, Lyn said that it is especially important for GLBT therapists to discuss guidelines for posttherapy encounters—confidentiality, limits on such interactions, how or whether to acknowledge each other—both at the beginning of therapy and on termination. Adams quoted a gay therapist who was a group leader for a weekend seminar for gay men and found during the weekend that two of his former clients had also been chosen as group leaders:

I had terminated with each of them relatively soon before that, and I feel like both of them have pretty good boundaries and are pretty respectful about that. It is something that I always talk about in my therapy with clients, so it's not news to them that something like this might happen. . . . It was just awkward because there we were as peers, in a sense, juxtaposed with this historical therapeutic relationship where we were definitely not peers. (p. 36)

Adams (1994) spoke with a lesbian therapist who described an uncomfortable situation in which the therapist and her partner were waiting for their own therapy appointment. She encountered a former client in the waiting room and felt uncomfortable that the client would know that the therapist and her partner were there for therapy. The lesbian therapist chose not to acknowledge the former client:

> Because we didn't make eye contact—I just saw her out of the corner of my eye, and I just kind of pretended that I was busy with these magazines. And I could, for some reason, sense that she—caught on that I was there, but did not approach me, and just kind of walked out. So I think that was probably the most difficult situation for me because it was so intimate, and it was also so revealing of something very personal about me. (p. 37)

Another of the therapists in Adams's (1994) study was surprised to find a former client at the therapist's regular 12-step meeting. The therapist chose to talk with the former client during the break and asked the former client to find another group because of the importance of anonymity for both of them within the 12-step group. In a self-help meeting, another lesbian therapist found herself unwilling to share personal issues with a former client present:

> After the break, she kind of asked me how I felt about her being there, which is really nice in a way, because otherwise, I would have just had to put up with her being there. And it was still tricky about how to handle it, but I did tell her that she has a right to be there, but I also did feel uncomfortable and self-conscious, and that if she could find another meeting that was good for her, then that would be great! (Adams, 1994, p. 37)

An especially difficult small-community, posttherapy situation proved very painful for a lesbian therapist in Adams's (1994) study. The therapist had to terminate the therapeutic relationship with a client who became romantically involved with the therapist's former lover:

So we went into the post-termination, and the struggle on what to do because this woman with whom I had been involved with not so long before that time—she and I periodically got together socially. . . . It was very difficult to maintain that friendship and to have to set the boundary, and in fact, we eventually just had to fade out of the friendship. It just left such big gaps that couldn't be discussed. . . . That was very painful for me. . . . That was not a humorous encounter—that was troubling to the core. (p. 43)

Lyn (1990) addressed the difficulty of avoiding social interaction, especially with former clients in small geographic communities with small GLBT populations and few therapists. She identified work, volunteer settings, and community social events as particularly complicated. Lyn quoted one of the respondents in her study:

I refuse to isolate myself by not being an active member of the local gay community, but am constantly faced with dilemmas of social encounters. Should I refuse to serve on a committee, do a panel presentation, or go to a party just because a current/former client is also involved? I believe not only would refusing be unhealthy for me, but also prove poor role modeling. For me, the key is avoiding intentional social relationships with clients. (pp. 95–96)

Interagency Issues: Working With Other Community Agencies, Groups, and Professionals

Gay, lesbian, bisexual, transgender clients may require services from other GLBT culture-specific agencies, and it is important for psychologists to work cooperatively with a range of resources. As with other small communities, news on the grapevine travels quickly. A psychologist's reputation can easily be enhanced or damaged by negative interactions with other professionals. Gay, lesbian, bisexual, transgender psychologists may also face the small-community dilemma of learning negative information about other professionals. They then struggle: Should they discourage clients from seeing those professionals, or should they confront other professionals within the community about concerns regarding the behavior? Both dilemmas prove difficult within a small-community context, especially because professionals may hesitate to share the community's dirty laundry with the broader heterosexual culture.

Religious Affiliation

Although it is rarely addressed in the professional literature, psychologists who live and practice within a religiously affiliated community often face issues that are similar to those of other small-community psychologists. Their personal, professional, and spiritual lives may be intertwined with those of their clients, which may be beneficial but also problematic.

Dilemmas Involving Professional Boundaries

Religiously affiliated psychologists are sometimes sought out by clients because they are of the same belief system. The result is the same small-community dilemma of permeable boundaries. Psychologists may then find themselves on church, synagogue, or mosque committees with clients, see different members of a family as clients, or provide therapy to people who have friendships with each other. Multiple-role relationships are likely to occur within the religious community, as therapists are often called on to counsel fellow members of the community (Case, McMinn, & Meek, 1997). In their study of nonromantic, nonsexual posttherapy relationships between psychologists and former clients, Anderson and Kitchener (1996) included the following example:

> A former client's family joined the religious institution to which I belonged and where I became an officer. The couple who had seen me in short-term family work around their child's problems became active in the institution and we wound up working together on . . . activities sharing responsibility for committee work and where they were often in a position of reporting directly to me on committee activities. (p. 63)

Geyer (1994) identified the challenge of confidentiality for psychologists practicing within a religiously affiliated community. He pointed out that psychologists may find themselves in situations in which clients are considered for positions of responsibility within the church or "situations in which the client's right to confidentiality and self-determination conflict with larger goals of the church" (Geyer, 1994, p. 190). Religiously affiliated psychologists may have to struggle with clients running into each other and discussing their respective therapies with the particular psychologist. They may also get requests from staff colleagues for therapy for themselves or for relatives (Geyer, 1994).

H. M. L. Miller and Atkinson (1988) identified potential conflicts of interest for clergypersons, some of which may also be true for psychologists within faith-based communities. There may be role confusion if psychologists perform a variety of functions within their religious community—teacher, committee member, worship leader—within which they interact with potential, current, or former clients. The psychologist must then honor a professional commitment to "function objectively, with confidentiality and client-centered focus during the counseling session itself" (H. M. L. Miller & Atkinson, 1988, p. 117). These overlapping roles hold the possibility of role confusion and conflict. Even if psychologists within religious communities remain objective, they may be perceived as otherwise by members of the congregation who may make judgments based on incomplete information— judgments that psychologists are unable to refute because of confidentiality obligations.

Another example of overlapping roles is the psychologist who is also an ordained member of the clergy. If the psychologist/ pastor, or other religious or spiritual leader, attempts to function simultaneously as both a spiritual counselor and a psychotherapist, it is highly likely that roles will become confused both for clients and for the psychologist/spiritual counselor (Koocher & Keith-Spiegel, 1998).

Limited Resources and Limits of Competence

Psychologists within religiously affiliated communities may feel pressure to be all things to all people within the community who are in need of assistance. They may have difficulty convincing clients to follow through on referrals to more appropriate providers outside the community (Geyer, 1994). A psychologist within a religiously affiliated community may be one of few mental health professionals within the community and may have personal values that differ from other psychologists outside of the community. Professional isolation, frequently experienced but rarely discussed, may result.

Community Expectations and Values Differences

Fear of stigma may occur for individuals who seek psychological services within a small, religiously based community. Geyer (1994) suggested that this "will especially be true in churches where trusting God and not needing to rely on professional services is seen to be a strength" (p. 190). The tendency to distrust outsiders is common within some denominations, which makes it even more likely that clients will seek out psychologists within their religious community (Geyer, 1994).

Mental health professionals who provide counseling within a religiously affiliated community may often learn of crises within the community indirectly from concerned others, who hope that the counselor will intervene. Because religious leaders would usually welcome such information and then contact those who are troubled or in crisis, the expectation may be that psychologists will do the same. In these situations, psychologists will need to tread carefully when reacting to follow-up questions from concerned others regarding personal issues of clients (Craig, 1991). Psychologists who preserve the confidentiality of clients are likely to encounter criticism within a community whose members often know a great deal about one another's personal lives.

Interagency Issues: Working With Other Community Agencies, Groups, and Professionals

It may be difficult for psychologists within religiously affiliated communities to successfully juggle healthy community relationships, sound professional judgment, and the avoidance of conflict within the community (Geyer, 1994). Disagreements may become common knowledge. Referrals may be dependent on adherence to similar religious values and stances. Psychologists who have disputes with others or negative information about other professionals within the community have to make difficult decisions. Should they compromise their own beliefs and values to work cooperatively? They may also need to disagree, both publicly and privately, for the greater good of clients and to promote client welfare.

Feminists

Psychologists who identify as feminists in their personal and professional lives constitute another small community. Clients may seek them out because of a perceived personal and political similarity of values and beliefs.

Dilemmas Involving Professional Boundaries

Some therapists within the feminist community believe that traditional boundaries are an unnecessary and harmful part of the power differential in therapy. However, Schoener and Luepker (1996) argued that within this small community it is essential that the therapist "define, establish, and . . . consistently implement the boundaries" (p. 376). The work of Gartrell (1992) and Brown (1994) supports Schoener and Luepker's admonition of the "dangers [that] lie in therapy by women therapists [who] are careless about boundaries or who don't realize that they are not immune from the risks in therapy simply by virtue of their gender or feminist orientation" (pp. 376–377).

Feminist therapists may be at risk for unethical overlapping relationships when they minimize their own vulnerability or downplay the power and symbolism of the therapeutic relationship (Adleman & Barrett, 1990). Although those who adhere to a feminist perspective may seek to calibrate this power differential, therapists still have significant information about clients, and clients may have very little information about their therapists (Biaggio & Greene, 1995).

Feminist therapists promote equality and a balance of power within the therapy relationship, which provides the challenge of how to balance power yet still maintain treatment boundaries (Brown, 1991). Brown (1991) identified threats to those treatment boundaries as invasive to clients' physical or emotional boundaries or as failure to protect clients from personal neediness or neglect of important treatment matters.

An important issue in feminist therapy is the ethical use of self-disclosure in therapy. Although intended to increase the equality of power issues in the therapeutic relationship, self-disclosure can also lead to boundary violations (Brown, 1991).

Mahalik, Van Ormer, and Simi (2000) promoted the recognition of a self-disclosure continuum within feminist therapy. They contended that information about the therapist is being transmitted to the client through observable characteristics of the therapist, the therapist's surroundings, and the therapist's involvement in public and community activities. This range of therapist self-disclosures, including within-therapy sharing of information, supports the principles of egalitarianism and connections that are intrinsic to feminist psychotherapy but that also provide potential pitfalls. The key issue is not the occurrence of self-disclosure but rather "*what* the therapist self-discloses and whether the therapist burdens the patient with personal problems in a manner that reverses the roles in the dyad" (Gutheil & Gabbard, 1998, p. 412; italics in original).

Simi and Mahalik (1997) addressed the possibility that self-disclosure in feminist therapy might result in boundary confusion and harmful overlapping relationships by proposing aspirational ethics around the use of therapist self-disclosure within feminist therapy. They advocated that feminist therapists help to preserve the client's power by using the following guidelines for self-disclosure: safeguarding the therapeutic relationship, self-care on the part of the therapist, preserving the voice of the client within therapy, and having a clear rationale for why self-disclosure and other therapeutic interventions are used. This approach supports the guidelines of the Feminist Therapy Institute Code of Ethics regarding self-disclosure: "A feminist therapist discloses information to the client that facilitates the therapeutic process. The therapist is responsible for using self-disclosure with purpose and discretion in the interests of the client" (Lerman & Porter, 1990, p. 39).

Clients and therapists within the feminist community may encounter each other in social settings, for example, on various committees. Adleman and Barrett (1990) indicated that clients typically choose a feminist therapist because they are part of the same community. Their shared world may include community events, professional organizations, and other activities. Adleman and Barrett suggested that discussion of mutual expectations within these overlaps is essential to avoid ethical compromises and to construct boundaries. This may become increasingly difficult after years of practice for the feminist therapist, who may take on leadership positions and who may also have many current and former clients within her own community and daily life. Clients may "inadvertently enter the therapist's personal and social life" (Brown, 1991, p. 327), and the therapist "accepts responsibility for monitoring such relationships to prevent potential abuse of or harm to the client" (Brown, 1991, p. 329). The feminist model also "requires the therapist to imagine the impact of her actions on the client, on that person in relationship to herself (the therapist) and on the interpersonal matrix in which they both participate" (Brown, 1991, p. 334).

Brown (1991) described the dilemma of feminist therapists as living in a fishbowl. She gave an example of a feminist therapist who was criticized for not taking on more no-fee clients, including a possible client who later attempted a very public suicide. Brown (1991) illustrated the complexity of such a dilemma in her description of "the therapist [who] found herself besieged by community members who were angry that the therapist had not rescued this woman, and the therapist [feeling] both angrier and guiltier" (p. 331) while dealing with the community condemnation of her attempt to balance conflicting personal and social needs.

Brown (1994) believes that feminist therapists move within a continuum of boundary violations during the course of professional practice. She recommended a consideration of the characteristics of boundary violations and evaluating whether they are likely to be present in a particular situation. Brown (1994) identified these characteristics as objectification of the client (satisfying the therapist's needs for power, recognition, affection, intimacy, entertainment, or education), impulsive gratification of the therapist's impulses, and consistent placement of the therapist's needs as primary. She described therapy as "always a pas de deux in which we are the supporting partner" (Brown, 1994, p. 36) and suggested that boundary violations occur "when the *relational* nature of therapy is forgotten, and work begins to center around the self and person of the therapist" (Brown, 1994, p. 37; italics in original). Because there may not always be clear rules about what constitutes a boundary violation, Brown (1994) reminds us of the importance for therapists, both feminist and others, "to create opportunities to do the purely human things in our lives outside of our work . . . that in therapy . . . would be considered boundary violations" (p. 37).

M. Hill (1990) contended that boundary violations within feminist therapy replicate the incest paradigm by therapists who want something that should never be a part of therapy. She identified sex, affirmation, friendship, and caretaking as possible violations and suggested that "Feminist therapists are particularly at risk in this area because we choose for philosophical and political reasons to be *people* (with human vulnerabilities, pain, and needs) as well as therapists with our clients" (p. 58; italics in original). She challenged feminist therapists to be clear about boundaries, especially with clients with whom they might have been friends or lovers had they met in a different context. Here, they experience the loss of being "in intimate relationships with people we genuinely like. Our job is to stay at this wonderful banquet of relationships and yet to taste none of it, no matter how hungry we may be" (M. Hill, 1990, p. 60).

Criminal Justice, Corrections, and Law Enforcement

Psychologists who practice in criminal justice, corrections, and law enforcement settings face challenges related to conflicting and overlapping roles. They may also face pressure, both external and internal, to take on client issues for which they have limited preparation and background in order to meet the needs of the closed systems in which they work.

Dilemmas Involving Professional Boundaries

Although many criminal justice agencies now rely on mental health resources outside of their department, some psychologists who work within the criminal justice system may be expected to perform potentially conflicting roles: preventive counseling, mental health treatment, assessment, teaching, and consulting with administrators (Dietz & Reese, 1986).

Psychologists within the criminal justice system may have different clients at different times—for example, seeing an inmate as a client and then being asked by a parole board to share information that may be damaging to that client (Saxton, 1986). Confidentiality may be limited in some instances, for example, within security prisons in which officers have the right and responsibility to search psychologists' files to obtain information about possible possession of weapons or other contraband (Saxton, 1986). As in other practice settings, clients need to be adequately informed of the limits to confidentiality at the beginning of the therapy session.

Koocher and Keith-Spiegel (1998) identified the necessity of clarification as to who the client is: the individual or the system. They claimed that psychologists who work within the criminal justice system need to be aware of possible role conflicts and address any conflicts directly with supervisors within the system. They presented an example of one such potential conflict involving an inmate client who reveals to a correctional psychologist an imminent plan by inmates that would involve the taking of hostages. The client then indicates that his own life would be in danger if the psychologist revealed this information. The correctional psychologist in this situation is faced with balancing conflicting ethical obligations to protect the rights of the client versus warning potential victims. Koocher and Keith-Spiegel included this example to illustrate the need to clarify expectations with prison officials ahead of time regarding reporting obligations of rule violations. The correctional psychologist would then be obligated to clarify with clients at the beginning of their psychotherapeutic relationship any restrictions on confidentiality.

Because concern for overall security in a correctional facility overrides the concern for the rights of individual inmates, psychologists in these facilities may be expected to "apply their expertise and skills to custody matters" (Weinberger & Sreenivasan, 2003, p. 362). Weinberger and Sreenivasan (2003) emphasized the possibility that inmates may view the therapy relationship as a way for the psychologist to glean information for later use in a parole board evaluation. Correctional psychologists should avoid such dual relationships, which may impair objectivity and exploit the inmate, whenever possible (Weinberger & Sreenivasan, 2003).

Weinberger and Sreenivasan (1994) believe that psychologists in the correctional system face troubling dilemmas primarily because "correctional personnel do not understand or support the standards and/or the psychologist's role as a mental health professional" (p. 163). Correctional psychologists may perform a variety of roles: administrative tasks, systemwide identification of and intervention on issues, critical incident stress debriefing to staff and their family members, training on a range of mental health topics, and other employee assistance roles (Weinberger & Sreenivasan, 2003).

Psychologists in correctional settings may also perform a law enforcement role in dealing with institutional disturbances, including "search[ing] for contraband, us[ing] a firearm, driv[ing] a perimeter patrol vehicle with a variety of firearms to prevent escapes, and coordinat[ing] inmate movement within the institution" (Weinberger & Sreenivasan, 2003, p. 362). Such roles are not the provision of psychological services and are likely conflicting roles, which "affects the way psychologists are viewed by both inmates and correctional personnel" (Weinberger & Sreenivasan, 2003, p. 370). Weinberger and Sreenivasan (2003) indicated that some correctional psychologists view these conflicting roles as actually beneficial in that they give psychologists a more accurate picture of the institutional environment and of the behavior of individual inmates. However,

> if the psychologist is perceived by the inmates as a cooperating member of the correctional staff who engages in security

work, this could well impair their ability to be seen by the inmate as objective professionals who will not exploit or harm them. (Weinberger & Sreenivasan, 2003, p. 371)

The duties of psychologists within correctional systems may vary widely across systems. These duties may include "assisting in inmate or cell searches, writing disciplinary reports, acting in administrative capacities, or quelling a riot" (White, 2003b, p. 20). The "grossly disproportionate degree of power and control that exists between inmates and staff" (White, 2003a, p. 14) inevitably complicates multiple-relationship issues within such settings, especially when psychologists are performing routine correctional tasks that take them outside of their clinical roles (White, 2003a). Although they might be problematic and "potential obstacles to maintaining or establishing a clinical relationship" (White, 2003a, p. 14), these overlapping relationships may not be unethical if clients are not being exploited.

Some duties may not be inherently unethical, for example, issuing rules violations for missed appointments. Others, however, such as strip searches and handcuffing, may seriously damage the psychologist's professional role. The critical ethical question revolves around the action's impact rather than the action itself—whether inmates are being harmed or exploited by the activities of psychologists (White, 2003b). Although correctional psychologists would be well advised to avoid nonclinical activities with clients whenever possible (White, 2003a), it is important to educate administrators regarding the important role that correctional psychologists play through their clinical expertise instead of being viewed simply as adjunct correctional officers (Weinberger & Sreenivasan, 2003).

Zelig's (1988) study of ethical dilemmas in police psychology indicated that confidentiality was mentioned most frequently as a dilemma. He identified the problem of "Who is the client?" especially in mandated referrals to a psychologist from within the department of an officer for evaluation or treatment, when "confidentiality between the officer and the psychologist is at most limited and often nonexistent" (Zelig, 1988, p. 336). Zelig pointed out that confidentiality may also be an issue regarding dangerousness and duty to warn when working with a client population of police officers. The police carry weapons and are often in situations in which they may be provoked by antagonistic citizens. He identified dual relationships as particularly troublesome and pervasive and gave the following example:

> A day in the life of a [police] psychologist may consist of conferring with detectives on a case with psychological implications, performing a fitness-for-duty evaluation, and administering inservice training. Any of the recipients of these services may also consult with the psychologist for other services, and it is understandable that they could misunderstand the role of the psychologist in their organization. (p. 337)

One of the most common and significant conflicts arises from psychologists not obtaining informed consent from the law enforcement agency, from individuals being treated or evaluated, or from collateral contacts. The possibility also exists that the psychologist's notes may be used forensically by an independent evaluator in ways that may have negative consequences for an inmate, even if the psychologist involved scrupulously avoids a dual role for him- or herself (Weinberger & Sreenivasan, 2003).

The 2002 APA Ethics Code addressed such conflicts in Standard 3.05, Multiple Relationships:

> (c) When psychologists are required by law, institutional policy, or extraordinary circumstances to serve in more than one role in judicial or administrative proceedings, at the outset they clarify role expectations and the extent of confidentiality and thereafter as changes occur (APA, 2002a, p. 1065);

and in Standard 3.10, Informed Consent:

> (c) When psychological services are court ordered or otherwise mandated, psychologists inform the individual of the nature of the anticipated services, including whether the services are court ordered or mandated and any limits of confidentiality, before proceeding (p. 1065);

as well as in Standard 4.02, Discussing the Limits of Confidentiality:

Psychologists discuss with persons. . . . and organizations with whom they establish a scientific or professional relationship (1) the relevant limits of confidentiality and (2) the foreseeable uses of the information generated through their psychological activities. (p. 1066)

The most significant and relevant change in the 2002 APA Ethics Code resulted from adding representation on the Ethics Code Task Force to ensure that issues relevant to psychologists practicing in the law enforcement system or the military would receive due consideration:

3.11 Psychological Services Delivered to or Through Organizations

(a) Psychologists delivering services to or through organizations provide information beforehand to clients and when appropriate those directly affected by the services about (1) the nature and objectives of the services, (2) the intended recipients, (3) which of the individuals are clients, (4) the relationship the psychologist will have with each person and the organization, (5) the probable uses of services provided and information obtained, (6) who will have access to the information, and (7) limits of confidentiality. As soon as feasible, they provide information about the results and conclusions of such services to appropriate persons.

(b) If psychologists will be precluded by law or by organizational roles from providing such information to particular individuals or groups, they so inform those individuals or groups at the outset of the service. (APA, 2002a, p. 1066)

Dietz and Reese (1986) suggested that police psychologists clearly disclose the ethical principles that will provide the basis for their work, identify their profession and clarify their role to anyone they interview, and limit the disclosure of confidential information to only that which is necessary. They included the following example to illustrate role confusion and improper behavior:

The Chief of a major department held a meeting with his director of psychological services and asked that the psycholo-

gist discreetly get in the company of the Deputy Chief, interview him, and determine whether he was an alcoholic. The
psychologist was ordered to bring that information back to
the Chief so that proper actions could be instituted if warranted. The Chief is highly influential in determining who oc-
cupies the position of Director of Psychological Services. Thereafter, the psychologist was often seen in the company of
department executives, particularly at luncheon meetings. He
assessed the Deputy Chief without the latter's knowledge.
Having determined that the Deputy Chief suffered from alcoholism, the psychologist provided treatment to the Deputy
Chief without advising him of his findings or the fact that his
apparently informal advice and counsel was actually treatment given at the direction of the Chief. (p. 390)

Limited Resources and Limits of Competence

In advising psychologists within law enforcement settings to disclose the limitations to their expertise, Dietz and Reese (1986) acknowledged that needs of law enforcement agencies involve a
range of skills and experiences contained across a variety of psychology specialties. A person may be asked to function as an in-
dustrial psychologist, a clinical psychologist, a community psychologist, and a forensic psychologist. Dietz and Reese urged law
enforcement psychologists to avoid trying to perform all of the
functions that may be needed and to disclose a lack of expertise if
asked to take on an activity for which they are unqualified.

Community Expectations and Values Differences

Dietz and Reese (1986) suggested that "Differences in attitudes,
values, techniques, and priorities produce situations in which
mental health professionals and law enforcement personnel can
easily find themselves at odds if neither group understands the
other's position and the assumptions that underlie it" (p. 386).
Both groups see themselves as helping people but may do so in
quite different and conflicting ways.

Although widely accepted in the academic community, public
debate and differences in approach are viewed as embarrassing

within law enforcement, which has a high need for unity (Dietz & Reese, 1986). Psychologists in law enforcement must comply with the agency standards of conduct while perhaps in disagreement with the agency regarding some of the standards of conduct. They must balance identification with law enforcement with commitment to psychology's norms and values (Dietz & Reese, 1986). Psychologists who work within law enforcement settings may experience some of the same stressors as police officers. They may have decreased contact with those outside law enforcement and may overidentify with police officers (Dietz & Reese, 1986). However, Dietz and Reese (1986) also point out that

> just as the psychotherapist who identifies too strongly with depressed patients because of his own depression is compromised in his treatment of such patients and incapable of the undistorted judgment his patients need, the mental health professional who identifies too strongly with law enforcement personnel is compromised in his ability to provide them with effective mental health services or undistorted consultative judgments. (p. 398)

As antidotes to overidentification with law enforcement personnel, Dietz and Reese (1986) advocated self-monitoring and ongoing participation in mental health activities outside of the specialization of law enforcement. Weinberger and Sreenivasan (2003) identified peer supervision and consultation as essential to high-quality practice in correctional settings, especially for the many psychologists who are the lone practitioners in their facilities.

Military

Military settings provide a unique set of small-community challenges for psychologists. Role confusion, limits to confidentiality, conflicts over client rights versus the needs of the larger system, overlapping relationships, limited resources and limits of competence, and values differences are among the areas where dilemmas can occur for military psychologists.

Dilemmas Involving Professional Boundaries

There are many opportunities for role confusion within a military setting. Military psychologists are part of a profession that encourages individual growth and privacy, but "they work for an entity that demands fidelity to rules and the collective interest" and where "following one set of rules often means breaking the other" (Sleek, 1995, p. 30). As Johnson, Ralph, and Johnson (2005) pointed out, a military unit is "often defined by boundary crossings and constant close quarters" (p. 73), which both enhances psychologists' opportunities to understand their clients and provides numerous opportunities for multiple-role dilemmas.

Staal and King (2000) indicated that there may only be one or two psychologists on many military bases. Because psychologists are also officers, their authority over enlisted members adds to the complications. Bases usually include many services—housing, stores, fitness and recreation facilities, restaurants, and so on—which makes it even more likely that lives and roles will overlap. Medical providers, administrators, and other individuals may be current or former clients.

Military psychologists are required to maintain state licensure and to adhere to the APA Ethics Code (T. B. Jeffrey, 1989; T. B. Jeffrey, Rankin, & Jeffrey, 1992). They face "the double burden of upholding the ethics code of psychologists while also supporting the mission" of the military (Orme & Doerman, 2001, p. 305). Loss of license or sanction for misconduct as a psychologist can result in loss of a military psychologist's job (T. B. Jeffrey et al., 1992). However, there are conflicts between those laws or principles and service regulations, especially in the area of confidentiality (T. B. Jeffrey, 1989; T. B. Jeffrey et al., 1992).

In a military environment, conflicts can arise over who the client is: the individual or the organization (Sleek, 1995; Staal & King, 2000). This can be especially difficult because few psychologists have received military-specific ethics education as part of their graduate ethics training (Staal & King, 2000). Military psychologists may be required to confirm to commanders whether an individual serviceperson is being seen for therapy (T. B. Jeffrey, 1989). "The military is uniquely different from many other organizations in that issues of national security must be considered in any discussion of the need to balance individual civil rights against public protection" (T. B. Jeffrey et al., 1992, p. 94). Although some in the military believe that any deviant behavior is a threat to national security, T. B. Jeffrey et al. (1992) maintained that "the reality is that the vast majority of clinical cases [are] not [threats]" (p. 94).

How do military psychologists best serve clients in the military? Do providers slant the information in charts to prevent a breach of confidentiality for the individual, taking into account the possibility that other medical or mental health personnel with access to the charts may, for example, discover that a client is GLBT and feel obligated to report? How do military psychologists deal with what Hines, Ader, Chang, and Rundell (1998) referred to as *divided loyalties* in dual agency, whereby psychologists sometimes have conflicting loyalties to clients and to the military? What should be included in any advance warning or informed consent given to military clients at the beginning of mental health treatment? Although military personnel know that medical and mental health confidentiality can be compromised for the greater good, they want to trust providers, and they tend to do so if not specifically warned (Howe, 1989). Psychologists, however, hold the authority to make decisions that can vitally affect the careers of others in the military through their diagnoses and recommendations (Orme & Doerman, 2001).

In Orme and Doerman's (2001) survey, a majority of the 263 U.S. Air Force psychologists who participated identified patient confidentiality and overlapping relationships as primary concerns. Their results identified an ongoing struggle to balance individual rights versus institutional need and right to know. The Air Force psychologists believed that sometimes they were coerced by those in authority to behave unethically. However, Orme and Doerman pointed out that providing appropriate client information to military agencies with a legitimate need to know was not an ethical violation provided proper informed consent had been given. However, military psychologists face "the difficult task of balancing the aims of national defense against the rights of the individual" (Orme & Doerman, 2001, p. 310).

Although Department of Defense and Army regulations may require release of information without a client's consent to officials with a need to know, no definition of *need to know* has been provided (T. B. Jeffrey et al., 1992). Servicepeople involved in sensitive or classified duties give up the right to privacy for both themselves and their families, which means that commanders may receive a report any time they or their families are seen by any health care practitioner. This ultimately results in a low utilization rate for mental health services (T. B. Jeffrey et al., 1992) and discomfort and anxiety for those who provide mental health services (Hines et al., 1998).

As an example of overlapping roles, military psychologists may be in a position to provide forensic evaluations and to treat individual servicepersons. In both situations, the military men and women being evaluated should know that there are limits to their confidentiality. Clients also need to be informed at the outset of therapy what kinds of information regarding their fitness for duty must be reported (Koocher & Keith-Spiegel, 1998).

Conversely, providers have to decide how they will or will not elicit information that may not be in the best interest of clients (Howe, 1989). The welfare of the military and the nation may be at stake. Howe (1989) suggested that not giving advance warning regarding the limited nature of confidentiality within the military is necessary in some cases to prevent exceptional harm and to protect the interests and safety of others within a military unit. Conversely, he suggested that military mental health providers avoid taking the position that any and all illegal activity by clients should be reported and that doing so may actually harm individual clients and the military in general.

Howe (1989), T. B. Jeffrey (1989), and T. B. Jeffrey et al. (1992) have advocated that advance warning/informed consent be given to all military clients and that confidentiality be violated only in situations in which extraordinary harm could occur. In addition, responses to requests for information should be limited to specific information for specific reasons, with disclosure usually occurring only with the written permission of the client (T. B. Jeffrey, 1989). Military psychologists must be especially aware of conditions under which they should or should not breach confidentiality, and they have a responsibility to society to breach confidentiality in serious situations (T. B. Jeffrey et al., 1992). The tension between the military psychologists' obligations to individual clients and to the larger organization may be reduced through careful informed consent, especially as those in the military "agree to adhere to various military regulations that provide specific standards and guidance as a condition of enlistment or commission as an officer. [These standards] include a compromise in some individual freedom and rights" (Staal & King, 2000, p. 704). It may also mean that military psychologists must take a professional stance that is unpopular with superior officers if demands are made to review all the information contained in client records when only part of the information is relevant to a particular investigation (Orme & Doerman, 2001).

It is highly likely that military psychologists will see as clients individuals whom they know in another context (Orme & Doerman, 2001). Like their rural colleagues, they may live and socialize within a small community where their lives frequently overlap with those of their clients. They may be asked to provide therapy for friends and colleagues, especially on bases located in remote areas. One respondent in Orme and Doerman's (2001) study gave the example of having to coordinate inpatient chemical dependency treatment for the wife of the commander, and another respondent told of providing therapy for colleagues and others within the psychologist's chain of command. One military psychologist who was the lone mental health officer on a base assumed dual roles as investigating and later treating clients involved in family abuse situations.

Johnson et al. (2005) highlighted the difficulties faced by military psychologists in embedded environments as members of a small team or unit. They identified the almost impossible task of simultaneous allegiance to ethical guidelines and federal statutes. Unlike their colleagues in most rural and other small communities, militarily embedded psychologists are rarely able to refuse service to clients and to avoid daily multiple roles. A psychologist in this situation "is always both care provider and commissioned officer with all the concomitant obligations" (Johnson et al., 2005, p. 75). They are agents of both the system and the individual, which "can create role strain for the psychologist and conflicting expectations for both individual and organizational clients" (Johnson et al., 2005, p. 75). These shifts between administrative and clinical duties are not easily predictable (Johnson et al., 2005).

Johnson et al. (2005) pointed out that overlapping relationships within a military context, although difficult to predict and negotiate, may have several benefits. Psychologists are better able to understand the culture and stressors faced by other members of their military unit. They also are seen as insiders and gain credibility through their visibility within the community. Such psychologists are also seen as more available and approachable by unit members with whom they interact on a daily basis.

Johnson (1995) provided the following suggestions in dealing with military ethical quandaries. Thinking of an APA–Department of Defense collaboration, he suggests the following:

- Operationalize the Department of Defense need-to-know policy. Clarify the definition of *need* and how psychologists can determine the validity of requests.
- Differentiate clinical and forensic roles. Create separate positions for clinical and forensic psychologists.
- Standardize informed-consent procedures and clarify for clients that confidentiality is not available within military health care settings.
- Develop standards for clinical documentation, including providing the minimum amount of required information and clarifying the legal requirements and benefits of psychologists maintaining private records.
- Provide continuing education on standards of practice for military psychologists, including strategies for handling conflicting demands, and offer a national hotline providing peer consultation.
- Lobby to modify the Department of Defense policy to reduce conflicts between competing demands and to protect the rights of consumers and providers without compromising the mission of the military.
- Coordinate research to study dilemmas of military psychologists, including trends and effectiveness of approaches.

As indicated earlier in this chapter, the most significant and relevant change in the 2002 APA Ethics Code for psychologists who practice in military settings resulted from adding relevant representation on the Ethics Code Task Force to ensure that issues relevant to psychologists practicing in the law enforcement system or the military would receive due consideration:

> 3.11 Psychological Services Delivered to or Through Organizations
>
> (a) Psychologists delivering services to or through organizations provide information beforehand to clients and when appropriate those directly affected by the services about (1) the nature and objectives of the services, (2) the intended recipients, (3) which of the individuals are clients, (4) the relationship the psychologist will have with each person and the organization, (5) the probable uses of services provided and information obtained, (6) who will have access to the information, and (7) limits of confidentiality. As soon as feasible, they provide information about the results and conclusions of such services to appropriate persons.
>
> (b) If psychologists will be precluded by law or by organizational roles from providing such information to particular individuals or groups, they so inform those individuals or groups at the outset of the service. (APA, 2002a, p. 1066)

Limited Resources and Limits of Competence

Military psychologists are sometimes pressured to provide services for which they have not been adequately trained, especially when other options are limited (Orme & Doerman, 2001). They struggle with not wanting to engage in psychological practices that may potentially harm clients while also striving to meet the needs of individual clients and of commanders who have insisted that particular clients be served. If they discover that previous treatment has been provided in negligent ways, military psychologists are faced with the dilemma of confronting other providers or reporting the provider to the appropriate licensing boards. Both choices could lead to myriad problems within the context of a small community in which people know each other and interact in various ways. Although it is preferable to informally approach negligent or unethical providers, that can be especially difficult in a military setting "if the offending provider is in the psychologist's chain of command or is of senior rank" (Orme & Doerman, 2001, p. 309).

Community Expectations and Values Differences

The current "don't ask, don't tell" policy surrounding gay men and lesbians in the military provides an example of potential values differences and conflicts between military psychologists and others within the military. Because ethical practice forbids discrimination based on sexual orientation, military psychologists have to grapple with ways to behave ethically and in the best interest of their clients within an overall military policy that contradicts professional standards. Because of the official stance that gay men and lesbians in the military are to be treated differently than others, psychologists are caught between not discriminating against their clients versus upholding military policy (Orme & Doerman, 2001). Clients who divulge homosexual behavior leave mental health providers struggling with ethical obligations to maintain confidentiality in the face of federal law that mandates disclosure of such behavior as a violation of military policy (Sleek, 1995). Military psychologists who make their views widely known risk censure themselves, as they practice in a setting in which open discussions of their views may be seen as insubordinate or threatening by their military superiors.

Other Small Communities: Chemical Dependency, Suburbs, Disability, Deaf–Hearing Impaired, and Therapists Who See Other Therapists

Dilemmas for psychologists in a variety of other small communities have many similarities to the communities we have already discussed. Overlapping relationships, limited resources, and interagency issues are all too real for therapists working within those small communities, especially if they are themselves members of the community.

Dilemmas Involving Professional Boundaries

There are countless examples of overlap between psychologists and clients in most of the small communities addressed in this section. Chemical dependency therapists who are also members of 12-step groups in which clients participate face the unfortunate dilemma of weighing what they disclose within a group, finding another group, or suggesting that clients find another group (Gonsiorek & Brown, 1986). They may attend large recovery-themed celebrations and patronize alcohol-free bars and coffeehouses where they are likely to interact with clients (Chapman, 1997; Schoener & Luepker, 1996). Chemical dependency counselors may have their boundaries stretched by working with clients who have issues and profiles similar to their own. They may also encounter dual relationships inherent in a field in which clients in recovery often choose to enter the substance abuse treatment field, which increases the likelihood of posttherapy contact between client and therapist (Chapman, 1997).

Psychologists who live and practice in a contained suburban setting face overlapping relationships in social and professional milieus. These issues have many similarities with those facing rural psychologists, especially overlapping dilemmas involving members of psychologists' own families. As an example, a psychologist may have enrolled her young daughter in a mother–daughter swimming class at the local community center only to find out that one or more of her clients are also in the class. When there are no other swimming classes that are close by or offered at times that fit into the psychologist's schedule, she is faced with the choice of taking her daughter out of the class or remaining in the pool with a client.

Well-respected psychologists may see other psychologists as clients and then interact with those same clients in professional organizations. They may have to evaluate whether to accept professional referrals from psychologist clients and may find themselves in work settings in which they are asked to supervise the professional work of a former client. Case consultation may prove challenging, as a psychologist strives to protect the identity of psychologist clients while never being sure if colleagues will recognize the description of a friend or associate.

Deaf psychologists may have a particularly difficult time, because much of their socializing is often within the deaf community in which their lives cross paths with those of their clients. They may also have a great deal of unsolicited out-of-therapy information about clients and others within the deaf community— information that they might wish they did not know and about which they may have to keep careful track. Because there are few deaf psychologists, they may find themselves having to make decisions about what constitutes the best interests of a client and about the wisdom of seeing several members of a family for individual therapy.

Limited Resources and Limits of Competence

When dealing with limited resources and limits of competence, deaf psychologists face issues similar to those facing their rural counterparts. They must be able to function as generalists within a small community in which they are perhaps the only psychologist available for clients, especially clients who are uncomfortable having sign language interpreters in therapy sessions.

Professional isolation can be a potential problem for psychologists within the deaf community, the community of individuals with disabilities, and other small communities in which the numbers of psychologists or other mental health professionals are small. Although they may have good professional relationships with other psychologists outside of their communities, it can be difficult to find another psychologist within the community with whom they can speak freely about client issues.

Community Expectations and Values Differences

Psychologists within these small communities may find themselves dealing with significant differences in values between themselves and their clients. Clients may expect that psychologists participate in community events, both professional and social, to an extent that is uncomfortable for individual psychologists. As in rural and other small communities, refusal to participate, or setting limits around one's participation, might leave psychologists open to criticism within the community or to accusations that a particular psychologist sees him- or herself as being above the daily lives of others within the community. Precisely because the community is so small, people may expect that a psychologist within that community must be available to meet the counseling and consultation needs of whomever asks.

The informal communication network may operate in ways similar to those of other small communities addressed earlier in this book. News about the work of a psychologist travels quickly, and sometimes inaccurately. The psychologist is in the difficult position of not being able to respond to protect the confidentiality of clients, even if the clients are making untrue statements about his or her work.

Interagency Issues: Working With Other Community Agencies, Groups, and Professionals

Even in small communities within larger communities or urban areas, psychologists must negotiate working relationships with relatively few resources for a specific population. As an example, there may be few social service agencies that work with blind clients. If a blind psychologist has difficulty with his or her own experiences with that agency, it would be problematic for him or her to refer clients to that same agency.

As in other small communities that we have discussed in this chapter, word travels fast. Both positive and negative experiences with a specific psychologist or other providers or agencies can quickly become public information within the community. Political differences of opinion on issues directly affecting the community are also sources of discussion and possible disapproval.

Chapter

6

Strategies to Minimize Risk

When dealing with ethical dilemmas in small communities, there are few absolute answers that can neatly resolve issues, particularly in the area of multiple relationships. Almost all standards and principles in ethics codes require the psychologist's informed judgment. Psychologists who practice in small communities need to be able to tolerate ambiguity and will not find security in the absolute answers that others may be quick to offer. Sometimes there is a "best" answer; other times, it may be better to consider more than one acceptable way to respond to ethical dilemmas (Herlihy & Corey, 1992). However, as Haas and Malouf (1989) posited, "the process of providing ethically appropriate and clinically sound services requires constant decision making" (p. 5).

Framing the right question is a large part of addressing an ethical issue. That frame should prompt one to be more vigilant, to act decisively, and to thoroughly address the issues at hand (Canter, Bennett, Jones, & Nagy, 1994). It is prudent to consider risks to both the client and the psychologist. The primary question to be weighed is whether the potential benefit of the relationship outweighs the potential for harm. Also, what are possible effects of the psychologist's decisions on other consumers, other professionals, the profession of psychology itself, and the larger society (Herlihy & Corey, 1992)?

Anne Hess (in a personal statement that does not officially reflect her membership on the American Psychological Association

[APA] Ethics Committee) highlighted what she termed "stealth" dilemmas. Hess described them as "situations that develop gradually, moving step by small step beyond once-firm professional boundaries. Although each step seemed harmless at the time, many practitioners later realize that they have landed themselves in deep trouble" (D. Smith, 2003b, p. 50).

Although setting appropriate boundaries is a professional imperative, flexibility in their maintenance is equally important. Given the individual differences among clients, fine adjustments may be required in nearly every case (D. Smith & Fitzpatrick, 1995). As the potential for harm increases, so should the prohibitions against engaging in that particular kind of behavior or relationship (Stockman, 1990).

Psychologists in small communities talk about being caught between what they experience as limited alternative resources and the profound needs of their clients. Thomas (1993) suggested that well-intentioned psychologists, when tempted to depart from standard ethics codes, consider the following factors before making a decision: "the client's history and therapeutic needs, the degree to which the considered action was motivated by the therapist's own needs, the potential for subsequent role confusion and possible harm to the therapeutic relationship" (p. 9).

Decision-Making Models

It is useful to have a framework in mind when faced with ethical dilemmas in small-community practice. Such a framework may be based on more general decision-making models but will also need to address issues common to small-community ethics. In this chapter, we highlight three general approaches to ethical decision making and then focus on issues that are specific to small communities.

Welfel (1998) outlined a complete, practical model for ethical decision making in her book, *Ethics in Counseling and Psychotherapy.* Welfel's model can be readily applied to decisions in a number of practice areas. It is especially helpful in taking the steps that are essential for a reasoned, professional response to a dilemma faced in everyday practice. The use of this framework may lessen the anxiety of psychologists who face a complicated dilemma, and it

provides the foundation for good basic practice. Welfel's protocol involved the following nine steps:[1]

1. *Develop ethical sensitivity.* Take courses and workshops that
    focus not only on ethical standards but also on how to fol-
    low a moral decision-making process. Continue to edu-
    cate yourself throughout your career. Discuss dilemmas
    with other psychologists and seek out the objective feed-
    back of others. Examine your own values and motivations
    for being a psychologist. Recognize that we face what
    Welfel described as "the commonness, complexity, and
    subtleties of ethical dilemmas" (p. 27) in everyday prac-
    tice. Establish methods of assessing the ethical dimensions
    of each case, possibly on the intake form or in case notes.
2. *Define the dilemma and the options.* Carefully examine pos-
    sible dilemmas and responses.
3. *Refer to professional standards.* See how standards and codes
    apply to a particular dilemma. Become so familiar with
    applicable standards that you can locate relevant sections
    quickly and easily. Refer to pertinent state and federal laws.
4. *Search out ethics scholarship.* Look for books and articles that
    address the same ethical issues that are of concern to you.
    Benefit from the perspective of experts and become more
    aware of aspects of an ethical dilemma that you may not
    have yet considered.
5. *Apply ethical principles to the situation.* Welfel pointed out
    that "The professional literature may narrow and clarify
    the options, but it rarely points to a single path" (p. 32).
    Look to the underlying principles that form the founda-
    tion of ethics codes. If applicable ethical principles conflict
    in a particular dilemma, keep client welfare uppermost in
    your concerns as you weigh conflicting principles to come
    to the best final decision.
6. *Consult your supervisor and respected colleagues.* Obtain ob-
    jective feedback from others to get additional information
    or points of view. Reduce emotional isolation by turning
    to trusted colleagues.
7. *Deliberate and decide.* After gaining the perspectives of oth-
    ers, and after seeking out the additional information that

[1]From *Ethics in Counseling and Psychotherapy: Standards, Research, and Emerging Issues* (p. 24), by E. R. Welfel, 1998, Pacific Grove, CA: Brooks/Cole. Copy-
right 1998 by Thomson Learning. Reprinted with permission of Wadsworth, a
division of Thomson Learning: www.thomsonrights.com.

you need, the responsibility rests with you to weigh all the
factors and come to an ethical decision. Even if the choice
and consequences cause you discomfort, you are upholding the standards of the profession and adding to your
confidence in making difficult ethical decisions.

8. *Inform your supervisor; implement and document your actions.*
Communicate first with your supervisor and then with
others who need to know of your decision, rationale, and
course of action. Document those factors in your case notes
or other necessary records.

9. *Reflect on the experience.* Once the immediate emotionality
and pressure have lifted, take the time to think back on
how and what you decided, along with how you may want
to deal with similar situations in the future.

Steinman, Richardson, and McEnroe (1998) proposed a seven-
step model that includes identification, consideration of consequences, resolution, feedback, and action. Like Welfel (1998), the
authors stressed the importance of thorough examination of alternatives, choices, and actions, along with the necessity of input
from and consultation with others to ensure that complicated
decisions are based on sound ethical principles. In the *Ethical
Decision-Making Manual for Helping Professionals,* Steinman et al.
(pp. 18–20) suggested the following seven steps:

1. Identify the ethical standard involved.
2. Determine ethical trap possibilities.
3. Frame a preliminary response.
4. Consider the consequences.
5. Prepare ethical resolution.
6. Get feedback.
7. Take action.

Koocher and Keith-Spiegel (1998, pp. 12–15) offered a model
that consists of eight steps, moving from consideration of issues,
to alternatives, to a final decision. These steps are as follows:

1. Determine that the matter is an ethical one.
2. Consult the guidelines already available that might apply to a specific identification and possible mechanism
for resolution.

3. Consider, as well as possible, all sources that might influence the kind of decision you will make.
4. Locate a trusted colleague whom you can consult.
5. Evaluate the rights, responsibilities, and vulnerability of all affected parties.
6. Generate alternative decisions.
7. Enumerate the consequences of making each decision.
8. Make the decision.

Minimizing Risk in Small Communities

These three decision-making models provide a sound basis for further elaboration and development of a model of ethical decision making that can be specifically applied to small-community ethical issues. In the following section, we use these models as the foundation for a set of factors designed to minimize practice risk for small-community psychologists. In the next sections of this chapter, we describe 16 strategies and provide more small-community specificity. When combined with any of the three general decision-making models, these factors contribute to a more complete decision-making protocol for small-community practice.

1. Recognize That Ethics Codes or Standards Are Necessary But Not Sufficient

Codes cannot cover every dilemma that psychologists face, especially within the complexity of small-community practice. We must be able to apply regulations but also make ethical decisions based on daily challenges. Psychologists must be knowledgeable regarding relevant standards and must also be able to take those guidelines and apply them to psychological situations that are usually not as clear-cut as the examples that are provided for or developed by traditionally trained urban colleagues. As Robert Kinscherf, former chair of the APA Ethics Committee, stated, "Instead of worrying about the ways [they] can get in trouble, psychologists should think about ethics as a way of asking 'How can I be even better in my practice?'" (D. Smith, 2003b, p. 50). (This statement by Kinscherf reflected his personal opinion and was not an official statement of the committee.)

2. Know Relevant Codes, Regulations, and Laws

Although it is a cliché, ignorance of the law is no excuse. Keep up to date with professional guidelines and standards and with state and national laws. Know the rules and regulations of the institution where you work.

3. Obtain Informed Consent

Obtaining informed consent is an ethically important first step that sets the tone of the professional relationship through an open, complete discussion of expectations, boundaries, and risks involved in therapy. D. Smith (2003b) suggested the following points for discussion:

- ☐ limits of confidentiality;
- ☐ how records are kept;
- ☐ your expertise, experience, and training;
- ☐ estimated length of therapy;
- ☐ alternative treatment approaches;
- ☐ fees and billing practices;
- ☐ emergency contacts;
- ☐ the client's right to terminate; and
- ☐ what services you will and will not provide.

Talk with clients directly about the plan of treatment and any ethical dilemmas that are involved for you as a psychologist. This discussion should include the very real possibility of overlapping relationships within the small community in which you practice (Tribbensee & Claiborn, 2003). Be sure that your case notes indicate the process of informed consent, along with documentation of any dual relationship or limits of competence and how treatment may possibly be affected. Describe relevant consultations with other mental health professionals. If there is a potential problematic dual relationship, discuss it as openly as possible with the client to ensure that he or she understands the reasoning behind not entering into a therapy relationship and the need for referral.

4. Involve Prospective Clients in Decision Making

Discuss with clients the implications of any overlapping social or business relationships, along with any concerns that you might have about where you will need to enhance your own professional background so you can work with these clients effectively. Give information about other available options and work together to decide whether you can enter into a therapy relationship. Document all of this in your case notes.

5. Talk Directly With Clients About the Likelihood of Out-of-Therapy Contact

Instead of waiting for that uncomfortable moment out in the community, discuss at the beginning of therapy the likelihood of out-of-therapy contact and reopen the issue as needed throughout the course of therapy (Barnett & Yutrzenka, 1995). Talk with clients about the uniqueness of the therapy relationship and how out-of-therapy interactions may be affected by that relationship (Stockman, 1990). Set clear limits with clients about the inappropriateness of discussing therapy when you meet each other in social or business settings.

Many psychologists in small communities are also involved in community organizations and events, which results in a kind of self-disclosure as to the psychologist's beliefs, values, and activities. An open discussion of how this information may affect a client can be a meaningful and necessary part of therapy (Faulkner & Faulkner, 1997).

6. Consider the Type and Severity of the Client's Presenting Problems

When deciding whether to see a client, consider how his or her specific problems may complicate the situation. For example, accepting a client who is presenting with problems of depression or anxiety may be different from seeing a client with a borderline personality disorder or with paranoia. Of course, in some remote settings, such decisions are a moot point. There may be no referral options available, or a client may be assigned to a particular agency as the primary service provider.

7. Set Clear Expectations

Kitchener (1988) warned, "As the incompatibility of expectations increases between roles, so will the potential for misunderstanding and harm" (p. 217). Discuss with clients what expectations they may have of you in the varying roles that you might play in the community. Clarify role obligations and expectations, and address problems as they arise (Kitchener, 1988). Any discrepancies between client expectations and the ability of the psychologist to meet these expectations should be clearly addressed (Stockman, 1990).

8. Set Clear Boundaries, Both Within Yourself and With Clients

Be clear with yourself as to what your limits are and communicate that clearly to clients from the beginning of the counseling relationship. Be clear from the beginning about the boundaries of the professional relationship and ways that personal interaction between you and clients in out-of-therapy situations could be affected.

Clear expectations and boundaries, whenever possible, strengthen the therapeutic relationship and may "provide a structure and safety for many patients that is a curative factor in itself" (Borys, 1994, p. 267). A mutual understanding of both can be a foundation "for a trusting, working alliance capable of resolving any boundary difficulties, identifying the process used to work through these and other difficulties, and learning the skills necessary to generalize this process to relationships or situations outside the therapy room" (Faulkner & Faulkner, 1997, p. 229). This is especially important in situations in which out-of-therapy contact cannot be closely controlled. In such situations, it is important for psychologists to be consistent between public and in-therapy presentation and behavior.

Thoughtful self-examination, along with an understanding of the reasons behind conventional boundaries and awareness of potential pitfalls, are necessary when weighing decisions about possible boundary alterations (Borys, 1994). D. Smith and Fitzpatrick (1995) suggested that any behavior "that might be construed as a boundary violation should be justified by sound clinical reasoning" (p. 505). Err on the side of caution when proceeding with a potentially overlapping relationship, and heed Roll and Millen's (1981) call to "rigidify" in dealing with other parameters of therapy (fees, cancellations of sessions, time limits, etc.). Rather than becoming more flexible about time, for example, it is useful to be less flexible. Roll and Millen cautioned that if it is impossible to avoid meeting clients outside of the therapy session, then the space of the therapy session will have to be as distinct as possible. Barnett and Yutrzenka (1995) urged compartmentalization of roles, not relationships, and stressed the importance of maintaining a constant interpersonal style, as psychologists in small-community settings cannot afford to be warm and caring in therapy and aloof and distant outside of therapy.

9. Be Scrupulous About Documentation

Scrupulous documentation protects us as psychologists and provides the opportunity to reexamine complicated events and issues in therapy. If entering into an overlapping relationship or stretching the limits of competency, document clearly in your case notes the rationale for entering into such a relationship. Failure to document such a relationship in case notes may leave psychologists open to accusations of carelessness and negligence (Pope, 1991). Record the procedures taken to maximize the potential benefit and minimize the potential risks, along with relevant discussions with consultants and clients themselves. In overlapping-relationship situations, it is also prudent to include information on relevant interactions, along with how the relationship may affect the client's "clinical status, prognosis, treatment plan, or response to the treatment plan" (Pope, 1991, p. 29).

Although we cannot foresee all possible circumstances in every relationship, good documentation can help support efforts to meet reasonable standards of care and to protect the best interests of clients (Barnett & Yutrzenka, 1995). It "is both a protection for the conscientious clinician and a further opportunity to examine the event itself" (D. Smith & Fitzpatrick, 1995, p. 505).

10. Be Especially Aware of Issues of Confidentiality

In a small community, even general discussions can be misinterpreted as being about specific clients. Because of overlaps in small communities, psychologists are at risk of forgetting where they heard personal news and need to be careful in conversations (Helbok, 2003). Discuss the limits of confidentiality with clients at the beginning of therapy and address the difference between confidentiality and privacy. Be sure that clients and others in the community understand that you cannot discuss the content of your therapy sessions with others or even verify that you may or may not be seeing a particular individual. However, you cannot guarantee that clients will not be seen coming or going from your office.

Explain to clients at the beginning of therapy what is done with their records and how the records are safely stored. Make sure that your office is sufficiently soundproof (D. Smith, 2003b).

Other professionals in a small community (physicians, attorneys, law enforcement, social service professionals, administrators, etc.) may adhere to different standards of confidentiality than those mandated for psychologists. Therefore, it is imperative for small-community psychologists to explain to other professionals the scope and limitations of confidentiality. Psychologists may meet with some resistance from other professionals, but clients in a small community will usually be relieved to know that psychologists will not routinely share information with others.

11. Be Aware of Broader Community Standards

Although personal or professional behaviors that differ from the norms of the community may go unnoticed or unquestioned in larger communities, they may readily become issues that reduce credibility and effectiveness in a small community. Try to anticipate dilemmas that might occur as you work with clients who either are or have been working with other, more traditional community service providers (Stockman, 1990). It may also be useful to involve or consult other providers, who may be able to provide valuable information about community values and culture.

Although ethical standards regarding confidentiality are a constant, it is important that psychologists in small communities understand the reactions of others. For example, physicians in small towns, religious leaders, administrators at small colleges, and community leaders in a variety of small communities may expect that information regarding clients be readily shared "for the greater good of the community" or to help specific individuals with whom you may both be working. Replying to such requests with a brusque, "You know that I can't share that information with you!" will undermine much-needed alliances and working relationships that can ultimately be beneficial to you and to your clients. It is important to be proactive in educating others about the scope and limits of your professional obligations. However, it is also important to be as collegial as possible. A response such as "I don't have any specific information that I can share with you, but let's talk about some other ways that I might be helpful" may still be met with a negative response, but the chances are greater that it will be accepted.

Personal behavior that differs from the norms of the community may leave small-community psychologists open to rumors and criticism. Psychologists who practice in a small-community setting will have to decide for themselves how to strike a balance among personal choices, integrity, and overall community standards. Stockman (1990) highlighted the possibility of a conflict of interests when one assumes a leadership role within a small community, for example, a psychologist who is also a member of the county board that votes to raise property taxes. She recommended being open to consultation from community members regarding general issues, community values, and typical ways that small-community members address problems.

12. Maintain a Hierarchy of Values

As we know, clients' needs should always come first, and decisions should be made on that basis. In assessing the potential risks of dual or overlapping relationships, it may be helpful to consider frequency and duration of out-of-therapy contact, setting (e.g., large groups, smaller groups, individual contact), and context (e.g., social, professional, workplace, evaluative/supervisory). Gottlieb (1993) suggested consideration of power, duration, and clarity of termination (likelihood that client and psychologist will have further contact) in advising dual relationships "only after the most careful consideration" (p. 47). If the decision is unclear, err on the side of caution and avoid boundary crossings. In particularly ambiguous situations, no matter how honorable your intentions, the behavior could potentially be viewed as unethical (D. Smith & Fitzpatrick, 1995). When the role of the psychologist conflicts with another social or professional role, then the alternate role, not the therapist role, should usually suffer (Roll & Millen, 1981).

This may entail sacrifice on the part of the psychologist and may result in some frustration on the part of both clients and psychologists. However, such sacrifice is a part of small-community practice and should be anticipated by psychologists who choose to work in that setting.

13. Know Yourself

Understand who you are, monitor your personal and professional needs, and be aware of how you may influence the lives of others. Work on your own blind spots, weaknesses, and prejudices (Barnett & Yutrzenka, 1995). We must be honest with ourselves and continue to ask "Whose needs are being met—the client's or our own?" (Herlihy & Corey, 1992, p. 225). As Michael Gottlieb, a member of the APA Ethics Committee, suggested (in a personal statement that cannot be considered an official statement of the committee), "Learning the Ethics Code and going to risk management workshops is not sufficient to avoid ethical problems. . . . Rather, we must look deeper and come to a better understanding of our emotional lives as well as our intellectual lives" (D. Smith, 2003a, p. 61).

Know the cues that indicate that your boundaries are slipping. Lack of adequate sleep, physical illness, increased self-disclosure, and overidentification with clients are only a few of the possibilities. Each of us must take the time and effort to recognize and react to personal and professional issues that might affect our work. Use social support to deal with burnout, which is likely to occur in working with the emotional intensity, ambiguity, and lack of easy solutions inherent to psychologists' work (Tamura, Guy, Brady, & Grace, 1994).

14. Participate in Ongoing Consultation and Discussion

Consultation is essential for good practice, not only because it helps us identify issues but also because it builds community among colleagues (Pope, 2003). Staff meetings, regularly scheduled supervision sessions, and informal consultation with colleagues are all valuable methods of professional development. It is also important to consult with colleagues who hold divergent views and who can challenge us to examine and learn from ethical challenges. Consultation, supervision, and personal therapy are especially important when the maintenance of appropriate boundaries and ethics proves difficult (D. Smith & Fitzpatrick, 1995).

Build networks and resources, attend conferences and workshops, and consult with others who can help you identify weaknesses or rationalizations. Openly discuss possible issues both when you suspect that an ethical dilemma may occur and on an ongoing basis. Seek immediate consultation when entering into an overlapping relationship, when the maintenance of appropriate boundaries is difficult, or when practicing outside your competency level. Continue that consultation periodically throughout the relationship. Reflect on and discuss conflicts and dilemmas that arise, especially regarding role expectations, role boundaries, and maintaining objectivity (Brownlee, 1996).

15. Continue to Educate Yourself

Few psychologists have received training during their graduate course work or internship placements on ethical issues in small-community practice. All too often, ethics education involved responding to dilemmas or scenarios with a "right" answer. Once a psychologist begins practicing in small communities, he or she quickly realizes the need for the development of ethical decision-making skills rather than quick answers to complicated situations. Therefore, it is especially important that one remain current on professional issues and on relevant research literature in the field of ethics. As Barnett and Yutrzenka (1995) suggested, "At a minimum, be a consumer of the professional literature" (p. 247). Psychologists need to participate in self-study and other more formal educational opportunities, along with being in a supportive environment in which ethical questions can be discussed and examined. Consulting with colleagues, attending conferences and other continuing education offerings, and reading journals and other publications are all ways to ensure the competence of your practice (D. Smith, 2003b).

16. Know When to Stop

Roll and Millen (1981) pointed out that there is a greater chance in overlapping relationships that the therapy contract will become unclear. They suggested that in such situations psychologists would be wise to refer the client elsewhere or terminate therapy too early, rather than keep a client in therapy too long, especially when the fine line between personal and professional relationships starts to blur within therapy sessions.

Posttherapy Relationships

Anderson and Kitchener (1996) provided a framework to assess the risks inherent in posttherapy relationships that is built on themes that emerged from data in their study of critical incidents of nonromantic, nonsexual relationships. Although the authors cautioned that good models do not necessarily result in clear answers, the four themes of their suggested framework outline a perspective that can be viewed as the basis for sound decision making:

1. *The therapeutic contract.* Was there a clear termination, processed by psychologist and client? Has enough time

elapsed since termination for both parties to take on new roles? Can the confidentiality of the therapy relationship be maintained? What was the nature of the client's presenting problems in terms of severity, chronicity, and diagnosis? Were presenting problems resolved to mutual satisfaction? If not, was the client appropriately referred? Is there a clear understanding by the client that a posttherapy relationship will probably preclude the possibility of a return to that particular therapist for later therapy?

2. *Dynamics of the bond.* How strong was the bond between psychologist and client, and were changes discussed before terminating? What were the power differential, client autonomy and independence, and transference? Would a posttherapy relationship present a possibility that accomplishments in therapy would be damaged or undone?

3. *Social roles.* Are role expectations similar or dissimilar between the therapeutic and posttherapy relationship? Are they realistic? Have they been discussed and clarified? How would in-therapy information affect the posttherapy relationship?

4. *Therapist motivation.* Has the psychologist sought out consultation? Will the client be exploited by a posttherapy relationship? How will the psychologist benefit, personally and professionally? Was therapy ended so that a posttherapy relationship could begin? How will the posttherapy relationship influence the client's or public's attitudes toward therapy?

One of the most important set of questions Anderson and Kitchener (1998) asked included "Is this posttherapy relationship avoidable, and if it is, why am I considering entering it? One year from now, will I be satisfied with my decision?" (p. 96). Those may be difficult questions for psychologists in small communities to answer, especially when posttherapy interactions are hard to avoid. Both possibilities—entering into or avoiding a posttherapy nonsexual relationship—may be awkward. However, our obligation to behave ethically is not ended with the termination of a therapy relationship.

7

The Challenge and Hope of Small-Community Psychology

The issues raised in the preceding chapters remind us that certainties are rare in the psychology profession. The following five recommendations are offered to address these small-community psychology uncertainties. Some of the recommendations are directed to individual psychologists, and some are directed to the profession of psychology in general.

Come Together to Address Issues and Changes

Psychologists from a range of small communities need to "enter the professional dialogue and be part of needed changes" (Barnett & Yutrzenka, 1995, p. 247). It would benefit all of psychology for psychologists from a variety of small communities to join together to help educate the broader profession about their daily practice dilemmas and choices. All psychologists need to be educated about those instances of practice that may differ from the wider standards but still constitute sound practice within small communities, for example, well-thought-out overlapping relationships. Ethics codes would do well to address more specifically the kinds of situations in which overlapping relationships would or clearly would not be unethical, along with underscoring the importance of consultation and supervision in such situations (Roll & Millen, 1981).

Examine the Content of Ethical Practice in Small-Community Psychology

In reporting the results of a national survey of ethical dilemmas encountered by members of the American Psychological Association (APA), Pope and Vetter (1992) called for ethical principles that "must address clearly and realistically the situations of those who practice in small towns, rural communities, and other remote locales" (p. 400). This call can be broadened to embrace the entire range of small communities in which psychologists practice.

An important step is to explicitly include the range of psychologists who practice in small communities—communities of color; gay, lesbian, bisexual, transgender; small colleges; therapists who see other therapists; law enforcement and corrections; military; disability; faith based; suburbs; and other small communities that can form even within the supposed anonymity of urban areas. Although there are some needs that are specific to certain populations, the conversations on appropriate ethical conduct should include the entire range of small communities. This is especially necessary in the area of nonsexual, posttherapy relationships. These relationships are not addressed explicitly by the 2002 APA Ethics Code (APA, 2002a), because of the First Amendment right to free association, which restricts what interactions the code can prohibit when therapy is concluded. By joining together across communities, psychologists can gain support for the difficulties that are a part of practicing ethically in small-community settings.

Engage in Open Discussion in Which the Risk of Censure Is Minimized

Hearing directly from small-community psychologists is the essential factor in accurately addressing relevant issues. Open discussions of the dilemmas of small-community practitioners need to be encouraged and supported. Roll and Millen (1981) went so far as to say that such discussions around multiple relationships "should be a matter of record and for exploration" (p. 186) to help the profession of psychology "understand what existing conditions are and help to determine what needs changing and how it might be changed" (p. 186). It is also important to consider the best interest of clients as primary, while encouraging "an open and accepting atmosphere for collegial inquiry and discussion" (Pollack, 2002, p. 59). Without such discussion, there is a potential danger that small-community psychologists may become more isolated, resulting in restricted input and an increased likelihood that self-protective barriers will be set up that prevent feedback. If fear of retribution from professional licensing boards in the helping professions, ethics committees, and professional organizations diminishes the opportunities for frank conversations about the realities of small-community practice, the resulting retreat into professional isolation may lead to a situation in which individual small-community psychologists become the sole arbiters of ethical decision making in their practices.

Although setting appropriate boundaries is a professional necessity, psychologists must also maintain a balance of flexibility in overlapping relationships (Herlihy & Corey, 1992). What constitutes sound ethical practice in traditional settings may not completely parallel the practice of small-community counterparts.

An open discussion of small-community/traditional-setting differences needs to take place in an atmosphere of mutual respect, free of recriminations and the fear of retribution. The intertwining of roles is complex; for example, many urban psychologists find themselves practicing in small communities within a larger urban setting. The needs of both small-community and traditional-setting clients deserve consideration and discussion when psychologists adapt guidelines for fair, ethical practice. A true collaboration between small-community and traditional-setting psychologists can be mutually beneficial and informative.

Include Small-Community Practice in Training Programs and Continuing Education

Schoener (1986) reminded readers that "Psychotherapy is a much more difficult business than the model we typically learn in graduate or medical school. Our own vulnerabilities put us at risk in many types of situations" (p. 287). Further attention in graduate training, research, and continuing education is an important method of illuminating the importance of ethical dilemmas and concerns in small-community psychology. Yet few psychologists have received any training on practice within small communities. There are countless examples of such dilemmas that could be taken from real life practice and used for discussion as part of graduate training in ethics, including what P. J. Miller (1994) identified as "a perpetual balancing act" (p. 6) in small-community practice. Gibson and Pope (1993) suggested that the behaviors about which practitioners are least certain might also be the behaviors most difficult to identify. They posited that a lack of confidence might be the result of a "lack of familiarity with the topic" (Gibson & Pope, 1993, pp. 330–331).

Because many graduate students cannot foresee where they will practice throughout their careers, they could benefit from learning about multiple-level relationships, how to creatively find and maintain collegiality, and how to develop the skills that go along with being a generalist in a small-community practice setting. The inclusion of small-community practice in psychology training programs and relevant continuing education opportunities, along with attention on how to weigh conflicting obligations, are other ways to elevate the importance of ethical practice.

One way to recruit psychologists to rural areas and other small communities might be to identify promising high school students and college undergraduates and then encourage them to bring their cultural perspective to the field of psychology. These might be people from within those small communities or others who are interested and able to integrate the complexities of context, race, culture, and ethics into their philosophical stance (Kersting, 2003b).

Ethical behavior is more than just learning from an academic course; it involves a set of skills that need to be developed and integrated throughout the entire scope of graduate training (Sell, Gottlieb, & Schoenfeld, 1986). Training programs "need to identify, through careful research, those factors that encourage ethical sensitivity and behavior in contrast with those that increase the likelihood that clinicians will act in ways that put their clients or others at risk for harm" (Borys & Pope, 1989, p. 292). It is important that faculty, training directors, and supervisors be sensitive to ethical issues and uphold those principles while serving as role models in their education of graduate students. They must also provide a safe and supportive environment in which to explore possible temptations or confusion (Borys & Pope, 1989).

Responsible ethics education does not end when graduate school is completed. Continuing education efforts need to specifically address the complexity of small-community ethics and practice by drawing on real-life examples that small-community psychologists face.

Weigh Importance When Conflicting Obligations Occur

The paradox of awareness and fluidity of boundaries, particularly in dual or overlapping relationships, leads to a constant examination and refinement of ethical codes in small-community practice. Psychologists may *know* the content of ethics codes and laws, but they often struggle in having to *choose* how to best apply codes and rules for client welfare. For example, rules that seem absolute are often subject to interpretation when the psychologist is faced with a dilemma (J. D. Woody, 1990). It is likely that identifying the relevant codes, laws, and policies "does not mark the end of the process, but rather the beginning of informed thinking about the specific instance at hand" (Pope, 2003, p. 35).

Fisher (2003) indicated that ethical decisions are a series of steps, based on the consequences of each previous step. Alternatives should consider risks and benefits, with sensitivity toward context and toward the persons who may be affected by these decisions. Unfortunately, most codes of ethics do not yet acknowledge conflicting obligations or offer instructions on how to weigh importance when obligations do conflict. The 2002 APA Ethics Code Task Force made a conscious decision not to include a model for the decision-making process in the Ethics Code, believing that the Ethics Code should provide aspirational guidelines and broad rules of conduct and that decision-making guidance should be provided separately.

An exception is the Canadian Psychological Association's (2000) Code of Ethics for Psychologists, which is structured on four overarching ethical principles that are to be considered and balanced when making ethical decisions. These four principles are (a) Respect for the Dignity of Persons, (b) Responsible Caring, (c) Integrity in Relationships, and (d) Responsibility to Society. The principles are clearly defined and ordered according to importance and relative weight, which addresses the reality of complex ethical situations when principles may conflict. In addition to providing a structure of importance, the Canadian Psychological Association's Code of Ethics for Psychologists explicitly includes a 10-step process for making decisions when ethical principles conflict, along with an expectation that difficult deliberations will include consultation with colleagues, advisory boards, or both.

Reexamination of Advantages of Small-Community Practice

A reexamination of the advantages of the practice of psychology in rural areas and other small communities is warranted. A study conducted by Kramen-Kahn and Hansen (1998) identified the following six categories of occupational rewards for psychotherapists: "feelings of effectiveness (e.g., helping clients improve); ongoing self-development; professional autonomy–independence; opportunities for emotional intimacy; professional–financial recognition and success; and flexible, diverse work" (p. 130). Most are readily available in small-community practice.

If managed professionally and ethically, overlapping relationships in a small-community setting may, in fact, be advantageous to both psychologist and client. Although this book and most other publications in the professional literature focus on the problems and dilemmas inherent to small-community practice (Hargrove, 1991), the picture presented by many small-community practitioners is much more positive. The lifestyle, opportunities, and sense of personal control make small-community psychologists valued contributors to the fabric of community life. More attention needs to be paid to the positive and life-enhancing qualities of small-community practice to offset the gloomy picture set forth in some of the literature and to counter the negative stereotypes possibly held by traditional, urban-based psychologists. Several of the advantages of small-community practice are addressed throughout the rest of this section. Although each could at times also be seen as a disadvantage, casting them in a positive light benefits all.

Lifestyle Advantages

Rural psychologists are quick to point out as advantages quality-of-life issues: clean air, recreational opportunities, community activities, beautiful natural surroundings, opportunities for genuine connections and friendships, lower cost of living, safety, and accessibility of schools. These are often the factors that drew psychologists to small communities and motivated them to remain there. One psychologist described it in this way:

> One of the positives of living in a community like this is that there is some institutional value of community spirit, honesty, friendliness, spirituality. . . . It's not like that all the time but definitely more than you see in larger cities. (Schank, 1994, p. 98)

Another said the following:

> One of the advantages is that it is a different kind of lifestyle—not the fast pace. It's the ability to identify with the value system. Ecologically and emotionally, it's being in a place where I appreciate the people that I live with. (p. 98)

The Variety and Challenge of Being a Generalist

In many small-community settings, psychologists must respond to a wide range of clients and client problems. Access to the Internet, telehealth resources, online journals, and other resources have increased the ability of psychologists outside of metropolitan areas to expand their knowledge and practice. They have an obligation to stay current on new information, trends, and practice issues and are often required to do so in response to client problems. Many thrive on the variety and challenge that are the basis for good general practice and are excited to be pushed to learn new approaches to therapy with specific client concerns. Generalists within small communities are able to do more things than urban specialists. They have more independence and may face less competition than their counterparts in traditional settings:

> The variety of clients that I have is wonderful. I do adolescents, couples, individuals, groups, and different issues—abuse, alcohol addiction, communication. I have such a wonderful variety, and I like that. I wouldn't like to narrow myself down into just doing [one thing]. I think you then would lose something of your own—life is not just one kind of narrow thing. (Schank, 1994, p. 98)

> You can do a lot, and there is a lot of variety. You are forced to use everything you have learned. (p. 98)

A Multifaceted View of Clients and Context

When managed well, the overlap in small-community psychology can be beneficial in that psychologists get to know their clients in a broader context and in a variety of ways, rather than just within the allotted 50-minute therapy hour. The therapeutic alliance may also be strengthened for clients who see a psychologist who is part of the same small community and who recognizes that community's shared values and beliefs (Catalano, 1997). Psychologists are able to know more about particular situations, interactions, people, and places that affect their clients in both positive and negative ways. Small-community psychologists may be able to have a more comprehensive understanding of their clients' needs and may be able to promote trust through already-established relationships (Perkins, Hudson, Gray, & Steward, 1998). Awareness of attachments between individuals and among groups can prove valuable in understanding the stressors and history of clients (Coakes & Bishop, 1996). This accessibility of information presents challenges but ultimately provides a far richer and more complete picture of clients' lives, as illustrated by the following examples:

> I think you see your patients more as human beings . . . you see them at their jobs or in the grocery store doing normal things. If you just saw your patients without that, you would kind of see them—you shouldn't, but—you would see them as a psychopathology. (Schank, 1994, p. 96)

> I think you can learn so much. You can . . . understand a lot of what clients bring you in their history and know what it means. I think that is a real plus. I think in some ways the interconnectedness of clients is a plus, even though it is stressful. But I can know more about what is going on, and my clients have more of a three-dimensional quality. (p. 96)

> It is just knowing your clients and their living situations—being able to have so much more information—and caring about the people. . . . I need some amount of connection to feel invested. . . . You really use the information to the max. . . . I like that. (p. 96)

Kersting (2003a) quoted a psychologist who had practiced in rural Wyoming:

> After a long struggle to feel effective and accepted, I believe the community started taking me into their hearts . . . Once that happens there's a tremendous loyalty that develops between the provider and the community. I felt like I provided a valuable service that wouldn't have existed without my presence as a frontier psychologist. (p. 68)

Building Relationships and Connections

The reciprocity and interdependence inherent in many small communities are attributes that small-community psychologists can use in the best interests of clients. Building these reciprocal relationships may take time and effort, but the benefits can enhance the personal and professional lives of practitioners and the clients with whom they work. It is important to be viewed as a team player and to have good relationships with other community agencies, religious leaders, local schools, social services, and medical professionals. As C. E. Hill and Fraser (1995) suggested, local resources can be tapped to provide more integrated services. Building a lay referral network can strengthen relationships between psychologists and communities while reciprocally channeling knowledge to and from appropriate resources. Knowing the available resources and being on a first-name basis with other service providers is clearly in the best interest of clients and probably adds to the job satisfaction of small-community psychologists. Familiarity with the resources and having personal contact with a wide range of other professionals and peer helpers means that a small-community psychologist can enhance the web of support for clients, and ultimately, for him- or herself.

Contacts between agencies may be more informal within small communities. Psychologists who can pick up the phone and call someone they know and trust may be more able to make a successful referral. In turn, when another professional needs assistance, the psychologist can return the favor. There may also be more opportunity to use peer helpers and to use informal, natural support networks as important parts of a treatment approach. Several small-community psychologists described it as follows:

> I think [resistance] was true initially. . . . But I spent a lot of time making connections and letting them get to know me. (Schank, 1994, p. 85)

> I have a good working relationship with the school. I think that is an advantage in a small community because you get to know people much more personally. So if I have a question or concern, it really is a call to talk directly with whom I need to talk and chat about and even kind of flex the rules when it is appropriate. (p. 82)

> There is a feeling that everybody needs everybody else. You can't afford to be all that standoffish because they need me, and there is going to be another day when I need them. [A] case in point—the director of children's social services for the county called me up one day. He had an emergency, and he needed me to fit a kid in right away who was suicidal. It was a real problem for me to do that, but I said to him, "Don't forget, because there is going to be a time when I need this back from you." Sure enough, not too much later, I had a cli-

ent that needed to go into a group home immediately because of an abusive situation. I called him and said, "I need you to do this. Cut through all the red tape. I don't want to hear any bureaucrat baloney. I need you to get this kid in right now." And he did. So we do depend on each other a lot. . . . Generally, it has been good. You can make a lot more happen for your clients. Not only that, but you have personal relationships with [other professionals]. We see them in church, in organizations, on the street, or wherever. So when I call someone to say, "I need this," it is hard for them to say no, just like it is hard for me to say no. . . . We expect each other to be there for each other. (pp. 83–84)

We collaborate with nontraditional providers a lot. Ministries are big ones, particularly because they have access to families that sometimes we don't. There is a level of trust with them that it not necessarily implicit with psychologists. They are like part of the extended family. I have done conjoint [therapy] with the pastors and clergy. I have had clients referred to me from clergy, and I have often referred clients back to their clergyperson if for some reason the person was not a willing participant in seeing a psychologist. Clergy working with clients call me and say, "I have this problem. What should I do?" Teachers, school counselors, social workers at the county who may not be clinicians by trade, county extension agents—anybody who is in a position of having some link to the family is a good ally to have. Because of the negative connotation for some people in seeing a psychologist, you can provide the service indirectly if you can do it through a trusted person like the clergy, etc. There is a bit of the negative attitude that you are nuts if you are seeing a psychologist, but you are not nuts if you go to your pastor or your doctor and talk about the same thing and get the same feedback—that's okay, very acceptable. So we do work with them a lot, more than I have ever worked anywhere else. That was kind of a little hump for me to get over because of a little bit of strutting my feathers, you know—"I'm the one who is trained to help you." (p. 84)

A network of community resources (e.g., self-help groups, people in other agencies, churches, organizations, indigenous healers) can provide helpful support and can assist small-community psychologists in moving outside a traditional clinical framework to collaborate with other support resources. This collaboration between resources can grow stronger over time, to the mutual benefit of all involved and the community in general.

Community Involvement and Acceptance

Psychologists who are involved in small communities are able to have an impact on the community—to the benefit of clients, the community, and the psychologist. Once accepted into the community, psychologists are seen as experts and imbued with the special power of their professional role (Kitchener, 1988). They are able to see the results of their work, have an impact on their community, take on leadership roles on various issues, and feel acknowledged and appreciated. They are known as more than just their jobs. In fact, it is often because of psychologists' participation in community activities that they are able to provide leadership and make other vital contributions (Coyle, 1999):

> Because I feel like I want to live in this community, I have a vested interest in these people and my relationship with them. . . . I have become extremely active in the community in developing a prevention program and a youth development and service program. . . . It has continued to keep me real interested in the community. . . . [Being involved in a lot of things] helps me to be a more qualified resource. (Schank, 1994, p. 76)

> You are seen as a leader in the community. . . . That is kind of neat. I think they feel . . . that if you have chosen to be here, that means you have something inside of you that is more genuine. (p. 76)

> I am accepted. I like my job, and I work with people that I really like. . . . People see me as an individual. I need to have people know me as a person. (p. 97)

> It is very rewarding. I can't explain enough that you can make such an impact in your own community because they are so appreciative to have you. (p. 96)

> I have this need to see that my efforts matter in some collective way. When I see my colleagues [in more traditional settings] and the anonymity, I don't know [that they see that what they do] makes a difference. . . . I like that—that sense of being

> valued. . . . You play a role in the fabric of the community . . .
> there is that symbolic aspect that you put in it, and it touches
> me. (p. 96)

Informal conversations with people in a small community are viewed as a common form of mental health education and may, in fact, be more useful than formal presentations (Heyman & VandenBos, 1989). With experience, small-community psychologists can become increasingly skilled at choosing the involvements that are most beneficial to their communities, their clients, and themselves. The increased visibility of psychologists in small communities can lead to further acceptance and trust of psychologists as individuals and knowledge about psychology as a profession.

Summary

Throughout this chapter, we have emphasized the challenges and hopes of psychologists who practice within small communities. All too often, psychologists focus on the difficulties and dilemmas and lose sight of the joys and rewards. The choices and changes that occur each day in the practice of small-community psychology provide the opportunity to examine the larger field of psychology, as we strive for standards of practice that provide the best care for clients and for however we define the community of which we are a part.

In the end, the ethical decisions that we make are a blend of guidelines and principles, contexts, and personal factors. As O'Neill (1989) suggested, "Many require compromises between competing values, must be made in the absence of perfect information, and require the courage to confront mistakes" (p. 339). Psychologists who recognize and accept these complexities and imperfections, who are willing to combine them with the strengths of the profession, and who are able to synthesize all this for the greater good of clients make an enormous contribution to the field and to the daily lives of the clients who trust us.

References

Adams, K. M. (1994). *When two worlds collide: Awkward or troubling post-termination encounters between therapists and clients.* Unpublished master's thesis, Augsburg College, Minneapolis, MN.

Adleman, J., & Barrett, S. E. (1990). Overlapping relationships: Importance of the feminist ethical perspective. In H. Lerman & N. Porter (Eds.), *Feminist ethics in psychotherapy* (pp. 87–91). New York: Springer.

Alexander, C. M., & Sussman, L. (1995). Creative approaches to multicultural counseling. In J. G. Ponterotto, J. M. Casas, L. A. Suzuki, & C. M. Alexander (Eds.), *Handbook of multicultural counseling* (pp. 375–384). Thousand Oaks, CA: Sage.

Amada, G. (1996). You can't please all of the people all of the time: Normative institutional resistances to college psychological services. *Journal of College Student Psychotherapy, 10*, 45–63.

American Psychological Association. (1953a). *Ethical standards of psychologists.* Washington, DC: Author.

American Psychological Association. (1953b). *Ethical standards of psychologists: A summary of ethical principles.* Washington, DC: Author.

American Psychological Association. (1992). Ethical principles of psychologists and code of conduct. *American Psychologist, 47*, 1597–1611.

American Psychological Association. (2002a). Ethical principles of psychologists and code of conduct. *American Psychologist, 57*, 1060–1073.

American Psychological Association. (2002b). *Guidelines on multicultural education, training, research, practice, and organizational change for psychologists.* Retrieved December 1, 2002, from http://www.apa.org/pi/multiculturalguidelines/formats.html

American Psychological Association, Office of Ethnic Minority Affairs. (1993). *Guidelines for providers of psychological services to ethnic, linguistic, and culturally diverse populations.* Retrieved March 23, 2002, from http://www.apa.org/pi/oema/guide.html

Anderson, S. K. (1993). A critical incident study of nonromantic–nonsexual relationships between psychologists and former clients. *Dissertation Abstracts International, 54*, 7B. (UMI No. 9333367)

Anderson, S. K., & Kitchener, K. S. (1996). Nonromantic, nonsexual posttherapy relationships between psychologists and former clients: An exploratory study of critical incidents. *Professional Psychology: Research and Practice, 27*, 59–66.

Anderson, S. K., & Kitchener, K. S. (1998). Nonsexual posttherapy relationships: A conceptual framework to assess ethical risks. *Professional Psychology: Research and Practice, 29,* 91–99.

Arredondo, P. (1999). Multicultural counseling competencies as tools to address oppression and racism. *Journal of Counseling & Development, 77,* 102–108.

Bachelor, A., & Horvath, A. (1999). The therapeutic relationship. In M. A. Hubble, B. L. Duncan, & S. D. Miller (Eds.), *The heart and soul of change: What works in therapy* (pp. 133–178). Washington, DC: American Psychological Association.

Backlar, P. (1996). Confidentiality and common sense. *Community Mental Health Journal, 32,* 513–518.

Baer, B. E., & Murdock, N. L. (1995). Nonerotic dual relationships between therapists and clients: The effects of sex, theoretical orientation, and interpersonal boundaries. *Ethics & Behavior, 5,* 131–145.

Bagarozzi, D. A. (1982). The family therapists' role in treating families in rural communities: A general systems approach. *Journal of Marital and Family Therapy, 8,* 51–58.

Baker, E. K. (2003). *Caring for ourselves: A therapist's guide to personal and professional well-being.* Washington, DC: American Psychological Association.

Barnett, J. E. (2004, January–February). Not all dual relationships unethical. *National Psychologist, 15.*

Barnett, J. E., & Yutrzenka, B. A. (1995). Nonsexual dual relationships in professional practice, with special applications to rural and military communities. *Independent Practitioner, 14,* 243–248.

Behnke, S. (2004, January). Multiple relationships and APA's new Ethics Code: Values and applications. *Monitor on Psychology, 35*(1), 66–67.

Behnke, S. (2005, April). Disclosing confidential information in consultations and for didactic purposes: Ethical Standards 4.06 and 4.07. *Monitor on Psychology, 36*(4), 76–77.

Bersoff, D. N. (1994). Explicit ambiguity: The 1992 Ethics Code as an oxymoron. *Professional Psychology: Research and Practice, 25,* 382–387.

Bersoff, D. N., & Koeppl, P. M. (1993). The relation between ethical codes and moral principles. *Ethics & Behavior, 3,* 345–357.

Biaggio, M., & Greene, B. (1995). Overlapping/dual relationships. In E. J. Rave & C. C. Larsen (Eds.), *Ethical decision making in therapy: Feminist perspectives* (pp. 88–123). New York: Guilford Press.

Birky, I., Sharkin, B. S., Marin, J., & Scappaticci, A. (1998). Confidentiality after referral: A study of how restrictions on disclosure affect relationships between therapists and referral sources. *Professional Psychology: Research and Practice, 29,* 179–182.

Borys, D. S. (1992). Nonsexual dual relationships. In L. VandeCreek, S. Knapp, & T. L. Jackson (Eds.), *Innovations in clinical practice* (Vol. 11, pp. 443–454). Sarasota, FL: Professional Resource Press.

Borys, D. S. (1994). Maintaining therapeutic boundaries: The motive is therapeutic effectiveness, not defensive practice. *Ethics & Behavior, 4*, 267–273.

Borys, D. S., & Pope, K. S. (1989). Dual relationships between therapist and
client: A national study of psychologists, psychiatrists, and social workers. *Professional Psychology: Research and Practice, 20*, 283–293.

Brodsky, A. M. (1989). Sex between patient and therapist: Psychology's data
and response. In G. O. Gabbard (Ed.), *Sexual exploitation in professional relationships* (pp. 15–25). Washington, DC: American Psychiatric Press.

Brown, L. S. (1991). Ethical issues in feminist therapy. *Psychology of Women Quarterly, 15*, 323–336.

Brown, L. S. (1994). Boundaries in feminist therapy: A conceptual formulation.
Women & Therapy, 15, 29–38.

Brownlee, K. (1996). Ethics of non-sexual dual relationships: A dilemma for the
rural mental health professional. *Community Mental Health Journal, 32*, 497–
503.

Butler, R. T. (1990, January). Dual relationships and therapy. *Minnesota Psychologist*, 23.

Canadian Psychological Association. (2000). *Canadian code of ethics for psychologists*. Retrieved December 6, 2003, from http://www.cpa.ca/ethics2000.html

Canter, M. B., Bennett, B. E., Jones, S. E., & Nagy, T. F. (1994). *Ethics for psychologists: A commentary on the APA Ethics Code*. Washington, DC: American
Psychological Association.

Case, P. W., McMinn, M. R., & Meek, K. R. (1997). Sexual attraction and religious therapists: Survey findings and implications. *Counseling and Values,
41*, 141–154.

Catalano, S. (1997). Challenges of clinical practice in small or rural communities: Case studies in managing dual relationships in and outside of therapy.
Journal of Contemporary Psychotherapy, 27, 23–35.

Chapman, C. (1997). Dual relationships in substance abuse treatment: Ethical
implications. *Alcoholism Treatment Quarterly, 15*, 73–79.

Coakes, S. J., & Bishop, B. J. (1996). Experience of moral community in a rural
community context. *Journal of Community Psychology, 24*, 108–117.

Corey, G., Corey, M. S., & Callanan, P. (1998). *Issues and ethics in the helping
professions*. Pacific Grove, CA: Brooks/Cole.

Coyle, B. R. (1999). Practical tools for rural psychiatric practice. *Bulletin of the
Menninger Clinic, 63*, 202–222.

Craig, J. D. (1991). Preventing dual relationships in pastoral counseling. *Counseling and Values, 36*, 49–54.

Crawford, N. (2003, June). Knocking down access barriers. *Monitor on Psychology, 34*(6), 64–65.

DeStefano, T., Clark, H., & Potter, T. (2005, Winter). Assessment of burnout
among rural mental health staff. *Rural Mental Health*, 18–24.

Dietz, P. E., & Reese, J. T. (1986). Perils of police psychology: 10 strategies for minimizing role conflicts when providing mental health services and consultation to law enforcement agencies. *Behavioral Sciences & the Law, 4*, 385–400.

Dittmann, M. (2003). Maintaining ethics in a rural setting. *Monitor on Psychology, 34*(6), 66.

Dunbar, E. (1982). Educating social workers for rural mental health settings. In H. A. Dengerink & H. J. Cross (Eds.), *Training professionals for rural mental health* (pp. 54–67). Lincoln: University of Nebraska Press.

Elkin, B., & Boyer, P. A. (1987). Practice skills and personal characteristics that facilitate practitioner retention in rural mental health settings. *Journal of Rural Community Psychology, 8*, 30–39.

Faulkner, K. K., & Faulkner, T. A. (1997). Managing multiple relationships in rural communities: Neutrality and boundary violations. *Clinical Psychology: Science and Practice, 4*, 225–234.

Fisher, C. B. (2003). *Decoding the Ethics Code: A practical guide for psychologists.* Thousand Oaks, CA: Sage.

Fisher, C. B., & Younggren, J. N. (1997). Value and utility of the 1992 Ethics Code. *Professional Psychology: Research and Practice, 28*, 582–592.

Flax, J. W., Wagenfeld, M. O., Ivens, R. E., & Weiss, R. J. (1979). *Mental health and rural America: An overview and annotated bibliography.* Rockville, MD: U.S. Department of Health, Education and Welfare.

Gabbard, G. O. (1994a). Reconsidering the American Psychological Association's policy on sex with former patients: Is it justifiable? *Professional Psychology: Research and Practice, 25*, 329–335.

Gabbard, G. O. (1994b). Teetering on the precipice: A commentary on Lazarus's "How certain boundaries and ethics diminish therapeutic effectiveness." *Ethics & Behavior, 4*, 283–286.

Gamm, L. D., Hutchison, L. L., Dabney, B. J., & Dorsey, A. M. (Eds.). (2003). *Rural Healthy People 2010: A companion document to Healthy People 2010.* College Station: Texas A&M University System Health Science Center, School of Rural Public Health, Southwest Rural Health Research Center.

Gartrell, N. K. (1992). Boundaries in lesbian therapy relationships. *Women & Therapy, 12*, 29–49.

Geyer, M. C. (1994). Dual role relationships and Christian counseling. *Journal of Psychology and Theology, 22*, 187–195.

Gibson, W. T., & Pope, K. S. (1993). Ethics of counseling: A national survey of certified counselors. *Journal of Counseling & Development, 71*, 330–336.

Gone, J. P. (2004). Mental health services for Native Americans in the 21st century United States. *Professional Psychology: Research and Practice, 35*, 10–18.

Gonsiorek, J. C., & Brown, L. S. (1986). Post therapy sexual relationships with clients. In G. R. Schoener, J. H. Milgrom, J. C. Gonsiorek, E. T. Leupker, &

R. M. Conroe (Eds.), *Psychotherapists' sexual involvement with clients* (pp. 289–309). Minneapolis, MN: Walk-In Counseling Center.

Gottlieb, M. C. (1993). Avoiding exploitive dual relationships: A decision-making model. *Psychotherapy, 30*, 41–48.

Gottlieb, M. C. (1994). Ethical decision making, boundaries, and treatment effectiveness: A reprise. *Ethics & Behavior, 4*, 287–293.

Green, S. L., & Hansen, J. C. (1989). Ethical dilemmas faced by family therapists. *Journal of Marital and Family Therapy, 2*, 149–158.

Gurnoe, S., & Nelson, J. (1990). Two perspectives in working with American Indian families: A constructivist–systemic approach. In E. Gonzalez-Santin & A. Lewis (Eds.), *Collaboration; the key: A model curriculum on Indian child welfare* (pp. 63–85). Tempe: Arizona State University School of Social Work.

Gutheil, T. G., & Gabbard, G. O. (1998). Misuses and misunderstandings of boundary theory in clinical and regulatory settings. *American Journal of Psychiatry, 155*, 409–414.

Haas, L. J., & Malouf, J. L. (1989). *Keeping up the good work: A practitioner's guide to mental health ethics.* Sarasota, FL: Professional Resource Exchange.

Haas, L. J., Malouf, J. L., & Mayerson, N. H. (1988). Personal and professional characteristics as factors in psychologists' ethical decision making. *Professional Psychology: Research and Practice, 19*, 35–42.

Hargrove, D. S. (1982). Mental health needs of rural America. In H. A. Dengerink & H. J. Cross (Eds.), *Training professionals for rural mental health* (pp. 14–26). Lincoln: University of Nebraska Press.

Hargrove, D. S. (1986). Ethical issues in rural mental health practice. *Professional Psychology: Research and Practice, 17*, 20–23.

Hargrove, D. S. (1991). Training PhD psychologists for rural service: A report from Nebraska. *Community Mental Health Journal, 27*, 293–298.

Hecker, L. L. (2003). Ethical, legal, and professional issues in marriage and family therapy. In L. L. Hecker & J. L. Wetchler (Eds.), *Introduction to marriage and family therapy* (pp. 493–511). New York: Haworth Clinical Practice Press.

Heinrich, R. K., Corbine, J. S., & Thomas, K. R. (1990). Counseling Native Americans. *Journal of Counseling & Development, 69*, 128–133.

Helbok, C. M. (2003). Practice of psychology in rural communities: Potential ethical dilemmas. *Ethics & Behavior, 13*, 367–384.

Herlihy, B., & Corey, G. (1992). *Dual relationships in counseling.* Alexandria, VA: American Association for Counseling and Development.

Heyman, S. R. (1982). Capitalizing on unique assets of rural areas for community interventions. *Journal of Rural Community Psychology, 3*, 35–48.

Heyman, S. R., & VandenBos, G. R. (1989). Developing local resources to enrich the practice of rural community psychology. *Hospital and Community Psychiatry, 40*, 21–23.

Hill, C. E., & Fraser, G. J. (1995). Local knowledge and rural mental health reform. *Community Mental Health Journal, 31,* 553–568.

Hill, M. (1990). On creating a theory of feminist therapy. In L. S. Brown & M. P. P. Root (Eds.), *Diversity and complexity in feminist therapy* (pp. 53–65). New York: Harrington Park Press.

Hines, A. H., Ader, D. N., Chang, A. S., & Rundell, J. R. (1998). Dual agency, dual relationships, boundary crossings, and associated boundary violations: A survey of military and civilian psychiatrists. *Military Medicine, 163,* 826–833.

Horst, E. A. (1989). Dual relationships between psychologists and clients in rural and urban areas. *Journal of Rural Community Psychology, 10,* 15–23.

Howe, E. G. (1989). Confidentiality in the military. *Behavioral Sciences & the Law, 7,* 317–337.

Human, J., & Wasem, C. (1991). Rural mental health in America. *American Psychologist, 46,* 232–239.

Ibrahim, F. A. (1996). A multicultural perspective on principle and virtue ethics. *The Counseling Psychologist, 24,* 78–85.

Ivey, A. E. (1987). Multicultural practice of therapy: Ethics, empathy, and dialectics. *Journal of Social and Clinical Psychology, 5,* 195–204.

Ivey, A. E., Ivey, M. B., & Simek-Morgan, L. (1997). *Counseling and psychotherapy: A multicultural perspective.* Boston: Allyn & Bacon.

Jeffrey, M. J., & Reeve, R. E. (1978). Community mental health services in rural areas: Some practical issues. *Community Mental Health Journal, 14,* 54–62.

Jeffrey, T. B. (1989). Issues regarding confidentiality for military psychologists. *Military Psychology, 1,* 49–56.

Jeffrey, T. B., Rankin, R. J., & Jeffrey, L. K. (1992). In service of two masters: The ethical–legal dilemma faced by military psychologists. *Professional Psychology: Research and Practice, 23,* 91–95.

Jennings, F. L. (1992). Ethics of rural practice. *Psychotherapy in Private Practice, 10,* 85–104.

Johnson, W. B. (1995). Perennial ethical quandaries in military psychology: Toward American Psychological Association–Department of Defense collaboration. *Professional Psychology: Research and Practice, 26,* 281–287.

Johnson, W. B., Ralph, J., & Johnson, S. J. (2005). Managing multiple roles in embedded environments: The case of aircraft carrier psychology. *Professional Psychology: Research and Practice, 36,* 73–81.

Jordan, A. E., & Meara, N. M. (1990). Ethics and the professional practice of psychologists: The role of virtues and principles. *Professional Psychology: Research and Practice, 21,* 107–114.

Kagle, J. D., & Giebelhausen, P. N. (1994). Dual relationships and professional boundaries. *Social Work, 39,* 213–220.

Keller, P. A. (1982). Training models for master's level community psychologists. In H. A. Dengerink & H. J. Cross (Eds.), *Training professionals for rural mental health* (pp. 40–51). Lincoln: University of Nebraska Press.

Keller, P. A., Murray, J. D., Hargrove, D. S., & Dengerink, H. A. (1983). Issues in training psychologists for rural settings. *Journal of Rural Community Psychology, 4,* 11–23.

Kenkel, M. B. (1986). Stress–coping–support in rural communities: A model for primary prevention. *American Journal of Community Psychology, 14,* 457–478.

Kersting, K. (2003a). Professional pioneering on the frontier. *Monitor on Psychology, 34*(6), 68.

Kersting, K. (2003b). Teaching self-sufficiency for rural practice. *Monitor on Psychology, 34*(6), 60–62.

Kessler, L. E., & Waehler, C. A. (2005). Addressing multiple relationships between clients and therapists in lesbian, gay, bisexual, and transgender communities. *Professional Psychology: Research and Practice, 36,* 66–72.

Kitchener, K. S. (1988). Dual role relationships: What makes them so problematic? *Journal of Counseling and Development, 67,* 217–221.

Kitchener, K. S., & Anderson, S. K. (2000). Ethical issues in counseling psychology: Old themes—new problems. In S. D. Brown & R. W. Lent (Eds.), *Handbook of counseling psychology* (pp. 50–82). New York: Wiley.

Kitchener, K. S., & Harding, S. S. (1990). Dual role relationships. In B. Herlihy & L. B. Golden (Eds.), *AACD ethical standards casebook* (4th ed., pp. 146–154). Alexandria, VA: American Association for Counseling and Development.

Klopfer, F. J. (1990). Emergency services outside the city: How "real life" works. *Human Services in the Rural Environment, 13,* 33–34.

Knapp, S., & VandeCreek, L. (2003). *Guide to the 2002 revision of the American Psychological Association's Ethics Code.* Sarasota, FL: Professional Resource Press.

Kofoed, L., & Cutler, D. L. (1982). Issues in rural community psychiatry training. In H. A. Dengerink & H. J. Cross (Eds.), *Training professionals for rural mental health* (pp. 70–82). Lincoln: University of Nebraska Press.

Koocher, G. P., & Keith-Spiegel, P. (1998). *Ethics in psychology: Professional standards and cases.* New York: Oxford University Press.

Kramen-Kahn, B., & Hansen, N. D. (1998). Rafting the rapids: Occupational hazards, rewards, and coping strategies of psychotherapists. *Professional Psychology: Research and Practice, 29,* 130–134.

Kutchins, H. (1991). The fiduciary relationship: The legal basis for social workers' responsibilities to clients. *Social Work, 36,* 106–113.

LaFromboise, T. D. (1988). American Indian mental health policy. *American Psychologist, 43,* 388–397.

Lamb, D. H., & Catanzaro, S. J. (1998). Sexual and nonsexual boundary violations involving psychologists, clients, supervisees, and students: Implications for professional practice. *Professional Psychology: Research and Practice, 29*, 498–503.

Lamb, D. H., Catanzaro, S. J., & Moorman, A. S. (2004). A preliminary look at
how psychologists identify, evaluate, and proceed when faced with possible multiple relationship dilemmas. *Professional Psychology: Research and
Practice, 35*, 248–254.

Lamb, D. H., Strand, K. K., Woodburn, J. R., Buchko, K. J., Lewis, J. T., & Kang,
J. R. (1994). Sexual and business relationships between therapists and
former clients. *Psychotherapy, 31*, 270–278.

Lazarus, A. A. (1998). How do you like *these* boundaries? *Clinical Psychologist,
51*, 22–25.

Lefley, H. P. (2002). Ethical issues in mental health services for culturally diverse communities. In P. Backlar (Ed.), *Ethics in community mental health
care: Commonplace concerns* (pp. 1–22). New York: Kluwer Academic/Ple-
num.

Lerman, H., & Porter, N. (Eds.). (1990). *Feminist ethics in psychotherapy.* New
York: Springer.

Libertoff, K. (1980). Natural helping networks in rural and youth family services. *Journal of Rural Community Psychology, 1*, 4–17.

Lloyd, A., & Hansen, J. (2003). Philosophical foundations of professional ethics.
In W. O'Donohue & K. Ferguson (Eds.), *Handbook of professional ethics for
psychologists: Issues, questions, and controversies* (pp. 17–33). Thousand Oaks,
CA: Sage.

Lyn, L. (1990). *Life in the fishbowl: Lesbian and gay therapists' social interactions with
clients.* Unpublished master's thesis, Southern Illinois University,
Carbondale.

Mabe, A. R., & Rollin, S. A. (1986). Role of a code of ethical standards in counseling. *Journal of Counseling & Development, 64*, 294–297.

MacKay, E., & O'Neill, P. (1992). What creates the dilemma in ethical dilemmas? Examples from psychological practice. *Ethics & Behavior, 2*, 227–244.

Mahalik, J. R., Van Ormer, A., & Simi, N. L. (2000). Ethical issues in using self-
disclosure in feminist therapy. In M. M. Brabeck (Ed.), *Practicing feminist
ethics in psychology* (pp. 189–201). Washington, DC: American Psychological Association.

Malley, P., Gallagher, R., & Brown, S. M. (1992). Ethical problems in university
and college counseling centers: A Delphi study. *Journal of College Student
Development, 22*, 238–244.

Mann, C. B., & Stein, T. C. (1993). Going it alone: The practice of psychology in
rural settings. *Rural Psychologist, 1*, 4–6.

Martin, S. (2002). APA's council adopts a new Ethics Code. *Monitor on Psychology*, *33*(10), 56–58.

May, R. (1994). "The centre cannot hold": Challenges in working psychodynamically in a college or university. *Psychodynamic Counselling*, *1*, 5–20.

McGoldrick, M. (1982). Ethnicity and family therapy: An overview. In M. McGoldrick, J. K. Pearce, & J. Giordano (Eds.), *Ethnicity and family therapy* (pp. 3–30). New York: Guilford Press.

McGuinness, T. P. (1987). Confidentiality: Professional and organizational influences. In R. P. Gallagher (Ed.), *Legal and ethical issues in university and college counselling centers* (IACS Monograph Series, No. 4, pp. 28–44). Alexandria, VA: International Association of Counseling Services.

Meara, N. M., Schmidt, L. D., & Day, J. D. (1996). Principles and virtues: A foundation for ethical decisions, policies, and character. *The Counseling Psychologist*, *24*, 4–77.

Miller, F. T. (1981). Mental health programming for the rural poor. *Journal of Rural Community Psychology*, *2*, 23–30.

Miller, H. M. L., & Atkinson, D. R. (1988). The clergyperson as counselor: An inherent conflict of interest. *Counseling and Values*, *32*, 116–123.

Miller, P. J. (1994). Dual relationships in rural practice: A dilemma of ethics and culture. *Human Services in the Rural Environment*, *18*, 4–7.

Moleski, S. M., & Kiselica, M. S. (2005). Dual relationships: A continuum ranging from the destructive to the therapeutic. *Journal of Counseling & Development*, *83*, 3–11.

Murray, J. D., & Keller, P. A. (1991). Psychology and rural America: Current status and future directions. *American Psychologist*, *46*, 220–231.

Nagayama Hall, G. C., Iwamasa, G. Y., & Smith, J. N. (2003). Ethical principles of the psychology profession and ethnic minority issues. In W. O'Donohue & K. Ferguson (Eds.), *Handbook of professional ethics for psychologists: Issues, questions, and controversies* (pp. 301–318). Thousand Oaks, CA: Sage.

Neukrug, E., Lovell, C., & Parker, R. J. (1996). Employing ethical codes and decision-making models: A developmental process. *Counseling and Values*, *40*, 98–106.

Nigro, T. (2004). Counselors' experiences with problematic dual relationships. *Ethics & Behavior*, *14*, 51–64.

O'Neill, P. (1989). Responsible to whom? Responsible for what? Some ethical issues in community intervention. *American Journal of Community Psychology*, *17*, 323–341.

Orme, D. R., & Doerman, A. L. (2001). Ethical dilemmas and U.S. Air Force clinical psychologists: A survey. *Professional Psychology: Research and Practice*, *32*, 305–311.

Parham, T. A. (1997). An African-centered view of dual relationships. In B. Herlihy & G. Corey (Eds.), *Boundary issues in counseling: Multiple roles and responsibilities* (pp. 109–111). Alexandria, VA: American Counseling Association.

Pearson, B., & Piazza, N. (1997). Classification of dual relationships in the helping professions. *Counselor Education and Supervision, 37,* 89–99.

Pedersen, P. B. (1995) Culture-centered ethical guidelines for counselors. In J. G. Ponterotto, J. M. Casas, L. A. Suzuki, & C. M. Alexander (Eds.), *Handbook of multicultural counseling* (pp. 34–49). Thousand Oaks, CA: Sage.

Pedersen, P. B. (1997a). *Culture-centered counseling interventions.* Thousand Oaks, CA: Sage.

Pedersen, P. B. (1997b). Cultural context of the American Counseling Association code of ethics. *Journal of Counseling & Development, 76,* 23–28.

Perkins, D. V., Hudson, B. L., Gray, D. M., & Steward, M. (1998). Decisions and justifications by community mental health providers about hypothetical ethical dilemmas. *Psychiatric Services, 49,* 1317–1322.

Perlman, B. (1977). Ethical concerns in community mental health. *American Journal of Community Psychology, 5,* 45–57.

Phillips, L. F., & Baker, M. J. (1983). The rural experience of psychotherapy with borderline patients. *Journal of Rural Community Psychology, 4,* 25–34.

Pipes, R. B. (1999). Nonsexual relationships between psychotherapists and their former clients: Obligations of psychologists. In D. Bersoff (Ed.), *Ethical conflicts in psychology* (pp. 254–256). Washington, DC: American Psychological Association.

Plaut, S. M. (1997). Boundary violations in professional–client relationships: Overview and guidelines for prevention. *Sexual and Marital Therapy, 12,* 77–94.

Pollack, D. (2002). Responding to boundary conflicts in community settings. In P. Backlar (Ed.), *Ethics in community mental health care: Commonplace concerns* (pp. 51–62). New York: Kluwer Academic/Plenum.

Pope, K. S. (1985). Dual relationships: A violation of ethical, legal, and clinical standards. *California State Psychologist, 20,* 1–3.

Pope, K. S. (1991). Dual relationships in psychotherapy. *Ethics & Behavior, 1,* 21–34.

Pope, K. S. (2003). Developing and practicing ethics. In M. J. Prinstein & M. D. Patterson (Eds.), *Portable mentor: Expert guide to a successful career in psychology* (pp. 33–43). New York: Plenum.

Pope, K. S., & Vasquez, M. J. T. (1998). *Ethics in psychotherapy and counseling: A practical guide* (2nd ed.). San Francisco: Jossey-Bass.

Pope, K. S., & Vetter, V. A. (1992). Ethical dilemmas encountered by members of the American Psychological Association: A national survey. *American Psychologist, 47,* 397–411.

Purtilo, R., & Sorrell, J. (1986). The ethical dilemmas of a rural physician. *Hastings Center Report, 16,* 24–28.

Rich, R. O. (1990). The American rural metaphor: Myths and realities in rural practice. *Human Services in the Rural Environment, 14*, 31–34.

Riddle, D. I. (1982). Training for rural mental health: Practicum training and supervision. In H. A. Dengerink & H. J. Cross (Eds.), *Training professionals for rural mental health* (pp. 83–89). Lincoln: University of Nebraska Press.

Ridley, C. R. (1995). *Overcoming unintentional racism in counseling and therapy.* Thousand Oaks, CA: Sage.

Roll, S., & Millen, L. (1981). A guide to violating an injunction in psychotherapy: On seeing acquaintances as patients. *Psychotherapy: Theory, Research and Practice, 18*, 179–187.

Rolland, M. F., & Hughes, C. S. (2004, Summer). Social workers as wisdom seekers: Consulting rural Alaska Native elders. *Rural Mental Health*, 19–21.

Sadeghi, M., Fischer, J. M., & House, S. E. (2003). Ethical dilemmas in multicultural counseling. *Journal of Multicultural Counseling and Development, 31*, 179–191.

Salisbury, W. A., & Kinnier, R. T. (1996). Posttermination friendship between counselors and clients. *Journal of Counseling & Development, 74*, 495–500.

Sanders Thompson, V. L., Bazile, A., & Akbar, M. (2004). African Americans' perceptions of psychotherapy and psychotherapists. *Professional Psychology: Research and Practice, 35*, 19–26.

Saxton, G. H. (1986). Confidentiality dilemmas for psychologists and psychiatrists in the criminal justice system. *American Journal of Forensic Psychology, 4*, 25–32.

Sawyer, D., & Beeson, P. G. (1998). *Rural mental health: 2000 & beyond.* St. Cloud, MN: National Association for Rural Mental Health.

Schank, J. A. (1994). *Ethical dilemmas of rural and small-community psychologists.* Unpublished doctoral dissertation, University of Minnesota, Minneapolis.

Schank, J. A. (1998). Ethical issues in rural counseling practice. *Canadian Journal of Counseling, 32*, 270–283.

Schank, J. A., & Skovholt, T. M. (1997). Dual relationship dilemmas of rural and small-community psychologists. *Professional Psychology: Research and Practice, 28*, 44–49.

Schank, J., Slater, R., Banerjee-Stevens, D., & Skovholt, T. (2003). Ethics of multiple and overlapping relationships. In W. O'Donohue & K. Ferguson (Eds.), *Handbook of professional ethics for psychologists: Issues, questions, and controversies* (pp. 181–193). Thousand Oaks, CA: Sage.

Schoener, G. R. (1986). Sexual involvement of therapists with clients after therapy ends: Some observations. In G. R. Schoener, J. H. Milgrom, J. C. Gonsiorek, E. T. Luepker, & R. M. Conroe (Eds.), *Psychotherapists' sexual involvement with clients* (pp. 265–287). Minneapolis, MN: Walk-In Counseling Center.

Schoener, G. R., & Luepker, E. T. (1996). Boundaries in group therapy: Ethical and practice issues. In B. DeChant (Ed.), *Women and group psychotherapy* (pp. 373–399). New York: Guilford Press.

Schopp, L. H., Johnstone, B., & Reid-Arndt, S. (2005). Telehealth brain injury training for rural behavioral health generalists: Supporting and enhancing rural service delivery networks. *Professional Psychology: Research and Practice, 36,* 158–163.

Sell, J. M., Gottlieb, M. C., & Schoenfeld, L. (1986). Ethical considerations of social–romantic relationships with present and former clients. *Professional Psychology: Research and Practice, 17,* 504–508.

Sharkin, B. S. (1995). Strains on confidentiality in college-student psychotherapy: Entangled therapeutic relationships, incidental encounters, and third-party inquiries. *Professional Psychology: Research and Practice, 26,* 184–189.

Sharkin, B. S., & Birkey, I. (1992). Incidental encounters between therapists and their clients. *Professional Psychology: Research and Practice, 23,* 326–328.

Sharkin, B. S., Scappaticci, A. G., & Birky, I. (1995). Access to confidential information in a university counseling center: A survey of referral sources. *Journal of College Student Development, 36,* 494–495.

Shernoff, M. (2001). Sexuality, boundaries, professional ethics, and clinical practice: Queering the issue. *Journal of Gay & Lesbian Social Services, 13,* 85–91.

Sherry, P., Teschendorf, R., Anderson, S., & Guzman, F. (1991). Ethical beliefs and behaviors of college counseling center professionals. *Journal of College Student Development, 32,* 350–358.

Shopland, S. N., & VandeCreek, L. (1991). Sex with ex-clients: Theoretical rationales for prohibition. *Ethics & Behavior, 1,* 35–44.

Simi, N., & Mahalik, M. R. (1997). Comparison of feminist versus psychoanalytic/dynamic and other therapists on self-disclosure. *Psychology of Women Quarterly, 21,* 465–483.

Simon, R. I., & Williams, I. C. (1999). Maintaining treatment boundaries in small communities and rural areas. *Psychiatric Services, 50,* 1440–1446.

Skovholt , T. M. (2001). *The resilient practitioner: Burnout prevention and self-care strategies for counselors, therapists, teachers and health professionals.* Boston: Allyn & Bacon.

Skovholt, T. M., & Jennings, L. (2004). *Master therapists: Exploring expertise in therapy and counseling.* Boston: Allyn & Bacon.

Sladen, B. J., & Mozdzierz, G. J. (1989). Distribution of psychologists in underserved areas: Changes over time, 1970–1981. *Professional Psychology: Research and Practice, 20,* 244–247.

Sleek, S. (1995). Military practice creates ethical squeeze. *APA Monitor, 26*(2), 30.

Smith, D. (2003a). In an ethical bind? *APA Monitor, 34*(1), 61.

Smith, D. (2003b). Ten ways practitioners can avoid frequent ethical pitfalls. *APA Monitor, 34*(1), 50.

Smith, D., & Fitzpatrick, M. (1995). Patient–therapist boundary issues: An integrative review of theory and research. *Professional Psychology: Research and Practice, 22,* 499–506.

Smith, T. S., McGuire, J. M., Abbott, D. W., & Blau, B. I. (1991). Clinical ethical decision making: An investigation of the rationale used to justify doing less than one believes one should. *Professional Psychology: Research and Practice, 22,* 235–239.

Sobel, S. B. (1984). Independent practice in child and adolescent psychotherapy in small communities: Personal, professional, and ethical issues. *Psychotherapy, 21,* 110–117.

Solomon, G. (1980). Rural human service delivery system: Entry issues. *Journal of Rural Community Psychology, 1,* 1–15.

Solomon, G., Hiesberger, J., & Winer, J. L. (1981). Confidentiality in rural community mental health. *Journal of Rural Community Psychology, 2,* 17–31.

Sonne, J. L. (1994). Multiple relationships: Does the new ethics code answer the right questions? *Professional Psychology: Research and Practice, 25,* 336–343.

Spooner, R. (1992). Dual relationships in college student personnel work. In B. Herlihy & G. Corey (Eds.), *Dual relationships in counseling* (pp. 157–160). Alexandria, VA: American Association for Counseling and Development.

St. Germaine, J. (1993). Dual relationships: What's wrong with them? *American Counselor, 2,* 25–30.

Staal, M. A., & King, R. E. (2000), Managing a multiple relationship environment: The ethics of military psychology. *Professional Psychology: Research and Practice, 31,* 698–705.

Steinman, S. O., Richardson, N. F., & McEnroe, T. (1998). *Ethical decision-making manual for helping professionals.* Pacific Grove, CA: Brooks/Cole.

Stockman, A. F. (1990). Dual relationships in rural mental health practice: An ethical dilemma. *Journal of Rural Community Psychology, 11,* 31–45.

Stone, G. L., & Lucas, J. (1990). Knowledge and beliefs about confidentiality on a university campus. *Journal of College Student Development, 31,* 437–444.

Sue, D. W. (1997). Multicultural perspectives on multiple relationships. In B. Herlihy & G. Corey (Eds.), *Boundary issues in counseling: Multiple roles and responsibilities* (pp. 106–109). Alexandria, VA: American Counseling Association.

Sue, D. W. (2004). Whiteness and ethnocentric monoculturalism: Making the "invisible" visible. *American Psychologist, 59,* 761–769.

Sue, D. W., Arredondo, P., & McDavis, R. J. (1995). Appendix III: Multicultural counseling competencies and standards: A call to the profession. In J. G. Ponterotto, J. M. Casas, L. A. Suzuki, & C. M. Alexander (Eds.), *Handbook of multicultural counseling* (pp. 624–644). Thousand Oaks, CA: Sage.

Sue, D. W., Bingham, R. P., Porche-Burke, L., & Vasquez, M. (1999). Diversification of psychology: A multicultural revolution. *American Psychologist, 54,* 1061–1069.

Sundet, P. A., & Mermelstein, J. (1984). Rural crisis intervention. *Human Services in the Rural Environment, 9,* 8–14.

Tamura, L. J., Guy, J. D., Brady, J. L., & Grace, C. (1994). Psychotherapists' management of confidentiality, burnout and affiliation needs: A national survey. *Psychotherapy in Private Practice, 13,* 1–17.

Thomas, J. (1993, July). Inquiries to the Ethics Committee: Focus on dual relationship and confidentiality dilemmas. *Minnesota Psychologist,* 9–10.

Thomason, T. C. (1991). Counseling Native Americans: An introduction for non-Native American counselors. *Journal of Counseling and Development, 69,* 321–327.

Tribbensee, N. E., & Claiborn, C. D. (2003). Confidentiality in psychotherapy and related contexts. In W. O'Donohue & K. Ferguson (Eds.), *Handbook of professional ethics for psychologists: Issues, questions, and controversies* (pp. 287–300). Thousand Oaks, CA: Sage.

Trimble, J. E. (2003). Cultural sensitivity and cultural competence. In M. J. Prinstein & M. D. Patterson (Eds.), *Portable mentor: Expert guide to a successful career in psychology* (pp. 13–32). New York: Plenum.

Vasquez, M. J. (1991). Sexual intimacies with clients after termination: Should a prohibition be explicit? *Ethics & Behavior, 1,* 45–61.

Vasquez, M. J. (2003). Ethical responsibilities in therapy: A feminist perspective. In M. Kopala & M. A. Keitel (Eds.), *Handbook of counseling women* (pp. 557–573). Thousand Oaks, CA: Sage.

Weinberger, L. E., & Sreenivasan, S. (1994). Ethical and professional conflicts in correctional psychology. *Professional Psychology: Research and Practice, 25,* 161–167.

Weinberger, L. E., & Sreenivasan, S. (2003). Ethical principles of correctional psychology. In W. O'Donohue & K. Ferguson (Eds.), *Handbook of professional ethics for psychologists: Issues, questions, and controversies* (pp. 359–375). Thousand Oaks, CA: Sage.

Welfel, E. R. (1998). *Ethics in counseling and psychotherapy: Standards, research, and emerging issues.* Pacific Grove, CA: Brooks/Cole.

White, T. W. (2003a, September–October). Managing dual relationships in correctional settings. *National Psychologist,* 14–15.

White, T. W. (2003b, November–December). Revisiting dual relationships in correctional settings. *National Psychologist,* 20.

Woody, J. D. (1990). Resolving ethical concerns in clinical practice: Toward a pragmatic model. *Journal of Marital and Family Therapy, 16,* 133–150.

Woody, R. H. (1998). Bartering for psychological services. *Professional Psychology: Research and Practice, 29,* 174–178.

Younggren, J. N., & Gottlieb, M. C. (2004). Managing risk when contemplating multiple relationships. *Professional Psychology: Research and Practice, 35*, 255–260.

Zelig, M. (1988). Ethical dilemmas in police psychology. *Professional Psychology: Research and Practice, 19*, 336–338.

Zipple, A. M., Langle, S., Spaniol, L., & Fisher, H. (1990). Client confidentiality and the family's need to know: Strategies for resolving the conflict. *Community Mental Health Journal, 26*, 533–545.

Author Index

Abbott, D. W., 9, 22
Adams, K. M., 136, 137, 138, 147, 148
Ader, D. N., 165
Adleman, J., 153, 155
Akbar, M., 135
Alexander, C. M., 135
Amada, G., 124, 125, 126
American Association of Marriage
    and Family Therapists
    (AAMFT), 36
American Counseling Association,
    36
American Mental Health Counselors
    Association (AMHCA), 36
American Psychological Association
    (APA), 5, 14, 15, 16, 17, 21, 24,
    25, 26, 27, 28, 29, 30, 33, 35, 36,
    48, 61, 62, 72, 89, 91, 124, 132,
    139, 161, 169, 192
American Psychological Association
    (APA), Office of Ethnic
    Minority Affairs, 62, 131
Anderson, S. K., 11, 39, 48, 55, 124,
    150, 188, 189
Arredondo, P., 127, 130
Atkinson, D. R., 151

Bachelor, A., 48
Backlar, P., 12
Baer, B. E., 39
Bagarozzi, D. A., 65, 67
Baker, E. K., 70
Baker, M. J., 65
Bannerjee-Stevens, D., 47
Barnett, J. E., 44, 77, 181, 183, 184,
    186, 188, 191
Barrett, S. E., 153, 155
Bazile, A., 135
Beeson, G. P., 110

Behnke, S., 5, 23, 33, 34, 39
Bennett, B. E., 24, 175
Bersoff, D. N., 12, 13, 14, 24, 26, 30
Biaggio, M., 153
Bingham, R. P., 62, 128
Birky, I., 119, 122, 123
Bishop, B. J., 198
Blau, B. I., 9, 22
Borys, D. S., 30, 40, 48, 49, 55, 182,
    183, 195
Boyer, P. A., 64
Brady, J. L., 187
Brodsky, A. M., 52
Brown, L. S., 53, 134, 136, 146, 153,
    154, 155, 156, 171
Brown, S. M., 122
Brownlee, K., 30, 75, 187
Butler, R. T., 50

Callanan, P., 50
Canadian Psychological Association,
    21
Canter, M. B., 24, 25, 26, 29, 175
Case, P. W., 150
Catalano, S., 46, 47, 59, 76, 77, 78, 83,
    198
Catanzaro, S. J., 35, 118
Chang, A. S., 165
Chapman, C., 42, 46, 171
Claiborn, C. D., 85, 180
Clark, H., 68
Coakes, S. J., 198
Corbine, J. S., 140
Corey, G., 36, 37, 38, 39, 41, 42, 43,
    50, 72, 175, 186, 193
Corey, M. S., 50
Coyle, B. R., 91, 92, 96, 101, 113, 114,
    202
Craig, J. D., 152

Subject Index

Abortion, value differences over, 96–97

Abuse
 reporting of (example), 103
 and value differences in rural practice, 97

Acquaintances, as clients, 40. *See also* Social relationships

Advantages of small-community practice, 196–203

African Americans, 135–137

Aircraft carrier, psychologist's multiple relationships on, 37, 59

Alternative methods
 in cultural-ethnic communities, 143–144
 and rural practice, 107–108
 See also Local healers; Natural helpers; Nontraditional providers; Peer helpers

Alternatives
 and culpability, 43
 in decision making model, 179

Ambiguity in psychology, 7
 about causing harm, 36
 about dual relationships, 36
 about identity of client (criminal justice), 157
 need to tolerate, 175
 stress from, 8

American Association of Marriage and Family Therapists (AAMFT), code of as varying from others, 36

American Counseling Association, code of, 130
 as varying from others, 36

American Mental Health Counsels Association (AMHCA), code of as varying from others, 36

American Psychologist, survey on ethical decision making in, 24

American Psychological Association
 Division 17 (Society of Counseling Psychology) of, 62
 Division 45 (Society for the Psychological Study of Ethnic Minority Issues) of, 62
 "Ethical Principles of Psychologists and Code of Conduct" of, 5
 Ethics Code Task Force, 132, 195
 Guidelines on Multicultural Education, Training, Research, Practice, and Organizational Change for Psychologists of, 62, 127, 132, 133–134
 Guidelines for Providers of Psychological Services to Ethnic, Linguistic, and Culturally Diverse Populations of, 131–132
 Office of Ethnic Minority Affairs of, 62
 and specialization 95
 survey by, 192

American Psychological Association Ethics Code(s). *See at* Ethics Code, American Psychological Association

Anonymity, lack of, 46. *See also* Privacy

APA Monitor, Ethics Code drafts in, 24

About the Authors

Janet A. Schank, PhD, is a licensed psychologist in Minnesota and has been a member and chair of the Minnesota Psychological Association Ethics Committee. Her professional publications and presentations in Minnesota, other states, and nationally have focused on ethical practice in psychology. Dr. Schank has directed mental health services in several settings, including a liberal arts college, a community mental health agency, and a large suburban school district. She has worked in small-community settings, including communities of color and a small private liberal arts college.

Dr. Schank maintains an independent therapy and consulting practice in Minneapolis–St. Paul, Minnesota. She has consulted and presented over the past 20 years on ethical issues in psychology, small community practice, dual relationships, and professional boundaries. Dr. Schank is a native of rural Nebraska.

Thomas M. Skovholt, PhD, is a professor of educational psychology at the University of Minnesota and a part-time practitioner. He is a fellow of the American Psychological Association and board certified by the American Board of Professional Psychology. Dr. Skovholt has won awards for research, teaching, and practice. His authored or coauthored publications include *The Resilient Practitioner, Evolving Professional Self,* and *Master Therapists.* Dr. Skovholt has been a Fulbright Professor in Turkey and has also worked in Singapore, Kuwait, Norway, and Korea.